普通高等院校英语专业"十四五"规划系列精品教材

英美文学简明教程
（下册　美国文学）
（第3版）

An Introductory Course Book of English and American Literatures
（Volume Two　American Literature）
（3rd Edition）

主　编　张　文　张伯香
编　者　罗　城　孙　平　徐莉红
　　　　向　菁　陈　娃　柯　倩

华中科技大学出版社
中国·武汉

内容提要

本书广泛比较了国内外现有同类教材,吸收了近几年国内外美国文学研究的最新成果,按照选取适合学生阅读又具代表性的常见作品为原则,并结合编者自己多年的教学和研究体会,以美国文学发展的历史为顺序,编选了各个历史时期主要作家的代表作品。在体裁上,注意了诗歌、小说、戏剧与散文的适当比例。每章的内容包括历史文化背景、作者简介、作品选读、注释和思考题等。与其他同类书相比,本书扩大了入选作者范围,调整了选读作品,增加了学习思考题,从而使教材内容更加充实,语言叙述更加简明,选读作品的难度也相对降低,这将有利于学生的理解与掌握。本书为普通高等院校英语专业教材,也可供独立学院、教育学院、广播电视大学、成人高等教育及社会上英语自学者学习使用。(本书为授课教师提供 ppt 课件,免费索取请洽 QQ:3307902061)

图书在版编目(CIP)数据

英美文学简明教程. 下册,美国文学/张文,张伯香主编. —3 版. —武汉:华中科技大学出版社,2020.9
(2025.1 重印)
ISBN 978-7-5680-4702-9

Ⅰ.①英… Ⅱ.①张… ②张… Ⅲ.①英语-阅读教学-高等学校-教材 ②文学史-美国 Ⅳ.①H319.37

中国版本图书馆 CIP 数据核字(2020)第 160025 号

英美文学简明教程(下册 美国文学)(第 3 版)　　　　　　　　　　　　张　文　张伯香　主编
Yingmei Wenxue Jianming Jiaocheng (Xiace　Meiguo Wenxue) (Di-3 Ban)

策划编辑:刘　平
责任编辑:刘　平
责任校对:封力煊
封面设计:刘　卉
责任监印:周治超

出版发行:华中科技大学出版社(中国·武汉)　　电话:(027)81321913
　　　　　武汉市东湖新技术开发区华工科技园　　邮编:430223
录　　排:华中科技大学惠友文印中心
印　　刷:武汉市籍缘印刷厂
开　　本:787mm×1092mm　1/16
印　　张:17.25
字　　数:556 千字
版　　次:2025 年 1 月第 3 版第 5 次印刷
定　　价:49.80 元

本书若有印装质量问题,请向出版社营销中心调换
全国免费服务热线:400-6679-118　　竭诚为您服务
版权所有　侵权必究

第3版前言

《英美文学简明教程》(上下)是一套用英语撰写的高校英语专业本科生教材。其编写目的在于通过阅读和分析英美文学作品,促进学生语言基本功和人文素质的提高,增强学生对西方文学及文化的了解,从而培养学生阅读、理解、欣赏英语文学原著的能力,掌握文学批评的基本知识和方法。

本教材选择了英美文学历史上各个时期主要作家的代表作品,包括诗歌、戏剧、小说、散文等,并对各个历史断代的主要历史背景、文学思潮、文学流派,以及具体作家的文学生涯、创作思想、艺术特色及其代表作品的主题、人物、结构、语言等作了简明扼要的介绍和评价。

本教材自2009年面世以来,多次重印。不少高校将它作为英语专业本科生文学课教材和硕士研究生入学考试参考书;许多自学考试英语专业本科生、英语专业函授本科生以及报考英美文学专业研究生的同学对本教材也表现出了极大的兴趣;同时,好些读者还给编者发来热情洋溢的信件,表达他们对使用教材后的感受和意见。为了更好地满足广大读者的需要,2013年我们在保留教材原有优点的基础上,对其进行了修订,扩大了入选作者的数量,调整了选读作品,增加了学习思考题,从而使教材内容更加充实,语言叙述更加简明。为方便教师备课和学生自学,我们又于2015年编写出版了《英美文学简明教程学习指南》。

随着改革开放的逐步深入和科学技术的飞速发展,教材也要与时俱进,富有时代气息,要有利于学生创新能力和人文素质的培养。为此,我们决定对这套文学教材进行第三次修订。这次修订的重点是利用二维码链接,将原《英美文学简明教程学习指南》的内容融入教材中,让学生根据个人的兴趣、爱好,利用手机扫码功能,进一步了解英美作家与作品知识,既不增加教材分量,又能满足学生自主学习的需求。

《英美文学简明教程》(第3版)的问世与华中科技大学出版社领导的关心与支持密不可分,更是出版社责任编辑辛勤劳动的结晶。在此,我谨代表所有编者向他们表示诚挚的谢意。

参加《英美文学简明教程》(第3版)上册编写工作的有江宝珠、路璐、张秀芳、孙灵、周厚银、万欣等老师,参加下册编写工作的有罗城、孙平、徐莉红、向菁、陈娃、柯倩等老师,他们在选材、撰稿、注释、校对等方面做了大量的工作。全书的内容设计、章节安排、文字修改和通读定稿都由主编负责。由于多人执笔,风格难以统一,各种错误也在所难免,敬请广大读者批评指正。

张伯香
2020年4月于珞珈山

Contents

Chapter 1　The Literature of the Colonial Period ⋯⋯⋯⋯⋯⋯ (1)

　1.1　An Introduction ⋯⋯⋯⋯⋯⋯⋯⋯⋯⋯⋯⋯⋯⋯⋯⋯⋯⋯⋯⋯ (1)
　1.2　Anne Bradstreet ⋯⋯⋯⋯⋯⋯⋯⋯⋯⋯⋯⋯⋯⋯⋯⋯⋯⋯⋯⋯ (3)
　1.3　Edward Taylor ⋯⋯⋯⋯⋯⋯⋯⋯⋯⋯⋯⋯⋯⋯⋯⋯⋯⋯⋯⋯ (5)

Chapter 2　The Literature of the Revolutionary Period ⋯⋯⋯⋯⋯⋯ (8)

　2.1　An Introduction ⋯⋯⋯⋯⋯⋯⋯⋯⋯⋯⋯⋯⋯⋯⋯⋯⋯⋯⋯⋯ (8)
　2.2　Benjamin Franklin ⋯⋯⋯⋯⋯⋯⋯⋯⋯⋯⋯⋯⋯⋯⋯⋯⋯⋯ (11)
　2.3　Patrick Henry ⋯⋯⋯⋯⋯⋯⋯⋯⋯⋯⋯⋯⋯⋯⋯⋯⋯⋯⋯⋯ (15)
　2.4　Thomas Jefferson ⋯⋯⋯⋯⋯⋯⋯⋯⋯⋯⋯⋯⋯⋯⋯⋯⋯⋯ (19)

Chapter 3　The Literature of the Romantic Period ⋯⋯⋯⋯⋯⋯ (25)

　3.1　An Introduction ⋯⋯⋯⋯⋯⋯⋯⋯⋯⋯⋯⋯⋯⋯⋯⋯⋯⋯⋯⋯ (25)
　3.2　Washington Irving ⋯⋯⋯⋯⋯⋯⋯⋯⋯⋯⋯⋯⋯⋯⋯⋯⋯⋯ (27)
　3.3　Edgar Allan Poe ⋯⋯⋯⋯⋯⋯⋯⋯⋯⋯⋯⋯⋯⋯⋯⋯⋯⋯⋯ (35)
　3.4　Ralph Waldo Emerson ⋯⋯⋯⋯⋯⋯⋯⋯⋯⋯⋯⋯⋯⋯⋯⋯ (38)
　3.5　Henry David Thoreau ⋯⋯⋯⋯⋯⋯⋯⋯⋯⋯⋯⋯⋯⋯⋯⋯ (43)
　3.6　Nathaniel Hawthorne ⋯⋯⋯⋯⋯⋯⋯⋯⋯⋯⋯⋯⋯⋯⋯⋯ (49)
　3.7　Herman Melville ⋯⋯⋯⋯⋯⋯⋯⋯⋯⋯⋯⋯⋯⋯⋯⋯⋯⋯ (57)
　3.8　Abraham Lincoln ⋯⋯⋯⋯⋯⋯⋯⋯⋯⋯⋯⋯⋯⋯⋯⋯⋯⋯ (64)
　3.9　Henry Wadsworth Longfellow ⋯⋯⋯⋯⋯⋯⋯⋯⋯⋯⋯⋯ (67)
　3.10　Walt Whitman ⋯⋯⋯⋯⋯⋯⋯⋯⋯⋯⋯⋯⋯⋯⋯⋯⋯⋯⋯ (71)
　3.11　Emily Dickinson ⋯⋯⋯⋯⋯⋯⋯⋯⋯⋯⋯⋯⋯⋯⋯⋯⋯⋯ (77)

Chapter 4　The Literature of the Realistic Period ⋯⋯⋯⋯⋯⋯ (82)

　4.1　An Introduction ⋯⋯⋯⋯⋯⋯⋯⋯⋯⋯⋯⋯⋯⋯⋯⋯⋯⋯⋯⋯ (82)
　4.2　Mark Twain ⋯⋯⋯⋯⋯⋯⋯⋯⋯⋯⋯⋯⋯⋯⋯⋯⋯⋯⋯⋯ (84)
　4.3　O. Henry ⋯⋯⋯⋯⋯⋯⋯⋯⋯⋯⋯⋯⋯⋯⋯⋯⋯⋯⋯⋯⋯⋯ (90)
　4.4　Henry James ⋯⋯⋯⋯⋯⋯⋯⋯⋯⋯⋯⋯⋯⋯⋯⋯⋯⋯⋯⋯ (97)
　4.5　Theodore Dreiser ⋯⋯⋯⋯⋯⋯⋯⋯⋯⋯⋯⋯⋯⋯⋯⋯⋯⋯ (104)

I

4.6　Robert Frost ……………………………………………………………… (114)
4.7　Willa Cather ……………………………………………………………… (120)
4.8　Sherwood Anderson ……………………………………………………… (145)
4.9　Katherine Anne Porter …………………………………………………… (155)

Chapter 5　The Literature of the Modernist Period ……………………… (165)
5.1　An Introduction ………………………………………………………… (165)
5.2　Ezra Pound ……………………………………………………………… (168)
5.3　William Carlos Williams ………………………………………………… (171)
5.4　Langston Hughes ………………………………………………………… (174)
5.5　E. E. Cummings ………………………………………………………… (176)
5.6　Ernest Hemingway ……………………………………………………… (178)
5.7　F. Scott Fitzgerald ……………………………………………………… (183)
5.8　William Faulkner ………………………………………………………… (195)
5.9　Eugene O'Neill ………………………………………………………… (204)

Chapter 6　The Literature since World War II …………………………… (214)
6.1　An Introduction ………………………………………………………… (214)
6.2　Saul Bellow ……………………………………………………………… (216)
6.3　Arthur Miller …………………………………………………………… (230)
6.4　J. D. Salinger …………………………………………………………… (235)
6.5　Elizabeth Bishop ………………………………………………………… (243)
6.6　Robert Lowell …………………………………………………………… (246)
6.7　Theodore Roethke ……………………………………………………… (250)
6.8　Allen Ginsberg …………………………………………………………… (251)
6.9　Sylvia Plath ……………………………………………………………… (257)
6.10　Robert Hayden ………………………………………………………… (259)

Appendix I　Sample Test Paper …………………………………………… (262)

Appendix II　Acknowledgments …………………………………………… (269)

Chapter 1　The Literature of the Colonial Period

1.1　An Introduction

Long before European settlers arrived in North America, Asians, known as the ancestors of American Indians or Native Americans, had been living there for thousands of years. They arrived across Bering Strait and immigrated into America. These Native Americans had composed rich literary works. Myths, legends, stories, lyrics, and other forms of literature were preserved in oral form and passed down from one generation to another through ceremonies and other community gatherings. Native American stories, for example, glow with reverence for nature as a spiritual as well as a physical mother. Nature is alive and endowed with spiritual forces; main characters may be animals or plants, often totems associated with a tribe, group, or individual. Among the richest set of Native American stories that survive are creation myths, descriptions of the beginnings of the universe and of the origin of humankind. The creation myths of Native American cultures share with the Genesis accounts of the Bible a concern with relationships among the divine, the human, and the world of animals and plants. But unfortunately much of this literature had disappeared with the destruction of Native American cultures that followed white settlement of the continent.

America was rediscovered by Christopher Columbus in 1492. With this discovery, America, the mysterious world, has become for many people a genuine hope of a new life, an escape from poverty and persecution, or a chance to start again. Over the time, large numbers of the Spanish, the Dutch, the Swedes, the French, the Irish, and the English rushed into this fascinating and strange continent in rapid succession and established their own colonies respectively. Although English quickly became the language of America, regional and ethnic dialects had enlivened and enriched the country's literature.

In 1620, a group of English men and women, led by William Bradford, arrived at Plymouth, Massachusetts on a ship called the *Mayflower*. They were very devout Christians who wanted to purify their lives and their church of what they saw as the corruptions of English society and its state religion, the Church of England. They called themselves Saints or Separatists, but they are now generally called Puritans.

The Puritans believed in an all-powerful God who freely granted to his "Saints" the gift of grace, which can be described as the spirit that would guarantee salvation — central happiness with God. In their daily lives the Puritans wanted to demonstrate at every moment that they were worthy of it. For the Puritans everything was, ideally, aimed at personal salvation and the building of a new, God-centered society. They were willing to risk their lives for such a world, which would be a place where they could practice their religion freely and raise their children free from the frivolities and temptations of the Old World. Life for the average Puritan in the New World was essentially a life of work and prayer. The Puritans worked long and hard under extremely difficult conditions so that their farms and trading enterprises would prosper. In fact they believed prosperity was a sign of election, or God's special favor. In the pursuit of virtue, the Puritans passed laws against many activities that could distract good souls from their real task. These Puritan codes of values, philosophy of life, and point of view have later become American Puritanism and, as an embedded strand in the American psyche, have been both positive and negative in shaping the American character.

Writing was an important part of Puritan life; it was often an extension of religion. The Puritan definition of good writing was one that brought home a full awareness of the importance of worshipping God and of the spiritual dangers that the soul faced on Earth. Life was seen as a test; failure led to eternal damnation and hellfire, and success to heavenly bliss. This world was an arena of constant battle between forces of God and those of Satan, a formidable enemy with many disguises. The Puritans interpreted all things and events as symbols with deeper spiritual meanings, and felt that in advancing their own profit and their community's well-being, they were also furthering God's plans. They did not draw lines of distinction between the secular and religious spheres: All of life was an expression of the divine will.

The Puritans sought to purify their language just as they sought to purify their lives. Everything they wrote avoided the complicated and decorative style of their European contemporaries. They preferred to write in what they called plain style, even as they strove for plainness in their architecture, clothing, food, and household furnishings. Plain style was meant simply to communicate ideas as clearly as possible. Writing was not a way of showing off cleverness or learning but a way of serving God and the community. The first work published in the Puritan colonies was the *Bay Psalm Book* (1640) and the first American writer was Captain John Smith whose reports of exploration and settlement have been described as the first American literature written in English.

Early English immigrants were drawn to the southern colonies because of economic opportunity rather than religious freedom. Life in the southern colonies, begun in 1607 with Jamestown, Virginia, developed quite differently from life in New England. Unlike the Puritans, who lived quite closely together, much of the southern population lived on farms or plantations that were distant from one another. Often like little colonies of their own, these plantations were largely self-sufficient. Those large plantations were owned and operated by wealthy and well-educated colonists who developed a more social and outgoing way of life than the Puritans. They carried on correspondence with friends who often lived at great distances from them, as well as with family and friends back in England. Many of the southern colonists belonged to the Church of England, and their

Chapter 1 The Literature of the Colonial Period

ties with the Old World were stronger. As a result, they did not have the reasons to create a literature of their own. Still, in their letters, journals, and public reports, southern writers recorded the details of their way of life. The realities of science and politics blend, in their writings, with a New World sense of excitement and discovery. Thus, the southern literature was aristocratic and secular, reflecting the dominant social and economic systems of the southern plantations. And the colonial South may fairly be linked with a light, worldly, informative, and realistic literary tradition. Imitative of English literary fashions, the southerners attained imaginative heights in witty, precise observations of distinctive New World conditions.

Generally, we can say that the American literature has its beginnings in Europe, for the roots of the American culture are grounded in the life of the Old World. In race and in civilization the Americans were merely transplanted Europeans, who brought to the colonies unchanged Old World speech, manners, politics, and religion. Yet from the very beginning, their Old World manner of life was modified by their new environment. Colonial literature was, therefore, the product of two basic forces: the European cultural heritage and the American environment. However, the American writings of the seventeenth century possess as a whole no great artistic merit. They are valuable today chiefly as a study in origins and as a complex mirror of early American experience.

For its early colonial years American literature reflected the settlement and growth of the American colonies, largely through diaries, travel books, letters, journals, sermons, and histories. Some of these early works reached the level of literature, as in the robust and perhaps truthful account of the adventures by Captain John Smith and the sober, tendentious journalistic histories of John Winthrop and William Bradford in New England. In our review of the colonial period we noted four classes of writers: (1) the annalists and historians, of whom Bradford and Byrd were selected as typical of writers who often appear in American literary histories or anthologies; (2) the poets, of whom Wigglesworth, Anne Bradstreet and Godfrey are the most notable; (3) a few characteristic books dealing with nature and the Indians, which served readers of those days in the place of fiction; and (4) theological writers, among whom Cotton Mather and Jonathan Edwards are the most conspicuous.

1.2 Anne Bradstreet

1.2.1 About the Author

Anne Bradstreet (1612-1672), who has been praised as the first noteworthy American poet, was born in Northampton, England, into the family of a sturdy Puritan. She came to Massachusetts in the Winthrop Puritan group in 1630 with her father, Thomas Dudley, and her husband, Simon Bradstreet, both later governors of the state. A dutiful Puritan wife who raised a large family, she nevertheless found time to write

poetry. In 1650 her first volume of verse, *The Tenth Muse Lately Sprung Up in America*, appeared in London. It was followed by *Several Poems* (Boston, 1678), which contains "Contemplations," probably her best work.

Her finest poems are those closest to her personal experience as a Puritan wife and mother living on the edge of the wilderness. Like other Puritans, she found similarities between the domestic details of daily life and the spiritual details of her religious life. For Bradstreet the everyday and the everlasting were simply two sides of the same experience.

Although Bradstreet wrote many poems on familiar British themes and produced skilled imitations of British forms, her most remarkable works responded directly to her experiences in colonial New England. They reveal her attraction to her new world, even as the discomforts of life in the wilderness sickened her. Her poetry contains a muted declaration of independence from the past and a challenge to authority. Her poetry also records early stirrings of female resistance to a social and religious system in which women are subservient to men. In "The Prologue" (1650), Bradstreet writes, "I am obnoxious to each carping tongue /Who says my hand a needle better fits, /[than] A poet's pen..." Bradstreet's instincts were to love this world more than the promised next world of Puritan theology, and her struggle to overcome her love for the world of nature energizes her poetry.

Today most of her poems have fallen into the obscurity of history, but her poem, "Contemplations," is still read. It compares the life of mankind with that of nonhuman nature and offers the reader an insight into the mentality of the early Puritan pioneering in a new world. In the ninth stanza, she wrote:

I heard the merry grasshopper then sing,
The black-clad cricket bear a second part;
They kept one tune and played on the same string,
Seeming to glory in their little art.
Shall creatures abject thus their voices raise.
And in their kind resound their Maker's praise.
Whilst, I as mute, can warble forth no higher lays?

1.2.2 "To My Dear and Loving Husband"

If ever two were one, then surely we. [1]
If ever man were loved by wife, then thee;
If ever wife was happy in a man,

Compare with me, ye women, if you can.
I prize thy love more than whole mines of gold
Or all the riches that the East² doth hold.
My love is such that rivers cannot quench,
Nor ought³ but love from thee give recompense.
Thy love is such I can no way repay.
The heavens reward thee manifold,⁴ I pray.
Then while we live, in love let's so persevere⁵
That when we live no more, we may live ever.

Notes

1. **we**: Anne's husband was Simon Bradstreet (1603-1697). They were married in England in 1628.
2. **the East**: East Indies.
3. **ought**: anything.
4. **manifold**: abundantly.
5. **persevere**: likely accented on the second syllable.

Study Questions

1. How would you characterize Bradstreet's feelings about her marriage?
2. How important is the simplicity of diction that distinguishes this love poem?
3. What does Bradstreet actually mean by the seeming paradox in the last line about living "no more" yet living "ever"?

1.3 Edward Taylor

1.3.1 About the Author

Edward Taylor (1642-1729), the best Puritan poet of colonial America, was born into the family of a dissenter in Coventry, England and began to suffer from religious persecution when he grew up. The persecution of 1662 led to his immigration to America. For fifty-eight years Taylor was both minister and physician to the people of Westfield, Massachusetts, bordering what he called the "howling wilderness." Because Taylor considered his poems a private record of his religious experience, he asked his heir never to publish them. As a result, the work of this major New England poet was unknown for 210 years after his death.

Taylor wrote metaphysical poems in the tradition of Donne and Herbert, treating religious themes and burning with an intense love for God. He was, first, and last, a Puritan poet, concerned about how his images speak for God. His poems use an extravagant imagery, which is not in the tradition of the Puritan plain style. Their emotion, however, is still the typically Puritan one of submissiveness and wonder in the face of God's grace and power. A good example is his poem, "Huswifery", a prayer in which the poet compares God's granting of grace to the work of a housewife who spins, weaves, and dyes a piece of cloth. By "huswifery," Taylor meant not only "housekeeping," but "managing well".

1.3.2 "Huswifery[1]"

Make me, O Lord, Thy spinning[2] wheel complete.
Thy holy word my distaff[3] make for me.
Make mine affections[4] Thy swift flyers[5] neat
And make my soul Thy holy spool to be.
My conversation make to be Thy reel
And reel the yarn thereon spun of Thy wheel.

Make me Thy loom then, knit therein this twine;
And make Thy holy spirit, Lord, wind quills[6];
Then weave the web Thyself. The yarn is fine.
Thine ordinances[7] make my fulling mills[8].
Then dye the same in heavenly colors choice,
All pinked[9] with varnished flowers of paradise.

Then clothe therewith mine understanding, will,
Affections, judgment, conscience, memory,
My words and actions, that their shine may fill
My ways with glory and Thee glorify.
Then mine apparel shall display before Ye
That I am clothed in holy robes for glory.

Notes

1. **Huswifery**: It denoted the full range of domestic tasks performed by Puritan housewives. In this poem, those tasks are narrowed to spinning and weaving.
2. **spinning**: making yarn by twisting woolen fibers.
3. **distaff**: A cleft staff about 3 feet long, on which … wool or flax was wound. It was held under the left arm, and the fibers of the material were drawn from it through the fingers of the left hand, and twisted spirally by the forefinger and thumb of the right, with the aid of the suspended spindle, round which the thread, as it was twisted or

Chapter 1 The Literature of the Colonial Period

spun, was wound.
4. **affections**: emotions.
5. **flyers**: later in machine spinning, the flyer twisted the thread as it led it to the bobbin and wound it therein.
6. **quills**: weaver's spindles.
7. **ordinances**: religious rites.
8. **fulling mills**: mills in which cloth is cleaned and thickened.
9. **pinked**: decorated.

Study Questions
1. What process is described in the poem?
2. What role does the poet play in the process? What role does God play?
3. Does Taylor believe one can achieve grace through one's own efforts, or must grace come as a gift from God? Supply evidence from the poem for your answer.

Chapter 2　The Literature of the Revolutionary Period

2.1　An Introduction

2.1.1　Historical Background

The eighteenth century was an important period in which the American national ideals were taking form. In the first half of the century, there were no radical political developments, no exciting struggles with the mother country. But in population, wealth, and racial stock, the period brought great changes. The middle colonies in particular, though founded later than Virginia and New England, grew rapidly. Into these colonies poured a large number of European immigrants, mixed in races and religions, who were attracted by the policy of religious toleration. Granted only that the immigrant should be industrious, American society could regenerate him by offering him a decent living, land, citizenship, and self-respect. In this unspoiled environment lived the typical American farmer, fortunate in his economic independence, in his warm, comfortable house, in his wild sports of country life, and in the affections of his family hearth. Here individuals of all nations were melted into a new race of men, whose labors and posterity would one day cause great changes in the world.

In this half century, a ragged line of colonies along the seaboard developed with rapid speed into a united and independent nation of five million people; a complex agrarian and mercantile society had grown up, supporting a wealthy class whose members moved with refined ease in the drawing rooms of Europe. And during this half-century, the people of the thirteen colonies had begun to prosper and started to communicate more with one another and to grow aware of their mutual problems and feelings.

In the second half of the eighteenth century, with the startling economic development in the thirteen colonies, the people wanted more rights to determine their own business. However, the British government wanted to bring the development under control and to collect more taxes from the colonies because defending the colonies against attacks by the French and others had cost the British a great deal of money. They thus decided to shift some of their financial burdens to the colonists. Thus came a series of infuriating laws and taxes. The Stamp Act in 1765 required that the colonists buy special stamps for newspapers, licenses, pamphlets, and many other documents. The Quartering Act in 1765 forced colonists to feed and house British soldiers in their own homes. The Townshend Acts in 1767 taxed tea, glass, lead, and paper. When some of the colonial assemblies refused to abide by the new laws, the British government declared those assemblies "dissolved." Violence was not far away. The Boston Massacre

Chapter 2 The Literature of the Revolutionary Period

erupted in 1770 when British troops fired on a taunting mob. In 1773 the British Parliament insisted again on its right and power to tax Americans. The tax on tea became a symbol, and the famous Boston Tea Party became a symbol too — a symbol of American resistance — as colonists dressed as Indians dumped a shipment of British tea into Boston Harbor.

Americans protested and petitioned King George Ⅱ for "no taxation without representation." They wanted only what was reasonable, they said. They wanted to share in their own government. Britain replied with the intolerable Acts of 1774, designed to punish Massachusetts for the Boston Tea Party. Many more rights that had been granted to the colonists in their charters were revoked. Then, when the British soldiers were spotted on their way to seize American arms at Concord, Americans responded with force. Thus, the War of Independence, also known as the American Revolution, began.

The second half of the eighteenth century was a time of swift and radical change, of action rather than reflection, and of the turning of many separate currents into one headlong stream. In January 1776, a public voice was widely heard in America demanding complete separation from Britain. The voice was that of Thomas Paine, whose pamphlet *Common Sense*, with its heated language, increased the growing demand for separation. It pointed the way toward the *Declaration of Independence* in July.

The hard-fought American Revolution against Britain (1775-1783) was the first modern war of liberation against a colonial power. The triumph of American independence seemed to many at the time a divine sign that America and her people were destined for greatness. Military victory fanned nationalistic hopes for a great new literature. Yet with the exception of outstanding political writing, few works of note appeared during or soon after the Revolution.

2.1.2 Cultural Background

During the eighteenth century, American literature underwent great changes in form, theme, and purpose as the colonies moved toward declaring their independence from Great Britain. As the century began, literature remained primarily religious in its endeavors to make sense of what still seemed a decidedly new world. As the century wore on, political thought — especially regarding the relationship between the colonies and the mother country — increasingly occupied American writers.

We will not be surprised to find that most American literature in the 18th century was political. Through newspapers, magazines, pamphlets, broadsides, and letters, colonial leaders discussed their ideas of human nature and of government. They began forging a new sense of national identity. Battles had to be fought before the thirteen colonies achieved independence. Nevertheless, for years before the first shot was fired, language was the source of growing American power. For those Americans, language became a weapon that could be used to fight for their independence.

The writings of this stormy period reflect the temper of two very different classes who were engaged in constant literary Party warfare. In the tense years the American people separated into two hostile parties: the Loyalists, who supported the mother country; and the Patriots, who insisted on the right of the colonies to manage their own affairs, and who furnished the armies that followed Washington in the War of Independence.

The Americans produced a great variety of unusual forms of literature: ballads, skits, broadsides, poems, editorials, essays, private and public letters, satires, pamphlets — written by people of every social class and almost every degree of skill. The energy of the age did not express itself in the usual forms with great original poetry, fiction, drama, music, or art. Yet a great number of Americans expressed themselves on the subjects of liberty, government, law, reason, and individual and national freedom. Throughout the land, weekly "Poet's Corners" in American newspapers never lacked locally written poems, songs, and satires. This writing was not sophisticated, but it was the writing of people whose lives were touched by the events of a turbulent time.

It is in the orations and pamphlets and state papers inspired by the Revolutionary agitation that we find the most satisfactory expression of the thought and feeling of that generation. Its typical literature is civic rather than aesthetic, a sort of writing which has been incidental to the accomplishing of some political, social, or moral purpose, and which scarcely regards itself as literature at all.

Many writers thought that the new nation possessed at least two unique subjects, two things no Europeans had experienced: the natural wilderness and the Revolution. They believed the majestic, awe-inspiring landscape provided a setting and even an antagonist that would be the basis of a great literature. They also believed that the Revolution provided stories of great human experiences and the beginning of an American mythology. They began to see the possibility of typical American characters in literature: The first American play, William Godfrey's *The Prince of Parthia* (1765), appeared during this period despite the moral censure accorded to theater in the colonies. It was followed by the first stage comedy, Royal Tyler's *The Contrast* (1787), which introduced Jonathan, the first stage Yankee.

Revolutions are expressions of the heart of the people; they grow gradually out of new sensibilities and wealth of experience. It would take 50 years of accumulated history for America to earn its cultural independence and to produce the first great generation of American writers: Washington Irving, James Fenimore Cooper, Ralph Waldo Emerson, Henry David Thoreau, Herman Melville, Nathaniel Hawthorne, Edgar Allan Poe, Walt Whitman, and Emily Dickinson.

2.1.3 The Enlightenment

The Enlightenment, conventionally seen as a European intellectual movement, was stimulated by the scientific revolution. It involved a new world view which explained the world and looked for answers in terms of reason rather than faith, and in terms of an optimistic, natural, humanistic approach rather than a fatalistic, supernatural one. During the Enlightenment, thinkers such as Voltaire, Montesquieu, Locke, Hobbes, and Rousseau made the radical proposition that reason and science could reveal the truth of life. Whatever the national or individual differences, the Enlightenment waged war on common enemies. In religion, it was against superstition, intolerance, and dogmatism; in politics, it was against tyranny; and in society, it was against prejudice, ignorance, inequality, and any obstacles to the realization of an individual's full intellectual and physical well-being.

This spirit of Enlightenment came rather late to the American colonies partly because of the cultural lag between dependencies and a mother country, partly because of the predominantly religious nature of the colonies, and partly because of the almost completely agrarian economy in America, which was not much concerned with scientific and technological development. Nevertheless, by the second half of the eighteenth century, the eastern seaboard cities had become centers of rationalistic thought. With its emphasis upon reason, its encouragement of scientific inquiry, and its almost childlike belief in the perfectibility of man and his world, the American Enlightenment marked a happy moving away from Puritan authoritarianism and produced a spirit of optimism especially fitting to the growing colonial culture. Many of the most distinguished leaders of the American Revolution — Jefferson, Washington, Franklin, Paine — were powerfully influenced by the European Enlightenment thought.

The American Enlightenment was categorized not only by knowledge of classical writings but also by an atmosphere where people craved new knowledge and wisdom. It was this craving that inspired people to make new developments in science, religion, and politics. Thomas Jefferson once said that a rational society is one that "informs the mind, sweetens the temper, cheers our spirits, and promotes health." Jefferson's attempt — a firm belief in progress, common sense, and the pursuit of happiness — is typical of the period we now call the Age of Reason.

2.2 Benjamin Franklin

2.2.1 About the Author

Benjamin Franklin (1706-1790) was born in Boston, the youngest son of a poor craftsman. As a child, Franklin had little formal education, but he taught himself by reading widely. When he was twelve, he was apprenticed to his half brother James, a printer and publisher. At the age of 17, he left his brother's employment and went to

 Philadelphia to work as a printer by himself. His qualities, industry and thrift, helped him to become a thriving printer.

As the owner and editor of *Pennsylvania Gazette* after 1730, Franklin made the periodical popular. Then he established a circulating library, organized a debating club that developed into the American Philosophical Society, and in 1751 helped to establish an academy that eventually became the University of Pennsylvania. In 1748 Franklin turned his printing business over to his foreman and devoted himself to his deepest interest — science. He did make substantial contributions to the scientific knowledge of his time. In fact, his work on lightning rods, earthquakes, bifocal eyeglasses, and electricity made him world famous.

Franklin was also one of the greatest statesmen of the American Revolution and of the newborn nation. He was a delegate to the Continental Congress. He was appointed to the committee that drafted the *Declaration of Independence*. He was chosen as one of the American diplomats to negotiate peace with Great Britain and laid the groundwork for the treaty. He also helped to direct the compromise that brought the Constitution of the United States into being. From 1757 until his final return to the United States in 1785, Franklin spent the vast majority of these years abroad, as a diplomat to Britain and France.

In 1771 when he was sixty-five, Franklin began to write an account of his life, which he intended for his son and was named as *The Autobiography*. The Puritan's emphasis on self-improvement, self-analysis, and moral and ethical values, along with the Enlightener's emphasis on rationalism, order, and education, could find fine expression in it. As the greatest literary artist in America in the Age of Enlightenment, Franklin helped establish a tradition in American writing of the simple, utilitarian style. It is the pattern of Puritan simplicity, directness, and concision. The lucidity of the narrative, the absence of ornaments in writing and of complex, involved structures in syntax and the Puritan abhorrence of paradox are demonstrated in the whole of the book.

2.2.2 An Excerpt from Chapter VIII of *The Autobiography*

It was about this time I conceived the bold and arduous project of arriving at moral perfection. I wished to live without committing any fault at any time; I would conquer all that either natural inclination, custom, or company might lead me into. As I knew, or thought I knew, what was right and wrong, I did not see why I might not always do the one and avoid the other. But I soon found I had undertaken a task of more difficulty than I had imagined. While my care was employed in guarding against one fault, I was often surprised by another; habit took the advantage of inattention; inclination was sometimes too strong for reason. I concluded, at length, that the mere speculative conviction that it was our interest to be completely virtuous, was not sufficient to prevent our slipping;

Chapter 2　The Literature of the Revolutionary Period

and that the contrary habits must be broken, and good ones acquired and established, before we can have any dependence on a steady, uniform rectitude of conduct. For this purpose I therefore contrived the following method.

In the various enumerations of the moral virtues I had met with in my reading, I found the catalogue more or less numerous, as different writers included more or fewer ideas under the same name. Temperance, for example, was by some confined to eating and drinking, while by others it was extended to mean the moderating every other pleasure, appetite, inclination, or passion, bodily or mental, even to our avarice and ambition. I proposed to myself, for the sake of clearness, to use rather more names, with fewer ideas annexed to each, than a few names with more ideas; and I included under thirteen names of virtues all that at that time occurred to me as necessary or desirable, and annexed to each a short precept,[1] which fully expressed the extent I gave to its meaning.

These names of virtues, with their precepts, were:

1. **Temperance.** Eat not to dullness; drink not to elevation.[2]
2. **Silence.** Speak not but what may benefit others or yourself; avoid trifling conversation.
3. **Order.** Let all your things have their places; let each part of your business have its time.
4. **Resolution.** Resolve to perform what you ought; perform without fail what you resolve.
5. **Frugality.** Make no expense but to do good to others or yourself; i. e., waste nothing.
6. **Industry.** Lose no time; be always employed in something useful; cut off all unnecessary actions.
7. **Sincerity.** Use no hurtful deceit; think innocently and justly, and, if you speak, speak accordingly.
8. **Justice.** Wrong none by doing injuries, or omitting the benefits that are your duty.
9. **Moderation.** Avoid extremes; forbear resenting injuries so much as you think they deserve.[3]
10. **Cleanliness.** Tolerate no uncleanliness in body, clothes, or habitation.
11. **Tranquillity.** Be not disturbed at trifles, or at accidents common or unavoidable.
12. **Chastity.** Rarely use venery but for health or offspring, never to dullness, weakness, or the injury of your own or another's peace or reputation.
13. **Humility.** Imitate Jesus and Socrates.[4]

My intention being to acquire the habitude of all these virtues, I judged it would be well not to distract my attention by attempting the whole at once, but to fix it on one of them at a time; and, when I should be master of that, then to proceed to another, and so on, till I should have gone thro' the thirteen; and, as the previous acquisition of some might facilitate the acquisition of certain others, I arranged them with that view, as they stand above. Temperance first, as it tends to procure that coolness and clearness of head, which is so necessary where constant vigilance was to be kept up, and guard maintained against the unremitting attraction of ancient habits, and the force of perpetual temptations. This being acquired and established, Silence would be more easy; and my desire being to gain knowledge at the same time that I improved in virtue, and considering that in conversation it was obtained rather by the use of the ears than of the tongue, and therefore wishing to break a habit I was getting into of prattling, punning, and joking, which only made me acceptable to trifling company, I gave Silence the second place. This and the next, Order, I expected would allow me more time for attending to my project and my studies. Resolution, once become habitual, would keep me firm in my endeavors to obtain all the subsequent virtues; Frugality and Industry freeing me from my remaining debt, and producing affluence and independence, would make more easy the practice of Sincerity and Justice, etc., etc. Conceiving then, that, agreeably to the advice of Pythagoras[5] in his Golden Verses, daily examination would be necessary, I contrived the following method for conducting that examination.

I made a little book, in which I allotted a page for each of the virtues. I ruled each page with red ink, so as to have seven columns, one for each day of the week, marking each column with a letter for the day. I crossed these columns with thirteen red lines, marking the beginning of each line with the first letter of one of the virtues, on which line, and in its proper column, I might mark, by a little black spot, every fault I found upon examination to have been committed respecting that virtue upon that day.

Form of the pages.

TEMPERANCE. *EAT NOT TO DULNESS; DRINK NOT TO ELEVATION.*							
	S.	M.	T.	W.	T.	F.	S.
T.							
S.	●●	●		●		●	
O.	●	●	●		●	●	●
R.			●			●	
F.		●			●		
I.				●			
S.							
J.							
M.							
C.							
T.							
C.							
H.							

Chapter 2　The Literature of the Revolutionary Period

　　I determined to give a week's strict attention to each of the virtues successively. Thus, in the first week, my great guard was to avoid every the least offence against Temperance, leaving the other virtues to their ordinary chance, only marking every evening the faults of the day. Thus, if in the first week I could keep my first line, marked T, clear of spots, I supposed the habit of that virtue so much strengthened and its opposite weakened, that I might venture extending my attention to include the next, and for the following week keep both lines clear of spots. Proceeding thus to the last, I could go thro' a course complete in thirteen weeks, and four courses in a year. And like him who, having a garden to weed, does not attempt to eradicate all the bad herbs at once, which would exceed his reach and his strength, but works on one of the beds at a time, and, having accomplished the first, proceeds to a second, so I should have, I hoped, the encouraging pleasure of seeing on my pages the progress I made in virtue, by clearing successively my lines of their spots, till in the end, by a number of courses, I should be happy in viewing a clean book, after a thirteen weeks' daily examination.

Notes
1. **precept**: rule.
2. **elevation**: slight drunkenness.
3. **forbear resenting injuries so much as you think they deserve**: refrain from resenting injuries, to whatever extent you think these injuries deserve resentment.
4. **Socrates**: Greek philosopher (B. C. 468-400) who initiated a question-and-answer method of teaching as a means of achieving self-knowledge. His theories of virtue and justice have survived through the writings of Plato, his most important pupil. Socrates was tried for corrupting the minds of Athenian youth and subsequently put to death.
5. **Pythagoras**: ancient Greek philosopher (B. C. 582-507). His teachings were influential for ages, but survive only in the tradition of his disciples. What Franklin refers to here is the Pythagorean discipline of "passionate intellectual contemplation."

Study Questions
1. Why does Franklin create his "method" for "moral perfection"?
2. What are the thirteen names of moral virtues that Franklin enumerated?
3. How can writing an autobiography contribute to self-knowledge?

2.3　Patrick Henry

2.3.1　About the Author
　　Patrick Henry (1736-1799) was born in Hanover County, Virginia. As a child, he had very little regular education. He was largely taught by his father, who had a good education. Later, Henry began his career as a storekeeper and tobacco farmer, but he

 was not successful. Then, when he was 18 he married Sarah Shelton and together they lived on a small farm. But in the meantime he acquired a taste for reading, of history especially.

Later Henry resolved to be a lawyer. He read and taught law to himself and surprisingly passed the bar examination. Within 3 years of practicing law, he had handled over 1100 cases. As a young lawyer, he astonished his courtroom audience in 1763 with an eloquent defense based on the idea of natural rights, the political theory that humans are born with certain inalienable rights. Simultaneously, he earned a reputation as a passionate and convincing speaker at once.

After having been elected to the Virginia House of Burgesses in 1765, he came to be a leader of the radical opposition to British rule. He opposed the Stamp Act, denounced George Ⅲ, called for united action by all the colonies against British "tyranny," and backed the boycott of British goods and the raising of a Continental army. During the second Virginia Convention in 1775, he delivered his most famous speech at St. John's Church in Richmond. His words became the clarion call that led the colonies into the Revolution. With courage and elegance, he cried, "I know not what course others may take, but as for me, give me liberty or give me death."

As the first governor of Virginia and as a state legislator, Henry continued to have profound influence on the development of the new nation. He also worked for the addition of the first ten amendments to the Constitution, which, known as the Bill of Rights, would guarantee certain freedoms, such as the freedom of speech and religion. Then Henry returned to his law practice and retired in 1794.

2.3.2 Speech in the Virginia Convention

Mr. President: No man thinks more highly than I do of the patriotism, as well as abilities, of the very worthy gentlemen who have just addressed the House. But different men often see the same subject in different lights; and, therefore, I hope it will not be thought disrespectful to those gentlemen if, entertaining as I do, opinions of a character very opposite to theirs, I shall speak forth my sentiments freely, and without reserve. This is no time for ceremony. The question before the House is one of awful moment[1] to this country. For my own part, I consider it as nothing less than a question of freedom or slavery; and in proportion to the magnitude of the subject ought to be the freedom of the debate. It is only in this way that we can hope to arrive at truth, and fulfil the great responsibility which we hold to God and our country. Should I keep back my opinions at such a time, through fear of giving offence, I should consider myself as guilty of treason towards my country, and of an act of disloyalty toward the majesty of heaven, which I revere above all earthly kings.[2]

Chapter 2 The Literature of the Revolutionary Period

  Mr. President, it is natural to man to indulge in the illusions of hope. We are apt to shut our eyes against a painful truth, and listen to the song of that siren till she transforms us into beasts.³ Is this the part of wise men, engaged in a great and arduous struggle for liberty? Are we disposed to be of the number of those who, having eyes, see not, and, having ears, hear not,⁴ the things which so nearly concern their temporal⁵ salvation? For my part, whatever anguish of spirit it may cost, I am willing to know the whole truth; to know the worst, and to provide for it.

  I have but one lamp by which my feet are guided; and that is the lamp of experience. I know of no way of judging of the future but by the past. And judging by the past, I wish to know what there has been in the conduct of the British ministry for the last ten years, to justify those hopes with which gentlemen have been pleased to solace themselves, and the House? Is it that insidious smile with which our petition has been lately received? Trust it not, sir; it will prove a snare to your feet. Suffer not yourselves to be betrayed with a kiss.⁶ Ask yourselves how this gracious reception of our petition comports with these war-like preparations which cover our waters and darken our land. Are fleets and armies necessary to a work of love and reconciliation? Have we shown ourselves so unwilling to be reconciled, that force must be called in to win back our love? Let us not deceive ourselves, sir. These are the implements of war and subjugation; the last arguments to which kings resort. I ask, gentlemen, sir, what means this martial array, if its purpose be not to force us to submission? Can gentlemen assign any other possible motive for it? Has Great Britain any enemy, in this quarter of the world, to call for all this accumulation of navies and armies? No, sir, she has none. They are meant for us; they can be meant for no other. They are sent over to bind and rivet upon us those chains which the British ministry have been so long forging. And what have we to oppose to them? Shall we try argument? Sir, we have been trying that for the last ten years. Have we anything new to offer upon the subject? Nothing. We have held the subject up in every light of which it is capable; but it has been all in vain. Shall we resort to entreaty and humble supplication? What terms shall we find which have not been already exhausted? Let us not, I beseech you, sir, deceive ourselves longer.

  Sir, we have done everything that could be done, to avert the storm which is now coming on. We have petitioned; we have remonstrated; we have supplicated; we have prostrated ourselves before the throne, and have implored its interposition⁷ to arrest the tyrannical hands of the ministry and Parliament. Our petitions have been slighted; our remonstrances have produced additional violence and insult; our supplications have been disregarded; and we have been spurned, with contempt, from the foot of the throne. In vain, after these things, may we indulge the fond⁸ hope of peace and reconciliation. There is no longer any room for hope. If we wish to be free if we mean to preserve inviolate those inestimable privileges for which we have been so long contending if we mean not basely to abandon the noble struggle in which we have been so long engaged, and which we have pledged ourselves never to abandon until the glorious object of our contest shall be obtained, we must fight! I repeat it, sir, we must fight! An appeal to arms and to the God of Hosts is all that is left us!

They tell us, sir, that we are weak; unable to cope with so formidable an adversary. But when shall we be stronger? Will it be the next week, or the next year? Will it be when we are totally disarmed, and when a British guard shall be stationed in every house? Shall we gather strength by irresolution and inaction? Shall we acquire the means of effectual resistance, by lying supinely on our backs, and hugging the delusive phantom of hope, until our enemies shall have bound us hand and foot? Sir, we are not weak if we make a proper use of those means which the God of nature has placed in our power. Three millions of people, armed in the holy cause of liberty, and in such a country as that which we possess, are invincible by any force which our enemy can send against us. Besides, sir, we shall not fight our battles alone. There is a just God who presides over the destinies of nations; and who will raise up friends to fight our battles for us. The battle, sir, is not to the strong alone;[9] it is to the vigilant, the active, the brave. Besides, sir, we have no election.[10] If we were base enough to desire it, it is now too late to retire from the contest. There is no retreat but in submission and slavery! Our chains are forged! Their clanking may be heard on the plains of Boston! The war is inevitable and let it come! I repeat it, sir, let it come.

It is in vain, sir, to extenuate the matter. Gentlemen may cry, Peace, Peace but there is no peace. The war is actually begun![11] The next gale that sweeps from the north[12] will bring to our ears the clash of resounding arms! Our brethren are already in the field! Why stand we here idle? What is it that gentlemen wish? What would they have? Is life so dear, or peace so sweet, as to be purchased at the price of chains and slavery? Forbid it, Almighty God! I know not what course others may take; but as for me, give me liberty or give me death!

Notes

1. **awful moment**: dreadful importance.
2. **I should consider myself as guilty of treason towards my country, and of an act of disloyalty toward the majesty of heaven, which I revere above all earthly kings**: Before the speech to the Second Virginia Convention, which was convened, among other reasons, to select delegates to the Continental Congress which would later declare American independence, Patrick Henry earned fame for his oratory as an attorney, as well as in the House of Burgesses (the Virginia Legislature), where, in 1765, he challenged a British tax (the Stamp Act), defying King George Ⅲ with the words "If this be treason, make the most of it."
3. **listen to the song of that siren till she transforms us into beasts**: In Homer's epic poem Odyssey, the enchantress Circe charms men with her song and then turns them into

swine.

4. **having eyes, see not, and, having ears, hear not**: In Ezekiel 12:2 the prophet addresses those "who have eyes to see, but see not, who have ears to hear, but hear not."
5. **temporal**: earthly.
6. **betrayed with a kiss**: In Luke 22:47-48 Judas betrays Jesus with a kiss.
7. **interposition**: intervention.
8. **fond**: foolish.
9. **The battle, sir, is not to the strong alone**: "The race is not to the swift, nor the battle to the strong" (Ecclesiastes 9:11).
10. **election**: choice.
11. **The war is actually begun**: This statement is a reference to the Boston Massacre of March 5, 1770, when British troops, occupying Boston to "keep order," killed five colonists at the head of an angry mob.
12. **the next gale that sweeps from the north**: In Massachusetts some colonists had already begun to show open resistance against the British.

Study Questions

1. What are the primary theme and mood of this speech?
2. What are the five main points in Patrick Henry's speech?
3. What did Patrick Henry say was Britain's purpose for sending a large army and navy to the colonies?
4. Why did Patrick Henry want a war?

2.4 Thomas Jefferson

2.4.1 About the Author

Thomas Jefferson (1743-1826) was born into a wealthy family in Virginia. When he was a boy he enjoyed hunting, fishing, riding horses and canoeing. He also loved music and learned to play the violin. He attended the College of William and Mary (1760-1762). After graduation, he studied law under George Wythe. He soon passed the bar exam and became a lawyer in Virginia. In 1769 he began six years of service as a representative in the Virginia House of Burgesses. In 1772 he married Martha Wayles Skelton, with whom he lived happily for ten years until her death.

Jefferson's reputation began to reach beyond Virginia in 1774, when he wrote a political pamphlet, A *Summary View of the Rights of British America*. Arguing on the basis of natural rights theory, Jefferson claimed that colonial allegiance to the king was voluntary. "The God who gave us life," he wrote, "gave us liberty at the same time: the hand of force may destroy, but cannot disjoin them."

Elected to the Second Continental Congress, meeting in Philadelphia, Jefferson was appointed on June 11, 1776, to head a committee of five in preparing the *Declaration of Independence*. That document, except for minor alterations by John Adams and Benjamin Franklin and some others made on the floor of Congress, was wholly the work of Jefferson. In spirit it reflects his debt to English political theorists, particularly John Locke, and to French and other continental philosophers.

In 1779, Jefferson succeeded Patrick Henry as governor of Virginia. In 1785 he succeeded Franklin as minister to France, and witnessed the beginning (1789) of the French Revolution. On his return (1790) he became Secretary of State. In 1796 he was elected as Vice-President of the United States. And in 1800 he was firstly elected as President of the Untied States and reelected in 1804. In the final 17 years of his life, Jefferson's major accomplishment was the founding of the University of Virginia (1819).

Jefferson was a scientist, an architect, and a philosopher-statesman, vitally interested in literature, the arts, and every phase of human activity. He passionately believed that a people enlightened by education, which must be kept free, could govern themselves better under democratic-republican institutions than under any other system. His most famous accomplishment was the writing of the *Declaration of Independence*. In this momentous decree, it was proclaimed that all men were created equal, regardless of birth, wealth, or status, and that the government is the servant, not the master, of the people. His writing style, shown in the *Declaration of Independence*, is simple, clear and powerful.

2.4.2 *Declaration of Independence*

When, in the course of human events, it becomes necessary for one people to dissolve the political bands which have connected them with another, and to assume among the powers of the earth, the separate and equal station to which the laws of nature and of nature's God entitle them, a decent respect to the opinions of mankind requires that they should declare the causes which impel them to the separation.

We hold these truths to be self-evident, that all men are created equal, that they are endowed by their Creator with certain unalienable[1] rights, that among these are life, liberty and the pursuit of happiness. That to secure these rights, governments are instituted among men, deriving their just powers from the consent of the governed. That whenever any form of government becomes destructive to these ends, it is the right of the people to alter or to abolish it, and to institute[2] new government, laying its foundation on such principles and organizing its powers in such form, as to them shall seem most likely to effect their safety and happiness. Prudence, indeed, will dictate that governments long established should not be changed for light and transient causes; and accordingly all experience hath shown that mankind are more disposed to suffer, while evils are sufferable, than to right[3] themselves by abolishing the forms to which they are accustomed. But when a long train of abuses and usurpations,[4] pursuing invariably the same object evinces a design to reduce them under absolute despotism,[5] it is their right, it is their duty, to throw off such government, and to provide new guards for their future security. — Such has been the patient sufferance of these colonies; and such is now the necessity which constrains[6] them to alter their former systems of government. The history of the present King of Great Britain is a history of repeated injuries and usurpations, all having in direct object the establishment of an absolute tyranny over these states. To prove this, let facts be submitted to a candid[7] world.

He has refused his assent to laws, the most wholesome and necessary for the public good.

He has forbidden his governors to pass laws of immediate and pressing importance, unless suspended in their operation till his assent should be obtained; and when so suspended, he has utterly neglected to attend to them.

He has refused to pass other laws for the accommodation of large districts of people, unless those people would relinquish the right of representation in the legislature, a right inestimable to them and formidable to tyrants only.

He has called together legislative bodies at places unusual, uncomfortable, and distant from the depository of their public records, for the sole purpose of fatiguing them into compliance with his measures.

He has dissolved representative houses repeatedly, for opposing with manly firmness his invasions on the rights of the people.

He has refused for a long time, after such dissolutions, to cause others to be elected; whereby the legislative powers, incapable of annihilation, have returned to the people at large for their exercise; the state remaining in the meantime exposed to all the dangers of invasion from without, and convulsions within.

He has endeavored to prevent the population of these states; for that purpose obstructing the laws for naturalization of foreigners; refusing to pass others to encourage their migration hither, and raising the conditions of new appropriations of lands.

He has obstructed the administration of justice, by refusing his assent to laws for establishing judiciary powers.

He has made judges dependent on his will alone, for the tenure of their offices, and the amount and payment of their salaries.

He has erected a multitude of new offices, and sent hither swarms of officers to harass our people, and eat out their substance.

He has kept among us, in times of peace, standing armies without the consent of our legislature.

He has affected to render the military independent of and superior to civil power.

He has combined with others to subject us to a jurisdiction foreign to our constitution, and unacknowledged by our laws; giving his assent to their acts of pretended legislation:

For quartering large bodies of armed troops among us:

For protecting them, by mock trial, from punishment for any murders which they should commit on the inhabitants of these states:

For cutting off our trade with all parts of the world:

For imposing taxes on us without our consent:

For depriving us in many cases, of the benefits of trial by jury:

For transporting us beyond seas to be tried for pretended offenses:

For abolishing the free system of English laws in a neighboring province,[8] establishing therein an arbitrary government, and enlarging its boundaries so as to render it at once an example and fit instrument for introducing the same absolute rule in these colonies:

For taking away our charters, abolishing our most valuable laws, and altering fundamentally the forms of our governments:

For suspending our own legislatures, and declaring themselves invested with power to legislate for us in all cases whatsoever.

He has abdicated government here, by declaring us out of his protection and waging war against us.

He has plundered our seas, ravaged our coasts, burned our towns, and destroyed the lives of our people.

He is at this time transporting large armies of foreign mercenaries to complete the works of death, desolation and tyranny, already begun with circumstances of cruelty and perfidy[9] scarcely paralleled in the most barbarous ages, and totally unworthy of the head of a civilized nation.

He has constrained our fellow citizens taken captive on the high seas to bear arms against their country, to become the executioners of their friends and brethren, or to fall themselves by their hands.

He has excited domestic insurrections amongst us, and has endeavored to bring on the inhabitants of our frontiers, the merciless Indian savages, whose known rule of warfare, is undistinguished destruction of all ages, sexes and conditions.

In every stage of these oppressions we have petitioned for redress[10] in the most humble terms: our repeated petitions have been answered only by repeated injury. A prince, whose character is thus marked by every act which may define a tyrant, is unfit

Chapter 2   The Literature of the Revolutionary Period

to be the ruler of a free people.

Nor have we been wanting in attention to our British brethren. We have warned them from time to time of attempts by their legislature[11] to extend an unwarrantable jurisdiction over us. We have reminded them of the circumstances of our emigration and settlement here. We have appealed to their native justice and magnanimity, and we have conjured[12] them by the ties of our common kindred to disavow these usurpations, which would inevitably interrupt our connections and correspondence. They too have been deaf to the voice of justice and of consanguinity.[13] We must, therefore, acquiesce in the necessity, which denounces[14] our separation, and hold them, as we hold the rest of mankind, enemies in war, in peace friends.

We, therefore, the representatives of the United States of America, in General Congress, assembled, appealing to the Supreme Judge of the world for the rectitude of our intentions, do, in the name, and by the authority of the good people of these colonies, solemnly publish and declare, that these united colonies are, and of right ought to be free and independent states; that they are absolved from all allegiance to the British Crown, and that all political connection between them and the state of Great Britain, is and ought to be totally dissolved; and that as free and independent states, they have full power to levy war, conclude peace, contract alliances, establish commerce, and to do all other acts and things which independent states may of right do. And for the support of this declaration, with a firm reliance on the protection of Divine Providence, we mutually pledge to each other our lives, our fortunes and our sacred honor.

Notes
1. **unalienable**: that cannot be taken away.
2. **institute**: to establish, organize.
3. **right**: to make reparation or amends for.
4. **usurpations**: unlawful seizures of power.
5. **despotism**: tyranny.
6. **constrain**: to force.
7. **candid**: impartial.
8. **abolishing the free system of English laws in a neighboring province**: In 1774 the British, having captured Quebec, forced strict laws on colonists there.
9. **perfidy**: betrayal of trust.
10. **redress**: just compensations for a wrong doing.
11. **legislature**: British Parliament.
12. **conjured**: solemnly appealed to.
13. **consanguinity**: blood relationship.
14. **denounces**: here announces.

Study Questions

1. According to the first paragraph, what does "a decent respect to the opinions of mankind" require?
2. According to the second paragraph, what truths are self-evident? What is the purpose of government, and when should a government be replaced?
3. In the final sentence of the Declaration, the signers pledge their "fortunes," or fate. What do you think their fate would have been if Britain had been the victor in the war?
4. What was the purpose of the *Declaration of Independence*?

Chapter 3　The Literature of the Romantic Period

3.1　An Introduction

　　Romanticism is a movement that marked a partial reaction in literature, philosophy, art, religion, and politics from the Neoclassicism of the preceding period. For romantics, the feelings, intuitions and emotions were more important than reason and common sense. The movement originated in Germany but quickly spread to England, France, and other countries. It reached America around the year 1820, when Washington Irving published *The Sketch Book*. It came to an end when the American Civil War broke out. Being a period of the great flowering of American literature, it is also called "the American Renaissance".

　　With the success of the American Revolution, the young Republic, unburdened with the inherited past and history, was flourishing into a politically, economically and culturally independent country. Historically, it was the time of westward expansion. The western boundary had reached to the Pacific by 1860; the number of its states had increased from the original thirteen at the time of its independence to twenty-one by the middle of the 19th century; its total population increased from four million people in 1790 to thirty million in 1860. Politically, democracy and equality became the ideal of the new nation, and the two-party system came into being. The Romantic spirit seemed particularly suited to American democracy. It stressed individualism, affirmed the value of the common people, and looked to the inspired imagination for its aesthetic and ethical values. Economically, the whole nation was experiencing an industrial revolution, which affected the rural as well as the urban life. The use of steam power in industry and agriculture, the erection of factories and textile mills, the demand of a large employment, and the technological innovations all helped restructure the economic life. In addition, the new tide of immigration gave a big push to the already booming industry. Besides, the level of education and literacy had increased significantly. Magazines, newspapers, journals appeared in ever-increased numbers. It is this fast development of American society that provides the fertile soil to American romantic literature.

　　Foreign influences, especially those from Great Britain, exerted a great impact on the writers of the new world. Born of the same cultural heritage, the American writers shared some common features with the English Romanticists. They both believed in man's being good in nature and corruption in society; they both stressed individualism and affirmed the inner life of the self; they both cherished strong interest in the past, especially the medieval, and were attracted by the wild, the indefinite, the exotic, the mysterious, and the strange. However, American romanticism exhibited from the very beginning some distinct features of its own. The national experience of "pioneering into the west" proved to be rich and unique resources for American writers. America's vast mountains, fertile plains and exotic landscapes inspired many native imaginations. In addition, American Puritanism as a very important cultural heritage also exerted a great influence over American literature. American moral values were essentially puritan. Compared with their European counterparts, American romantic writers tended more to moralize than to entertain in their works.

The phase of New England Transcendentalism is the summit of American Romanticism. It was, in essence, romanticism on Puritan soil. This transcendental movement, based on a fundamental belief in the unity of the world and God, was first flourished in New England from the 1830s to the Civil War. Transcendentalism emphasized the power of intuition, believing that people could learn things both from the outside world by means of the five senses and from the inner world by intuition. As romantic idealism, it placed spirit first and matter second. It believed that spirit transcended matter, and the permanent reality was the spiritual one. It took nature as symbolic of spirit of God. All things in nature were symbols of the spiritual, of God's presence. It believed that the individual was the most important element in society and that the ideal kind of individual was self-reliant and unselfish. Transcendentalism was also an ethical guide to life for the young nation of America. It preached the positive life and appealed to the best side of human nature. Therefore, it advocated the tolerance of difference in religious opinion and the free control of its own affairs by each congregation, and to go forward to the development of a new and distinctly American culture. The two greatest advocates of the movement were Ralph Waldo Emerson and Henry David Thoreau.

In this romantic period, there came up a great number of important writers, among whom the better known are poets such as Philip Freneau, William Cullen Bryant, Henry Wordsworth Longfellow, Edgar Ellen Poe, and, especially, Walt Whitman, whose *Leaves of Grass* established him as the most popular American poet of the 19th century. The fiction of the American Romantic period is an original and diverse body of work. It ranges from the comic fables of Washington Irving to the Gothic tales of Edgar Allen Poe, from the frontier adventures of James Fenimore Cooper to the narrative quests of Herman Melville, from the psychological romances of Nathaniel Hawthorne to the social realism of Rebecca Harding Davis. American Romanticists also differed in their understanding of human nature. To the transcendentalists such as Emerson and Thoreau, man is divine in nature and therefore forever perfectible; but to Hawthorne and Melville, everybody is potentially a sinner, and great moral courage is therefore essential for the improvement of human nature, as is shown in Hawthorne's *The Scarlet Letter*.

3.2 Washington Irving

3.2.1 About the Author

Washington Irving (1783-1859) was born in New York City. Early in his life he developed a passion for books, though he did not have much formal education. After elementary school, Irving began to study law, but his studies were interrupted by an illness. From 1804 to 1806, he traveled widely in Europe. When he returned home, he was called to the bar. However, he made little effort to practice his profession, preferring to amuse himself with literary ventures. Irving was engaged to Matilda Hoffman, but unfortunately his fiancée died before they got married. After that Irving kept unmarried all his life.

Irving's career as a writer started in journals and newspapers. He contributed to the *Morning Chronicle* (1802-1803) and published *Salmagundi* (1807-1808). Irving enjoyed visiting different places and a large part of his life was spent in Europe. He often wrote about the places he visited. However, in spite of his foreign travels, Irving's imagination frequently drew upon his childhood memories of New York State. In 1819-1820 he published *The Sketch Book of Geoffrey Crayon*, which includes his best known stories. In 1832, Irving established his home Sunnyside in Tarrytown. After seventeen years' absence, he found his name a household word, and himself universally honored as the first American who had won for his country recognition on equal terms in the literary world. And Sunnyside was visited by many artists, politicians, writers, and other influential people.

Irving was a proliferate writer and wrote a large number of books. His diverse works include *The Life and Voyages of Christopher Columbus* (1828), *The Alhambra* (1832), *A Tour of the Prairies* (1835), and *The Adventures of Captain Bonneville U. S. A.* (1837). However, his *Sketch Book*, which included the two famous stories, "Rip Van Winkle" and "The Legend of Sleepy Hollow," remains his most recognized and influential contribution to American literature.

Irving was admired as a leading American author during his lifetime. His work reflected the shift in American literature from the rationalism of the 18th century to the sentimental romanticism of the 19th century. But his taste was essentially conservative. He always exalted a disappearing past. In "Rip Van Winkle," Irving skillfully presented to us paralleled juxtapositions of two totally different worlds before and after Rip's 20 year's sleep. By moving Rip back and forth from a noisy world with his wife on the farm to a wild but peaceful natural world in the mountains, Irving described Rip's response and reaction in a dramatic way. Besides, Irving tried to associate a certain place with the inward movement of a person and to charge his sentences with emotion so as to create a true and vivid character. And his style and choice of subjects greatly influenced future writers in America.

3.2.2 An Excerpt from *Rip Van Winkle*

On waking, he found himself on the green knoll whence he had first seen the old man of the glen. He rubbed his eyes — it was a bright sunny morning. The birds were hopping and twittering among the bushes, and the eagle was wheeling aloft, and breasting the pure mountain breeze. "Surely," thought Rip, "I have not slept here all night." He recalled the occurrences before he fell asleep. The strange man with a keg of liquor — the mountain ravine — the wild retreat among the rocks — the woe-begone[1] party at ninepins — the flagon — "Oh! that flagon! that wicked flagon!" thought Rip — "what excuse shall I make to Dame Van Winkle!"

He looked round for his gun, but in place of the clean well-oiled fowling-piece, he found an old firelock lying by him, the barrel incrusted with rust, the lock falling off, and the stock worm-eaten. He now suspected that the grave roysterers[2] of the mountain had put a trick upon him, and having dosed him with liquor, had robbed him of his gun. Wolf, too, had disappeared, but he might have strayed away after a squirrel or partridge. He whistled after him and shouted his name, but all in vain; the echoes repeated his whistle and shout, but no dog was to be seen.

He determined to revisit the scene of the last evening's gambol, and if he met with any of the party, to demand his dog and gun. As he rose to walk, he found himself stiff in the joints, and wanting in his usual activity. "These mountain beds do not agree with me," thought Rip; "and if this frolic should lay me up with a fit of the rheumatism, I shall have a blessed time with Dame Van Winkle." With some difficulty he got down into the glen: he found the gully up which he and his companion had ascended the preceding evening; but to his astonishment a mountain stream was now foaming down it, leaping from rock to rock, and filling the glen with babbling murmurs. He, however, made shift to scramble up its sides, working his toilsome way through thickets of birch, sassafras,[3] and witch-hazel,[4] and sometimes tripped up or entangled by the wild grapevines that twisted their coils or tendrils from tree to tree, and spread a kind of network in his path.

At length he reached to where the ravine had opened through the cliffs to the amphitheatre; but no traces of such opening remained. The rocks presented a high impenetrable wall over which the torrent came tumbling in a sheet of feathery foam, and fell into a broad deep basin, black from the shadows of the surrounding forest. Here, then, poor Rip was brought to a stand. He again called and whistled after his dog; he was only answered by the cawing of a flock of idle crows, sporting high in air about a dry tree that overhung a sunny precipice; and who, secure in their elevation, seemed to look down and scoff at the poor man's perplexities. What was to be done? The morning was passing away, and Rip felt famished for want of his breakfast. He grieved to give up his dog and gun; he dreaded to meet his wife; but it would not do to starve among the mountains. He shook his head, shouldered the rusty firelock, and, with a heart full of trouble and anxiety, turned his steps homeward.

As he approached the village he met a number of people, but none whom he knew, which somewhat surprised him, for he had thought himself acquainted with every one in the country round. Their dress, too, was of a different fashion from that to which he was accustomed. They all stared at him with equal marks of surprise, and whenever they cast their eyes upon him, invariably stroked their chins. The constant recurrence of this gesture induced Rip, involuntarily, to do the same, when to his astonishment, he found his beard had grown a foot long!

He had now entered the skirts of the village. A troop of strange children ran at his heels, hooting after him, and pointing at his gray beard. The dogs, too, not one of which he recognized for an old acquaintance, barked at him as he passed. The very village was altered; it was larger and more populous. There were rows of houses which he had never seen before, and those which had been his familiar haunts had disappeared. Strange names were over the doors — strange faces at the windows — every thing was strange. His mind now misgave him; he began to doubt whether both he and the world around him were not bewitched. Surely this was his native village, which he had left but the day before. There stood the Kaatskill mountains — there ran the silver Hudson at a distance — there was every hill and dale precisely as it had always been — Rip was sorely perplexed — "That flagon last night," thought he, "has addled my poor head sadly!"

It was with some difficulty that he found the way to his own house, which he approached with silent awe, expecting every moment to hear the shrill voice of Dame Van Winkle. He found the house gone to decay — the roof fallen in, the windows shattered, and the doors off the hinges. A half-starved dog that looked like Wolf was skulking about it. Rip called him by name, but the cur snarled, showed his teeth, and passed on. This was an unkind cut indeed — "My very dog," sighed poor Rip, "has forgotten me!"

He entered the house, which, to tell the truth, Dame Van Winkle had always kept in neat order. It was empty, forlorn, and apparently abandoned. This desolateness overcame all his connubial[5] fears — he called loudly for his wife and children — the lonely chambers rang for a moment with his voice, and then all again was silence.

He now hurried forth, and hastened to his old resort, the village inn — but it too was gone. A large rickety wooden building stood in its place, with great gaping windows, some of them broken and mended with old hats and petticoats, and over the door was painted, "The Union Hotel, by Jonathan Doolittle." Instead of the great tree that used to shelter the quiet little Dutch inn of yore,[6] there now was reared a tall naked pole, with something on the top that looked like a red night-cap, and from it was fluttering a flag, on which was a singular assemblage of stars and stripes[7] — all this was strange and incomprehensible. He recognized on the sign, however, the ruby face of King George, under which he had smoked so many a peaceful pipe; but even this was singularly metamorphosed. The red coat was changed for one of blue and buff, a sword was held in the hand instead of a sceptre, the head was decorated with a cocked hat, and underneath was painted in large characters, General Washington.

There was, as usual, a crowd of folk about the door, but none that Rip recollected. The very character of the people seemed changed. There was a busy, bustling, disputatious tone about it, instead of the accustomed phlegm and drowsy tranquility. He looked in vain for the sage Nicholas Vedder, with his broad face, double chin, and fair long pipe, uttering clouds of tobacco-smoke instead of idle speeches; or Van Bummel, the schoolmaster, doling forth the contents of an ancient newspaper. In place of these, a lean, bilious-looking[8] fellow, with his pockets full of handbills, was haranguing[9] vehemently about rights of citizens — elections — members of congress — liberty — Bunker's Hill — heroes of seventy-six — and other words, which were a perfect Babylonish jargon[10] to the bewildered Van Winkle.

The appearance of Rip, with his long grizzled beard, his rusty fowling-piece, his uncouth dress, and an army of women and children at his heels, soon attracted the attention of the tavern politicians. They crowded round him, eyeing him from head to foot with great curiosity. The orator bustled up to him, and, drawing him partly aside, inquired "on which side he voted?" Rip stared in vacant stupidity. Another short but busy little fellow pulled him by the arm, and, rising on tiptoe, inquired in his ear, "Whether he was Federal or Democrat?" Rip was equally at a loss to comprehend the question; when a knowing, self-important old gentleman, in a sharp cocked hat, made his way through the crowd, putting them to the right and left with his elbows as he passed, and planting himself before Van Winkle, with one arm akimbo,[11] the other resting on his cane, his keen eyes and sharp hat penetrating, as it were, into his very soul, demanded in an austere tone, "what brought him to the election with a gun on his shoulder, and a mob at his heels, and whether he meant to breed a riot in the village?"
— "Alas! gentlemen," cried Rip, somewhat dismayed, "I am a poor quiet man, a native of the place, and a loyal subject of the king, God bless him!"

Here a general shout burst from the by-standers — "A tory! a tory! a spy! a refugee! hustle him! away with him!" It was with great difficulty that the self-important man in the cocked hat restored order; and, having assumed a tenfold austerity of brow, demanded again of the unknown culprit, what he came there for, and whom he was seeking? The poor man humbly assured him that he meant no harm, but merely came there in search of some of his neighbors, who used to keep about the tavern.

"Well — who are they? — name them."

Rip bethought himself a moment, and inquired, "Where's Nicholas Vedder?"

There was a silence for a little while, when an old man replied, in a thin piping voice, "Nicholas Vedder! why, he is dead and gone these eighteen years! There was a wooden tombstone in the church-yard that used to tell all about him, but that's rotten and gone too."

"Where's Brom Dutcher?"

"Oh, he went off to the army in the beginning of the war; some say he was killed at the storming of Stony Point[12] — others say he was drowned in a squall at the foot of Antony's Nose.[13] I don't know — he never came back again."

"Where's Van Bummel, the schoolmaster?"

"He went off to the wars too, was a great militia general, and is now in congress."

Rip's heart died away at hearing of these sad changes in his home and friends, and finding himself thus alone in the world. Every answer puzzled him too, by treating of such enormous lapses of time, and of matters which he could not understand: war — congress — Stony Point; — he had no courage to ask after any more friends, but cried out in despair, "Does nobody here know Rip Van Winkle?"

"Oh, Rip Van Winkle!" exclaimed two or three, "Oh, to be sure! that's Rip Van Winkle yonder, leaning against the tree."

Rip looked, and beheld a precise counterpart of himself, as he went up the mountain: apparently as lazy, and certainly as ragged. The poor fellow was now completely confounded. He doubted his own identity, and whether he was himself or another man. In the midst of his bewilderment, the man in the cocked hat demanded who he was, and what was his name?

"God knows," exclaimed he, at his wit's end; "I'm not myself — I'm somebody else — that's me yonder — no — that's somebody else got into my shoes — I was myself last night, but I fell asleep on the mountain, and they've changed my gun, and every thing's changed, and I'm changed, and I can't tell what's my name, or who I am!"

The by-standers began now to look at each other, nod, wink significantly, and tap their fingers against their foreheads. There was a whisper also, about securing the gun, and keeping the old fellow from doing mischief, at the very suggestion of which the self-important man in the cocked hat retired with some precipitation. At this critical moment a fresh comely woman pressed through the throng to get a peep at the gray-bearded man. She had a chubby child in her arms, which, frightened at his looks, began to cry. "Hush, Rip," cried she, "hush, you little fool; the old man won't hurt you." The name of the child, the air of the mother, the tone of her voice, all awakened a train of recollections in his mind. "What is your name, my good woman?" asked he.

"Judith Gardenier."

"And your father's name?"

"Ah, poor man, Rip Van Winkle was his name, but it's twenty years since he went away from home with his gun, and never has been heard of since — his dog came home without him; but whether he shot himself, or was carried away by the Indians, nobody can tell. I was then but a little girl."

Rip had but one question more to ask; but he put it with a faltering voice:

"Where's your mother?"

"Oh, she too had died but a short time since; she broke a blood-vessel in a fit of passion at a New-England peddler."

There was a drop of comfort, at least, in this intelligence. The honest man could contain himself no longer. He caught his daughter and her child in his arms. "I am your father!" cried he — "Young Rip Van Winkle once — old Rip Van Winkle now! — Does nobody know poor Rip Van Winkle?"

All stood amazed, until an old woman, tottering out from among the crowd, put her hand to her brow, and peering under it in his face for a moment, exclaimed, "Sure enough! it is Rip Van Winkle — it is himself! Welcome home again, old neighbor — Why, where have you been these twenty long years?"

Rip's story was soon told, for the whole twenty years had been to him but as one night. The neighbors stared when they heard it; some were seen to wink at each other, and put their tongues in their cheeks: and the self-important man in the cocked hat, who, when the alarm was over, had returned to the field, screwed down the corners of his mouth, and shook his head — upon which there was a general shaking of the head throughout the assemblage.

It was determined, however, to take the opinion of old Peter Vanderdonk, who was seen slowly advancing up the road. He was a descendant of the historian of that name, who wrote one of the earliest accounts of the province. Peter was the most ancient inhabitant of the village, and well versed in all the wonderful events and traditions of the neighborhood. He recollected Rip at once, and corroborated his story in the most satisfactory manner. He assured the company that it was a fact, handed down from his ancestor the historian, that the Kaatskill mountains had always been haunted by strange beings. That it was affirmed that the great Hendrick Hudson, the first discoverer of the river and country, kept a kind of vigil there every twenty years, with his crew of the Half-moon; being permitted in this way to revisit the scenes of his enterprise, and keep a

Chapter 3 The Literature of the Romantic Period

guardian eye upon the river, and the great city called by his name. That his father had once seen them in their old Dutch dresses playing at nine-pins in a hollow of the mountain; and that he himself had heard, one summer afternoon, the sound of their balls, like distant peals of thunder.

To make a long story short, the company broke up, and returned to the more important concerns of the election. Rip's daughter took him home to live with her; she had a snug, well-furnished house, and a stout cheery farmer for a husband, whom Rip recollected for one of the urchins that used to climb upon his back. As to Rip's son and heir, who was the ditto[14] of himself, seen leaning against the tree, he was employed to work on the farm; but evinced an hereditary disposition to attend to anything else but his business.

Rip now resumed his old walks and habits; he soon found many of his former cronies,[15] though all rather the worse for the wear and tear of time; and preferred making friends among the rising generation, with whom he soon grew into great favor.

Having nothing to do at home, and being arrived at that happy age when a man can be idle with impunity, he took his place once more on the bench at the inn door, and was reverenced as one of the patriarchs of the village, and a chronicle of the old times "before the war." It was some time before he could get into the regular track of gossip, or could be made to comprehend the strange events that had taken place during his torpor. How that there had been a revolutionary war — that the country had thrown off the yoke of old England — and that, instead of being a subject of his Majesty George the Third, he was now a free citizen of the United States. Rip, in fact, was no politician; the changes of states and empires made but little impression on him; but there was one species of despotism under which he had long groaned, and that was — petticoat government.[16] Happily that was at an end; he had got his neck out of the yoke of matrimony, and could go in and out whenever he pleased, without dreading the tyranny of Dame Van Winkle. Whenever her name was mentioned, however, he shook his head, shrugged his shoulders, and cast up his eyes; which might pass either for an expression of resignation to his fate, or joy at his deliverance.

He used to tell his story to every stranger that arrived at Mr. Doolittle's hotel. He was observed, at first, to vary on some points every time he told it, which was, doubtless, owing to his having so recently awaked. It at last settled down precisely to the tale I have related, and not a man, woman, or child in the neighborhood, but knew it by heart. Some always pretended to doubt the reality of it, and insisted that Rip had been out of his head, and that this was one point on which he always remained flighty. The old Dutch inhabitants, however, almost universally gave it full credit. Even to this day they never hear a thunderstorm of a summer afternoon about the Kaatskill, but they say Hendrick Hudson and his crew are at their game of nine-pins; and it is a common wish of all hen-pecked husbands in the neighborhood, when life hangs heavy on their hands, that they might have a quieting draught out of Rip Van Winkle's flagon.

Notes
1. **the woe-begone**: the depressed.
2. **roysterers**: people who play and drink at the same time.
3. **sassafras**: A deciduous eastern North American tree having irregularly lobed leaves and aromatic bark, leaves, and branches.
4. **witch-hazel**: type of Asian or North American tree with yellow flowers.
5. **connubial**: relating to marriage or the married state.
6. **of yore**: long ago.
7. **... fluttering a flag, on which was a singular assemblage of stars and stripes**: refers to American National flag.
8. **bilious-looking**: short-tempered; ill-humored.
9. **haranguing**: serious and angry.
10. **Babylonish jargon**: Genesis11. 1-9, Babel being confused with Babylon. Here it means confusing words.
11. **with one arm akimbo**: with one arm on the hip.
12. **Stony Point**: site of a fort in the Revolutionary War, on the west bank of the Hudson south of West Point. On July 15th, 1779, American defeated British army here, now it's a state historic site for tourists.
13. **Antony's Nose**: mountain near West Point, another fortified.
14. **ditto**: copy, duplicate.
15. **cronies**: friends, partners.
16. **petticoat government**: control of women.

Study Questions
1. What historical events did Rip Van Winkle sleep through?
2. Why was Rip Van Winkle so surprised when he returned to the village?
3. What do the war and the death of Rip's wife have in common in terms of how Rip will live the rest of his life?
4. What comparison is Irving implying when he states at the end of the story that Dame Van Winkle's death has released Rip from "petticoat government"?
5. How much effect did American Revolution have on daily life of the common people?

Essay Topics
1. Analyze the humorous elements in "Rip Van Winkle".
2. How can the story be seen as dealing with the change from a British monarchy to an American democracy?

3.3 Edgar Allan Poe

3.3.1 About the Author

Edgar Allan Poe (1809-1849) was born in Boston, Massachusetts. Both his parents died before he was 3 years old. The poor orphan was taken into the home of John Allan, a prosperous merchant in Richmond. When Poe was 6, he went to school in England for 5 years. He learned Latin and French, as well as math and history. Returning to Virginia, he continued his education and attended the University of Virginia in 1826. He showed remarkable scholastic ability in classical languages but was forced to leave the university after only eight months because of quarrels with Allan over his gambling debts. Allan later  disowned him. Lacking any means of support, Poe enlisted himself in the army. In 1830, Poe entered West Point as a cadet, but his stay there was short-lived.

Poe next took up residence in Baltimore with his widowed aunt and her daughter, Virginia, and started a career as a journalist and an editor for various magazines. In 1836, Edgar married his cousin, Virginia. In order to support his family, Poe began to place short stories in magazines. His first volume of short stories, *Tales of the Grotesque and Arabesque* was published in 1839. It was during this period that Poe wrote some of his best stories and poetry. When his poem, "The Raven", was published in 1845, fame came to him swiftly, but there was still never enough money to make his family financially secure. In early 1847, Poe's young wife, Virginia, died of consumption. During the years following his wife's death, Poe's life was taking a steady turn downward. He began to lose his struggle with drinking and drugs. At the age of 40, his wretched and painful life finally came to an end.

A master of symbolism, Poe is considered to be the father of the detective story, and he remains one of the most timeless and extraordinary of all American creative artists. And his stories, such as "The Fall of the House of Usher" (1839), "Murders in the Rue Morgue" (1841), and "The Goldbug" (1843), would later be regarded as classics of their genre. His poems, including "To Helen," "The Raven," "The City in the Sea," "The Bells," and "Annabel Lee," are rich with musical phrases and sensuous images. By his influential literary contribution, Poe holds a unique position in the history of American literature. His popularity in the world is also ever-increasing.

3.3.2 "To Helen[1]"

Helen, thy beauty is to me
Like those Nicean barks[2] of yore
That gently, over a perfumed sea,
The weary, way-worn wanderer bore
To his own native shore.

On desperate seas long wont to roam,
Thy hyacinth hair, thy classic face,
Thy Naiad[3] airs have brought me home
To the glory that was Greece,
And the grandeur that was Rome.

Lo, in yon brilliant window-niche[4]
How statue-like I see thee stand,
The agate[5] lamp within thy hand,
Ah! Psyche,[6] from the regions which
Are Holy Land!

Notes

1. "**To Helen**": This is a poem often praised as a near-perfect statement of the Romantics' idealized love of pure beauty. Poe claimed that the mother of a school friend was the inspiration for Helen. However, the poem is not about any actual woman but about an ideal of beauty that can exist only in the imagination.
2. **Nicean barks**: Poe may be referring to boats from the shipbuilding city of Nicea in Asia Minor near the Trojan War site. It is likely, however, that he created the phrase for its melodious sound.
3. **Naiad**: in classical mythology, nymphs of quite fresh water. "Naiad airs" probably suggest restfulness.
4. **window-niche**: a recess in a wall, as for holding a statue.
5. **agate**: a hard stone with bands of different colors, used in jewellery. In antiquity, lamps made of agate were associated with immortality.
6. **Psyche**: a mortal loved by Cupid, she disobeyed his command not to try to find out who he was. He fled. Eventually reunited with him, she was changed into an immortal who personified "the breath of life, the human spirit or soul."

Study Questions

1. What does the title of the poem mean to you?
2. What words or phrases are direct or indirect references to ancient beliefs and stories?

What do these allusions contribute to Helen's meaning in the poem?
3. What is the theme of this poem?

3.3.3 "Annabel Lee[1]"

It was many and many a year ago,
In a kingdom by the sea,
That a maiden there lived whom you may know
By the name of ANNABEL LEE;
And this maiden she lived with no other thought
Than to love and be loved by me.

I was a child and she was a child,
In this kingdom by the sea;
But we loved with a love that was more than love —
I and my Annabel Lee;
With a love that the winged seraphs[2] of heaven
Coveted[3] her and me.

And this was the reason that, long ago,
In this kingdom by the sea,
A wind blew out of a cloud, chilling
My beautiful Annabel Lee;
So that her highborn kinsman came
And bore her away from me,
To shut her up in a sepulcher[4]
In this kingdom by the sea.

The angels, not half so happy in heaven,
Went envying her and me —
Yes! — that was the reason (as all men know,
In this kingdom by the sea)
That the wind came out of the cloud by night,
Chilling and killing my Annabel Lee.

But our love it was stronger by far than the love
Of those who were older than we —
Of many far wiser than we —
And neither the angels in heaven above,

> Nor the demons down under the sea,
> Can ever dissever[5] my soul from the soul
> Of the beautiful Annabel Lee.
>
> For the moon never beams without bringing me dreams
> Of the beautiful Annabel Lee;
> And the stars never rise but I feel the bright eyes
> Of the beautiful Annabel Lee;
> And so, all the night-tide, I lie down by the side
> Of my darling — my darling — my life and my bride,
> In the sepulcher there by the sea,
> In her tomb by the sounding sea.

Notes

1. **Annabel Lee**: It is Poe's last poem, believed to have been dedicated to the memory of his wife. But several women known to Poe have claimed to the real-life Annabel Lee. However, the likelihood might be that the poet was dramatizing a universal situation common in earlier times when parents arranged marriages and took harsh measures against daughters who did not cooperate.
2. **seraphs**: one kind of angels that protects the seat of God according to the bible.
3. **coveted**: to have a very strong desire to have something that someone else has.
4. **sepulcher**: a small room or building in which the bodies of dead people were put.
5. **dissever**: to separate a person or thing from another.

Study Questions

1. What is the function of the repetition of the line "In this kingdom by the sea"?
2. In what sense does the poem read like a story?
3. What personal images help the reader to grasp the speaker's intense feelings of loss?
4. How does the speaker describe his love for Annabel Lee?

3.4 Ralph Waldo Emerson

3.4.1 About the author

Ralph Waldo Emerson (1803-1882) was born in Boston, Massachusetts. He was educated in Boston and Harvard. While at Harvard, he began keeping a journal, which became a source of his later lectures, essays, and books. Between the years of 1821 and 1825 upon graduating Harvard, Emerson took a job in teaching in the Boston area. Although he found little pleasure in his work as a teacher, he did enjoy walking tours and attempting poetry. In 1829 Emerson married the seventeen-year-old Ellen Louisa Tucker, who died in 1831 from tuberculosis. Emerson's first and only settlement was at the important Second Unitarian Church of Boston, where he became sole pastor in 1830. Emerson traveled to Europe in 1832. He met William Wordsworth, Samuel Taylor Coleridge, and Thomas Carlyle, with whom he corresponded for half a century. After returning to the United States, Emerson lectured on natural history, biology, and history. In 1835 Emerson married Lydia Jackson and settled with her at the east end of the village of Concord, Massachusetts, where he then spent the rest of his life.

Emerson's first book, *Nature*, a collection of essays, appeared in 1836 when he was thirty-three. Emerson emphasized individualism and rejected traditional authority. He invited the world to "enjoy an original relation to the universe" and emphasized "the infinitude of the private man." The book was regarded as the Bible of New England Transcendentalism. It made a tremendous impact on the intellectual life of America. His lectures *The American Scholar* (1837) and *Address at Divinity College* (1838) challenged the Harvard intelligentsia and warned about a lifeless Christian tradition. In the 1850s he started to gain success as a lecturer and his books became a source of moderate income. His *English Traits*, a summary of English character and history, appeared in 1856. Other later works include *Conduct of Life* (1860), *Society and Solitude* (1870), a selection of poems called *Parnassus* (1874), and *Letters and Social Aims*, edited by J. Elliot Cabot (1876). Emerson's heath started fail after the partial burning of his house in 1872. He made his last tour abroad in 1872-1873, and then withdrew more and more from public life. Emerson died on April 27, 1882 in Concord.

As an essayist Emerson was a master of style. Many of his phrases have long since passed into common English parlance. His essays have speech-like characteristics and a prophetic tone, a sermon like quality, often linked to his practice as a Unitarian minister. Emerson's influence on American literature cannot be exaggerated. His importance lies in the fact that he embodied a new nation's desire and struggle to assert its' own identity in its' formative period.

3.4.2 An excerpt from Chapter one of *Nature*

To go into solitude,[1] a man needs to retire as much from his chamber as from society. I am not solitary whilst I read and write, though nobody is with me. But if a man would be alone, let him look at the stars. The rays that come from those heavenly worlds, will separate between him and what he touches. One might think the atmosphere was made transparent[2] with this design, to give man, in the heavenly bodies, the perpetual[3] presence of the sublime.[4] Seen in the streets of cities, how great they are! If the stars should appear one night in a thousand years, how would men believe and adore; and preserve for many generations the remembrance[5] of the city of God which had been shown! But every night come out these envoys[6] of beauty, and light the universe with their admonishing[7] smile.

The stars awaken a certain reverence,[8] because though always present, they are inaccessible; but all natural objects make a kindred[9] impression, when the mind is open to their influence. Nature never wears a mean[10] appearance. Neither does the wisest man extort[11] her secret, and lose his curiosity by finding out all her perfection. Nature never became a toy to a wise spirit. The flowers, the animals, the mountains, reflected the wisdom of his best hour, as much as they had delighted the simplicity of his childhood.

When we speak of nature in this manner, we have a distinct but most poetical sense in the mind. We mean the integrity of impression made by manifold natural objects. It is this which distinguishes the stick of timber of the wood-cutter, from the tree of the poet. The charming landscape which I saw this morning, is indubitably[12] made up of some twenty or thirty farms. Miller owns this field, Locke that, and Mannin[13] the woodland beyond. But none of them owns the landscape. There is a property in the horizon which no man has but he whose eye can integrate all the parts, that is, the poet. This is the best part of these men's farms, yet to this their warranty-deeds[14] give no title. [15]

To speak truly, few adult persons can see nature. Most persons do not see the sun. At least they have a very superficial seeing. The sun illuminates only the eye of the man, but shines into the eye and the heart of the child. The lover of nature is he whose inward and outward senses are still truly adjusted to each other; who has retained the spirit of infancy even into the era of manhood. His intercourse with heaven and earth, becomes part of his daily food. In the presence of nature, a wild delight runs through the man, in spite of real sorrows. Nature says, — he is my creature, and maugre[16] all his impertinent griefs, he shall be glad with me. Not the sun or the summer alone, but every hour and season yields its tribute[17] of delight; for every hour and change corresponds to and authorizes a different state of the mind, from breathless noon to grimmest midnight. Nature is a setting that fits equally well a comic or a mourning piece. In good health, the air is a cordial[18] of incredible virtue. Crossing a bare common, [19] in snow puddles, at twilight, under a clouded sky, without having in my thoughts any occurrence of special good fortune, I have enjoyed a perfect exhilaration. [20] I am glad to the brink[21] of fear. In the woods too, a man casts off his years, as the snake his slough, [22] and at what period soever of life, is always a child. In the woods, is perpetual youth. Within these plantations of God, a decorum[23] and sanctity[24] reign, a perennial[25] festival is dressed, and the guest sees not how he should tire of them in a thousand years. In the woods, we return to reason and faith. There I feel that nothing can befall me in life, — no disgrace, no calamity, (leaving me my eyes,) which nature cannot repair. Standing on the bare ground, — my head bathed by the blithe[26] air, and uplifted into infinite space, — all mean egotism[27] vanishes. I become a transparent eye-ball; I am nothing; I see all; the currents of the Universal Being circulate through me; I am part or particle of God. The name of the nearest friend sounds then foreign and accidental: to be brothers, to be acquaintances, — master or servant, is then a trifle and a disturbance. I am the lover of uncontained[28] and immortal beauty. In the wilderness, I find something more dear and connate[29] than in streets or villages. In the tranquil landscape, and especially in the distant line of the horizon, man beholds somewhat as beautiful as his own nature.

The greatest delight which the fields and woods minister,[30] is the suggestion of an occult[31] relation between man and the vegetable. I am not alone and unacknowledged. They nod to me, and I to them. The waving of the boughs in the storm, is new to me and old. It takes me by surprise, and yet is not unknown. Its effect is like that of a higher thought or a better emotion coming over me, when I deemed I was thinking justly or doing right.

Yet it is certain that the power to produce this delight, does not reside in nature, but in man, or in a harmony of both. It is necessary to use these pleasures with great temperance[32] For, nature is not always tricked[33] in holiday attire, but the same scene which yesterday breathed perfume and glittered as for the frolic[34] of the nymphs, is overspread with melancholy today. Nature always wears the colors of the spirit. To a man laboring under calamity, the heat of his own fire hath sadness in it. Then, there is a kind of contempt of the landscape felt by him who has just lost by death a dear friend. The sky is less grand as it shuts down[35] over less worth in the population.

Notes
1. **solitude**: the state or quality of being alone or remote from others.
2. **transparent**: capable of transmitting light so that objects or images can be seen as if there were no intervening material.
3. **perpetual**: lasting for eternity.
4. **sublime**: inspiring awe; impressive.
5. **remembrance**: something remembered; a reminiscence.
6. **envoys**: messengers; agents.
7. **admonishing**: to reprove gently but earnestly.
8. **reverence**: a feeling of profound awe and respect and often love.
9. **kindred**: having a similar or related origin, nature, or character.
10. **mean**: shabby; miserly; ignoble.
11. **extort**: obtain something by violence or threats.
12. **indubitably**: undoubtedly.
13. **Miller owns this field, Locke that, and Mannin...**: Here, Miller, Locke and Mannin stand for ordinary farmers.
14. **warranty-deeds**: a covenant by which the seller of land binds himself or herself and

his or her heirs to defend the security of the estate conveyed.
15. **title**: a legitimate right.
16. **maugre**: in spite of.
17. **tribute**: a gift, payment, declaration, or other acknowledgment of gratitude, respect, or admiration.
18. **cordial**: stimulating medicine or drink.
19. **common**: area of open public land.
20. **exhilaration**: the state of being stimulated, refreshed.
21. **brink**: edge.
22. **slough**: a depression or hollow, usually filled with deep mud or mire.
23. **decorum**: rightness; harmony.
24. **sanctity**: holiness of life or disposition; saintliness.
25. **perennial**: lasting an indefinitely long time; enduring.
26. **blithe**: happy and carefree.
27. **egotism**: state of mind in which one is always thinking about oneself and what is best for oneself.
28. **uncontained**: boundariless.
29. **connate**: closely related.
30. **minister**: to give active service or help to something or somebody.
31. **occult**: beyond the realm of human comprehension; inscrutable.
32. **temperance**: moderation and self-restraint, as in behavior or expression.
33. **tricked**: dressed.
34. **frolic**: lively and enjoyable activity.
35. **shut down**: close; stop working.

Study Questions

1. According to paragraph 1, what does Emerson say would happen if the stars appeared one night in a thousand years?
2. According to paragraph 2, why does Emerson believe the stars awaken a reverence in people?
3. According to paragraph 3, how does Emerson describe the lover of nature?
4. Why does Emerson think few adult persons can see nature?

Essay Topics

1. What does Emerson mean when he says he becomes "a transparent eye-ball"?
2. How does Emerson's essay combine philosophical and poetic insight?

Chapter 3　The Literature of the Romantic Period

3.5　Henry David Thoreau

3.5.1　About the Author

Henry David Thoreau (1817-1862) was born in Concord, Massachusetts. He was educated first at Concord Academy and then at Harvard University. After graduation, he joined with his brother to establish his own school in Concord. Thoreau lived a simple and relatively quiet life, making his living briefly as a teacher and pencil maker, but mostly as a land surveyor. He loved nature and spent most of his free time exploring the local countryside. A decisive turning point in Thoreau's life came when he met Ralph Waldo Emerson. Although the two American thinkers had a turbulent relationship due to serious philosophical and personal differences, they had a profound and lasting effect upon one another.

In 1845 Thoreau built himself a house in the woods on land owned by Emerson. He lived there until 1847, keeping detailed records of his daily activities, observations of nature, and spiritual meditations. From his experiences he produced his famous work *Walden*. Thoreau viewed his existential quest as a venture in philosophy, because it was motivated by an urgent need to find a reflective understanding of reality that could inform a life of wisdom. Thoreau also wrote and lectured against slavery. He was a member of the Underground Railway for many years. His most famous essay, *Civil Disobedience* (1849), was a result of an overnight visit in 1846 in a jail, where he ended after refusing to pay his taxes in protest against the Mexican War and the extension of slavery. Most of Thoreau's work was published after his death. This included *Excursions* (1863), *The Maine Woods* (1864), *Cape Cod* (1865) and *A Yankee in Canada* (1866).

Thoreau had intimate bonds with his family and friends, and remained single although he was deeply in love at least twice. Thoreau was a man of "simple and high thinking" and his writings proved to have more of an impact on the men of the 20th century than those of his own time.

3.5.2　An Excerpt from *Walden*

...

At a certain season of our life we are accustomed to consider every spot as the possible site of a house. I have thus surveyed the country on every side within a dozen miles of where I live. In imagination I have bought all the farms in succession, for all were to be bought and I knew their price. I walked over each farmer's premises, tasted his wild apples, discoursed on husbandry with him, took his farm at his price, at any price, mortgaging it to him in my mind; even put a higher price on it, — took everything but a deed of it, — took his word for his deed, for I dearly love to talk, — cultivated it, and him too to some extent, I trust, and withdrew when I had enjoyed it long enough, leaving him to carry it on. This experience entitled me to be regarded as a sort of real-estate broker by my friends. Wherever I sat, there I might live, and the landscape radiated from me accordingly. What is a house but a sedes,[1] a seat? — better if a country seat. I discovered many a site for a house not likely to be soon improved, which some might have thought too far from the village, but to my eyes the village was too far from it. Well, there I might live, I said; and there I did live, for an hour, a summer and a winter life; saw how I could let the years run off, buffet the winter through, and see the spring come in. The future inhabitants of this region, wherever they may place their houses, may be sure that they have been anticipated. An afternoon sufficed to lay out the land into orchard woodlot, and pasture, and to decide what fine oaks or pines should be left to stand before the door, and whence each blasted tree could be seen to the best advantage; and then I let it lie, fallow perchance, for a man is rich in proportion to the number of things which he can afford to let alone.

My imagination carried me so far that I even had the refusal[2] of several farms, — the refusal was all I wanted, — but I never got my fingers burned by actual possession. The nearest that I came to actual possession was when I bought the Hollowell place,[3] and had begun to sort my seeds, and collected materials with which to make a wheelbarrow to carry it on or off with; but before the owner gave me a deed of it, his wife — every man has such a wife — changed her mind and wished to keep it, and he offered me ten dollars to release him. Now, to speak the truth, I had but ten cents in the world, and it surpassed my arithmetic to tell, if I was that man who had ten cents, or who had a farm, or ten dollars, or all together. However, I let him keep the ten dollars and the farm too, for I had carried it far enough; or rather, to be generous, I sold him the farm for just what I gave for it, and, as he was not a rich man, made him a present of ten dollars, and still had my ten cents, and seeds, and materials for a wheelbarrow left. I found thus that I had been a rich man without any damage to my poverty. But I retained the landscape, and I have since annually carried off what it yielded without a wheelbarrow. With respect to landscapes, —

"I am monarch of all I *survey*,

My right there is none to dispute."[4]

I have frequently seen a poet withdraw, having enjoyed the most valuable part of a farm, while the crusty farmer supposed that he had got a few wild apples only. Why, the owner does not know it for many years when a poet has put his farm in rhyme, the most admirable kind of invisible fence, has fairly impounded it, milked it, skimmed it, and got all the cream, and left the farmer only the skimmed milk.

...

Chapter 3 The Literature of the Romantic Period

  I was seated by the shore of a small pond, about a mile and a half south of the village of Concord and somewhat higher than it, in the midst of an extensive wood between that town and Lincoln, and about two miles south of that our only field known to fame, Concord Battle Ground; but I was so low in the woods that the opposite shore, half a mile off, like the rest, covered with wood, was my most distant horizon. For the first week, whenever I looked out on the pond it impressed me like a tarn[5] high up on the side of a mountain, its bottom far above the surface of other lakes, and, as the sun arose, I saw it throwing off its nightly clothing of mist, and here and there, by degrees, its soft ripples or its smooth reflecting surface was revealed, while the mists, like ghosts, were stealthily withdrawing in every direction into the woods, as at the breaking up of some nocturnal conventicle. The very dew seemed to hang upon the trees later into the day than usual, as on the sides of mountains.

  This small lake was of most value as a neighbor in the intervals of a gentle rain storm in August, when, both air and water being perfectly still, but the sky overcast, mid-afternoon had all the serenity of evening, and the wood thrush sang around, and was heard from shore to shore. A lake like this is never smoother than at such a time; and the clear portion of the air above it being shallow and darkened by clouds, the water, full of light and reflections, becomes a lower heaven itself so much the more important. From a hill top near by, where the wood had been recently cut off, there was a pleasing vista southward across the pond, through a wide indentation in the hills which form the shore there, where their opposite sides sloping toward each other suggested a stream flowing out in that direction through a wooded valley, but stream there was none. That way I looked between and over the near green hills to some distant and higher ones in the horizon, tinged with blue. Indeed, by standing on tiptoe I could catch a glimpse of some of the peaks of the still bluer and more distant mountain ranges in the north-west, those true-blue coins from heaven's own mint, and also of some portion of the village. But in other directions, even from this point, I could not see over or beyond the woods which surrounded me. It is well to have some water in your neighborhood, to give buoyancy to and float the earth. One value even of the smallest well is, that when you look into it you see that earth is not continent but insular. This is as important as that it keeps butter cool. When I looked across the pond from this peak toward the Sudbury meadows, which in time of flood I distinguished elevated perhaps by a mirage in their seething valley, like a coin in a basin, all the earth beyond the pond appeared like a thin crust insulated and floated even by this small sheet of intervening water, and I was reminded that this on which I dwelt was but dry land.

  ...

  We must learn to reawaken and keep ourselves awake, not by mechanical aids, but by an infinite expectation of the dawn, which does not forsake us in our soundest sleep. I know of no more encouraging fact than the unquestionable ability of man to elevate his life by a conscious endeavor. It is something to be able to paint a particular picture, or to carve a statue, and so to make a few objects beautiful; but it is far more glorious to carve and paint the very atmosphere and medium through which we look, which morally we can do. To affect the quality of the day, that is the highest of arts. Every man is tasked to make his life, even in its details, worthy of the contemplation of his most elevated and critical hour. If we refused, or rather used up, such paltry information as we get, the oracles would distinctly inform us how this might be done.

I went to the woods because I wished to live deliberately, to front[6] only the essential facts of life, and see if I could not learn what it had to teach, and not, when I came to die, discover that I had not lived. I did not wish to live what was not life, living is so dear; nor did I wish to practise resignation, unless it was quite necessary. I wanted to live deep and suck out all the marrow of life, to live so sturdily and Spartan-like[7] as to put to rout all that was not life, to cut a broad swath and shave close, to drive life into a corner, and reduce it to its lowest terms, and, if it proved to be mean, why then to get the whole and genuine meanness of it, and publish its meanness to the world; or if it were sublime, to know it by experience, and be able to give a true account of it in my next excursion. For most men, it appears to me, are in a strange uncertainty about it, whether it is of the devil or of God, and have somewhat hastily concluded that it is the chief end of man here to "glorify God and enjoy him forever."[8]

Still we live meanly, like ants; though the fable tells us that we were long ago changed into men;[9] like pygmies we fight with cranes;[10] it is error upon error, and clout upon clout, and our best virtue has for its occasion a superfluous and evitable wretchedness. Our life is frittered away by detail. An honest man has hardly need to count more than his ten fingers, or in extreme cases he may add his ten toes, and lump the rest. Simplicity, simplicity, simplicity! I say, let your affairs be as two or three, and not a hundred or a thousand; instead of a million count half a dozen, and keep your accounts on your thumb nail. In the midst of this chopping sea of civilized life, such are the clouds and storms and quicksands and thousand-and-one items to be allowed for, that a man has to live, if he would not founder and go to the bottom and not make his port at all, by dead reckoning,[11] and he must be a great calculator indeed who succeeds. Simplify, simplify. Instead of three meals a day, if it be necessary eat but one; instead of a hundred dishes, five; and reduce other things in proportion. Our life is like a German Confederacy,[12] made up of petty states, with its boundary forever fluctuating, so that even a German cannot tell you how it is bounded at any moment. The nation itself, with all its so called internal improvements, which, by the way are all external and superficial, is just such an unwieldy and overgrown establishment, cluttered with furniture and tripped up by its own traps, ruined by luxury and heedless expense, by want of calculation and a worthy aim, as the million households in the land; and the only cure for it as for them is in a rigid economy, a stern and more than Spartan simplicity of

Chapter 3 The Literature of the Romantic Period

life and elevation of purpose. It lives too fast. Men think that it is essential that the Nation have commerce, and export ice, and talk through a telegraph, and ride thirty miles an hour, without a doubt, whether they do or not; but whether we should live like baboons or like men, is a little uncertain. If we do not get out sleepers,[13] and forge rails, and devote days and nights to the work, but go to tinkering upon our lives to improve them, who will build railroads? And if railroads are not built, how shall we get to heaven in season? But if we stay at home and mind our business, who will want railroads? We do not ride on the railroad; it rides upon us. Did you ever think what those sleepers are that underlie the railroad? Each one is a man, an Irishman, or a Yankee man. The rails are laid on them, and they are covered with sand, and the cars run smoothly over them. They are sound sleepers, I assure you. And every few years a new lot is laid down and run over; so that, if some have the pleasure of riding on a rail, others have the misfortune to be ridden upon. And when they run over a man that is walking in his sleep, a supernumerary sleeper in the wrong position, and wake him up, they suddenly stop the cars, and make a hue and cry about it, as if this were an exception. I am glad to know that it takes a gang of men for every five miles to keep the sleepers down and level in their beds as it is, for this is a sign that they may sometime get up again.

...

Let us spend one day as deliberately as Nature, and not be thrown off the track by every nutshell and mosquito's wing that falls on the rails. Let us rise early and fast, or break fast, gently and without perturbation; let company come and let company go, let the bells ring and the children cry, — determined to make a day of it. Why should we knock under and go with the stream? Let us not be upset and overwhelmed in that terrible rapid and whirlpool called a dinner, situated in the meridian shallows. Weather this danger and you are safe, for the rest of the way is down hill. With unrelaxed nerves, with morning vigor, sail by it, looking another way, tied to the mast like Ulysses.[14] If the engine whistles, let it whistle till it is hoarse for its pains. If the bell rings, why should we run? We will consider what kind of music they are like. Let us settle ourselves, and work and wedge our feet downward through the mud and slush of opinion, and prejudice, and tradition, and delusion, and appearance, that alluvion[15] which covers the globe, through Paris and London, through New York and Boston and Concord, through Church and State, through poetry and philosophy and religion, till we come to a hard bottom and rocks in place, which we can call reality, and say, This is, and no mistake; and then begin, having a point d'appui,[16] below freshet and frost and fire, a place where you might found a wall or a state, or set a lamp-post safely, or perhaps a gauge, not a Nilometer, but a Realometer,[17] that future ages might know how deep a freshet of shams and appearances had gathered from time to time. If you stand right fronting and face to face to a fact, you will see the sun glimmer on both its surfaces, as if it were a cimeter,[18] and feel its sweet edge dividing you through the heart and marrow, and so you will happily conclude your mortal career. Be it life or death, we crave only reality. If we are really dying, let us hear the rattle in our throats and feel cold in the extremities; if we are alive, let us go about our business.

Time is but the stream I go a-fishing in. I drink at it; but while I drink I see the sandy bottom and detect how shallow it is. Its thin current slides away, but eternity remains. I would drink deeper; fish in the sky, whose bottom is pebbly with stars. I cannot count one. I know not the first letter of the alphabet. I have always been regretting that I was not as wise as the day I was born. The intellect is a cleaver; it discerns and rifts its way into the secret of things. I do not wish to be any more busy with my hands than is necessary. My head is hands and feet. I feel all my best faculties concentrated in it. My instinct tells me that my head is an organ for burrowing, as some creatures use their snout and fore-paws, and with it I would mine and burrow my way through these hills. I think that the richest vein is somewhere hereabouts; so by the divining rod[19] and thin rising vapors I judge; and here I will begin to mine.

Notes

1. **a sedes**: a seat (in Latin).
2. **refusal**: the opportunity or right to accept or reject something before it is offered elsewhere.
3. **the Hollow Place**: an old farm near Concord.
4. **"I am monarch of all I survey, My right there is none to dispute"**: The lines are from William Cowper's *Verses Supposed to Be Written by Alexander Selkirk*, with the pun italicized by Thoreau.
5. **tarn**: lake.
6. **front**: face.
7. **Spartan-like**: simple, hardy, and disciplined, like the life of the Spartans of ancient Greece.
8. **"glorify God and enjoy him forever"**: answer to the question "what is the chief end of man?" in the New England Primer.
9. **Still we live meanly, like ants; though the fable tells us that we were long ago changed into men**: in a Greek fable Zeus transforms ants into men.
10. **pygmies we fight with cranes**: in the *Iliad* the Trojans are compared to cranes.
11. **dead reckoning**: navigating without sighting the stars.
12. **a German Confederacy**: group of European states unified under Prince Otto Von Bismarck (1851-1898), the first chancellor of the German Empire.
13. **sleepers**: wooden railroad ties that support the rails. A pun is used here. It refers to dead men underground or idlers.
14. **Ulysses**: Roman name for Odysseus, character in Homer's *Iliad* and *Odyssey*. "**tied to the mast like Ulysses**": to resist the temptation of Sirens, sea nymphs whose

singing can lure ships to destruction, Ulysses covered his fellows' ears with wax and had himself tied to the mast in order to hear the music and not to have the ship destroyed.

15. **alluvion**: the increasing of land area along a shore by deposited alluvium or by the recession of water.
16. **a point d'appui**: this is French, it means "point of support."
17. **not a Nilometer, but a Realometer**: Nilometer is a gauge used to measure the rise of the Nile River. Realometer is a coined word by Thoreau on imitating Nilometer.
18. **cimeter**: scimitar, a curved Asian sword with the edge on the convex side.
19. **divining rod**: forked stick that supposedly reveals the presence of underground minerals or water.

Study Questions

1. What audience does Thoreau imagine for his work?
2. What complaints does Thoreau have about American life?
3. Why does Thoreau want to live in the woods?

Essay Topics

1. How is *Walden* an expression of the transcendentalist vision?
2. Discuss the seasonal metaphor that thematically unifies *Walden*.

3.6 Nathaniel Hawthorne

3.6.1 About the Author

Nathaniel Hawthorne (1804-1864) was born in Salem, Massachusetts, to a family that had been prominent in the area since colonial times. When the boy was four, his father died. But his maternal relatives financed his education at Bowdoin College. After graduation, Hawthorne returned to his mother's house in Salem for the express purpose of writing. For twelve years he led a rather lonely existence, reading books of those literary master minds, especially Bunyan, Spenser and Shakespeare, which were essential for his formation as a writer.

Hawthorne began his career, first as a magazine editor and then as a clerk in the Boston Customs House. He also stayed for some time at Concord and Lenox, where he met the principal literary figures of the time, Emerson and Thoreau and Melville. In 1842 Hawthorne married Peabody, an active participant in the Transcendentalist movement, and settled with her in Concord.

But soon a growing family and mounting debts compelled their return to Salem. During these years, Hawthorne wrote and published the best of his works. Among them, the tales collected in *Mosses from an Old Manse* (1846) and *The Snow-Image and Other Twice-Told Tales* (1851) best demonstrate Hawthorne's early obsession with the moral and psychological consequences of pride, selfishness, and secret guilt; *The Scarlet Letter* (1850), always regarded as the best of his works, tells a simple but very moving story in which four people living in a Puritan community are involved in and affected by the sin of adultery in different ways; *The House of the Seven Gables* (1851) was based on the tradition of a curse pronounced on the author's family when his great-grandfather was a judge in the Salem witchcraft trials; *The Blithedal Romance* (1852) is a novel he wrote to reveal his own experiences on the Brook Farm and his own methods as a psychological novelist. In the following years, Hawthorne went to Europe and worked as American consul to Liverpool, then traveled as a tourist in France and Italy, the experience of which helped him produce another book, *The Marble Faun* (1860).

Hawthorne was the first American novelist to develop truly native and American settings, characters, and even plots in his works. He answered the requests of Emerson and Longfellow for a native literature instead of one based and characterized on that of Europe. With modern psychological insight, Hawthorne probed the secret motivations in human behavior and the guilt and anxiety that he believed resulted from all sins against humanity.

As a writer of literary craftsmanship, Hawthorne is extraordinary. The structure and the form of his writings are always carefully worked out to cater for the thematic concern. He is a great allegorist and almost every story can be read allegorically, as is the case in "Young Goodman Brown". Hawthorne is also a master of symbolism, which he took from the Puritan tradition and bequeathed to American literature in a revivified form. His emphasis on allegory and symbolism often makes his characters seem shadowy and unreal, but his best characters reveal the emotional and intellectual ambivalence he felt to be inseparable from the Puritan heritage of America. Hawthorne's writings have remained alive and his artistic reputation has continued through more than a century of changing literary taste.

3.6.2 Chapter 23 from *The Scarlet Letter*

The eloquent voice,[1] on which the souls of the listening audience had been borne aloft, as on the swelling waves of the sea, at length came to a pause. There was a momentary silence, profound as what should follow the utterance of oracles. Then ensued a murmur and half-hushed tumult; as if the auditors, released from the high spell that had transported them into the region of another's mind, were returning into themselves, with all their awe and wonder still heavy on them. In a moment more, the crowd began to gush forth from the doors of the church. Now that there was an end, they needed other breath, more fit to support the gross and earthly life into which they relapsed, than that atmosphere which the preacher had converted into words of flame, and had burdened with the rich fragrance of his thought.

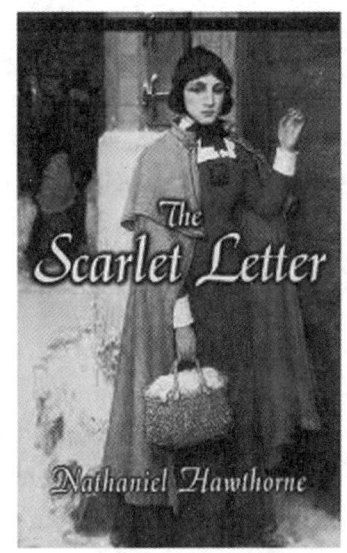

In the open air their rapture broke into speech. The street and the market-place absolutely babbled, from side to side, with applauses of the minister. His hearers could not rest until they had told one another of what each knew better than he could tell or hear. According to their united testimony, never had man spoken in so wise, so high, and so holy a spirit, as he that spake this day; nor had inspiration ever breathed through mortal lips more evidently than it did through his. Its influence could be seen, as it were, descending upon him, and possessing him, and continually lifting him out of the written discourse that lay before him, and filling him with ideas that must have been as marvelous to himself as to his audience. His subject, it appeared, had been the relation between the Deity and the communities of mankind, with a special reference to the New England which they were here planting in the wilderness. And, as he drew towards the close, a spirit as of prophecy had come upon him, constraining him to its purpose as mightily as the old prophets of Israel[2] were constrained; only with this difference, that, whereas the Jewish seers had denounced[3] judgments and ruin on their country, it was his mission to foretell a high and glorious destiny for the newly gathered people of the Lord. But, throughout it all, and through the whole discourse, there had been a certain deep, sad undertone of pathos, which could not be interpreted otherwise than as the natural regret of one soon to pass away. Yes; their minister whom they so loved — and who so loved them all, that he could not depart heavenward without a sigh — had the foreboding of untimely death upon him, and would soon leave them in their tears! This idea of his transitory stay on earth gave the last emphasis to the effect which the preacher had produced; it was as if an angel, in his passage to the skies, had shaken his bright wings over the people for an instant, — at once a shadow and a splendor, — and had shed down a shower of golden truths upon them.

Thus, there had come to the Reverend Mr. Dimmesdale — as to most men, in their various spheres, though seldom recognized until they see it far behind them — an epoch of life more brilliant and full of triumph than any previous one, or than any which could hereafter be. He stood, at this moment, on the very proudest eminence of superiority, to which the gifts of intellect, rich lore, prevailing eloquence, and a reputation of whitest sanctity, could exalt a clergyman in New England's earliest days, when the professional character was of itself a lofty pedestal. Such was the position which the minister occupied, as he bowed his head forward on the cushions of the pulpit at the close of his Election Sermon. Meanwhile, Hester Prynne was standing beside the scaffold of the pillory, with the scarlet letter still burning on her breast!

Now was heard again the clangor of the music, and the measured tramp of the military escort, issuing from the church-door. The procession was to be marshaled thence to the town-hall, where a solemn banquet would complete the ceremonies of the day.

Once more, therefore, the train of venerable and majestic fathers was seen moving through a broad pathway of the people, who drew back reverently, on either side, as the Governor and magistrates, the old and wise men, the holy ministers, and all that were eminent and renowned, advanced into the midst of them. When they were fairly in the market-place, their presence was greeted by a shout. This — though doubtless it might acquire additional force and volume from the childlike loyalty which the age awarded to its rulers — was felt to be an irrepressible outburst of the enthusiasm kindled in the auditors by that high strain of eloquence which was yet reverberating in their ears. Each felt the impulse in himself, and, in the same breath, caught it from his neighbor. Within the church, it had hardly been kept down; beneath the sky, it pealed upward to the zenith. There were human beings enough, and enough of highly wrought and symphonious feeling, to produce that more impressive sound than the organ-tones of the blast, or the thunder, or the roar of the sea; even that mighty swell of many voices, blended into one great voice by the universal impulse which makes likewise one vast heart out of the many. Never, from the soil of New England, had gone up such a shout! Never, on New England soil, had stood the man so honored by his mortal brethren as the preacher.

How fared it with him then? Were there not the brilliant particles of a halo in the air about his head? So etherealized by spirit as he was, and so apotheosized by worshipping admirers, did his footsteps in the procession really tread upon the dust of earth?

As the ranks of military men and civil fathers moved onward, all eyes were turned towards the point where the minister was seen to approach among them. The shout died into a murmur, as one portion of the crowd after another obtained a glimpse of him. How feeble and pale he looked amid all his triumph! The energy — or say, rather, the inspiration which had held him up, until he should have delivered the sacred message that brought its own strength along with it from heaven — was withdrawn, now that it had so faithfully performed its office. The glow, which they had just before beheld burning on his cheek, was extinguished, like a flame that sinks down hopelessly among the late-decaying embers. It seemed hardly the face of a man alive, with such a deathlike hue; it was hardly a man with life in him, that tottered on his path so nervelessly, yet tottered, and did not fall!

One of his clerical brethren, — it was the venerable John Wilson, — observing the state in which Mr. Dimmesdale was left by the retiring wave of intellect and sensibility, stepped forward hastily to offer his support. The minister tremulously, but decidedly, repelled the old man's arm. He still walked onward, if that movement could be so described, which rather resembled the wavering effort of an infant, with its mother's arms in view, outstretched to tempt him forward. And now, almost imperceptible as were the latter steps of his progress, he had come opposite the well-remembered and weather-darkened scaffold, where, long since, with all that dreary lapse of time between, Hester Prynne had encountered the world's ignominious stare. There stood Hester, holding little Pearl by the hand! And there was the scarlet letter on her breast! The minister here made a pause; although the music still played the stately and rejoicing march to which the procession moved. It summoned him onward, — onward to the festival! — but here he made a pause.

Bellingham, for the last few moments, had kept an anxious eye upon him. He now left his own place in the procession, and advanced to give assistance; judging from Mr. Dimmesdale's aspect that he must otherwise inevitably fall. But there was something in the latter's expression that warned back the magistrate, although a man not readily obeying the vague intimations that pass from one spirit to another. The crowd, meanwhile, looked on with awe and wonder. This earthly faintness was, in their view, only another phase of the minister's celestial strength; nor would it have seemed a miracle too high to be wrought for one so holy, had he ascended before their eyes, waxing dimmer and brighter, and fading at last into the light of heaven!

He turned towards the scaffold, and stretched forth his arms.

"Hester," said he, "come hither! Come, my little Pearl!"

It was a ghastly look with which he regarded them; but there was something at once tender and strangely triumphant in it. The child, with the bird-like motion which was one of her characteristics, flew to him, and clasped her arms about his knees. Hester Prynne — slowly, as if impelled by inevitable fate, and against her strongest will — likewise drew near, but paused before she reached him. At this instant old Roger Chillingworth thrust himself through the crowd, — or, perhaps, so dark, disturbed, and evil was his look, he rose up out of some nether region, — to snatch back his victim from what he sought to do! Be that as it might, the old man rushed forward and caught the minister by the arm.

"Madman, hold! What is your purpose?" whispered he. "Wave back that woman! Cast off this child! All shall be well! Do not blacken your fame, and perish in dishonor! I can yet save you! Would you bring infamy on your sacred profession?"

"Ha, tempter! Methinks thou art too late!" answered the minister, encountering his eye, fearfully, but firmly. "Thy power is not what it was! With God's help, I shall escape thee now!" He again extended his hand to the woman of the scarlet letter.

"Hester Prynne," cried he, with a piercing earnestness, "in the name of Him[4], so terrible and so merciful, who gives me grace, at this last moment, to do what — for my own heavy sin and miserable agony — I withheld myself from doing seven years ago, come hither now, and twine thy strength about me! Thy strength, Hester; but let it be guided by the will which God hath granted me! This wretched and wronged old man is opposing it with all his might! — with all his own might and the fiend's! Come, Hester, come! Support me up yonder scaffold!"

The crowd was in a tumult. The men of rank and dignity, who stood more immediately around the clergyman, were so taken by surprise, and so perplexed as to the purport of what they saw, — unable to receive the explanation which most readily presented itself, or to imagine any other, — that they remained silent and inactive spectators of the judgment which Providence seemed about to work. They beheld the minister, leaning on Hester's shoulder and supported by her arm around him, approach the scaffold, and ascend its steps; while still the little hand of the sin-born child was clasped in his. Old Roger Chillingworth followed, as one intimately connected with the drama of guilt and sorrow in which they had all been actors, and well entitled, therefore, to be present at its closing scene.

"Hadst thou sought the whole earth over," said he, looking darkly at the clergyman, "there was no one place so secret, — no high place nor lowly place, where thou couldst have escaped me, — save on this very scaffold!"

"Thanks be to Him who hath led me hither!" answered the minister.

Yet he trembled, and turned to Hester with an expression of doubt and anxiety in his eyes, not the less evidently betrayed, that there was a feeble smile upon his lips.

"Is not this better," murmured he, "than what we dreamed of in the forest?"[5]

"I know not! I know not!" she hurriedly replied. "Better? Yea; so we may both die, and little Pearl die with us!"

"For thee and Pearl, be it as God shall order," said the minister; "and God is merciful! Let me now do the will which he hath made plain before my sight. For, Hester, I am a dying man. So let me make haste to take my shame upon me."

Partly supported by Hester Prynne, and holding one hand of little Pearl's, the Reverend Mr. Dimmesdale turned to the dignified and venerable rulers; to the holy ministers, who were his brethren; to the people, whose great heart was thoroughly appalled, yet overflowing with tearful sympathy, as knowing that some deep life-matter — which, if full of sin, was full of anguish and repentance likewise — was now to be laid open to them. The sun, but little past its meridian, shone down upon the clergyman, and gave a distinctness to his figure, as he stood out from all the earth to put in his plea of guilty at the bar of Eternal Justice.[6]

"People of New England!" cried he, with a voice that rose over them, high, solemn, and majestic, — yet had always a tremor through it, and sometimes a shriek, struggling up out of a fathomless depth of remorse and woe, — "ye, that have loved me!

Chapter 3 The Literature of the Romantic Period

— ye, that have deemed me holy! — behold me here, the one sinner of the world! At last! — at last! — I stand upon the spot where, seven years since, I should have stood; here, with this woman, whose arm, more than the little strength wherewith I have crept hitherward, sustains me, at this dreadful moment, from grovelling down upon my face! Lo, the scarlet letter which Hester wears! Ye have all shuddered at it! Wherever her walk hath been, — wherever, so miserably burdened, she may have hoped to find repose,—it hath cast a lurid gleam of awe and horrible repugnance round about her. But there stood one in the midst of you, at whose brand of sin and infamy ye have not shuddered!"

It seemed, at this point, as if the minister must leave the remainder of his secret undisclosed. But he fought back the bodily weakness, — and, still more, the faintness of heart, — that was striving for the mastery with him. He threw off all assistance, and stepped passionately forward a pace before the woman and the child.

"It was on him!" he continued, with a kind of fierceness; so determined was he to speak out the whole. "God's eye beheld it! The angels were for ever pointing at it! The Devil knew it well, and fretted it continually with the touch of his burning finger! But he hid it cunningly from men, and walked among you with the mien of a spirit, mournful, because so pure in a sinful world! — and sad, because he missed his heavenly kindred! Now, at the death-hour, he stands up before you! He bids you look again at Hester's scarlet letter! He tells you, that, with all its mysterious horror, it is but the shadow of what he bears on his own breast, and that even this, his own red stigma, is no more than the type of what has seared his inmost heart! Stand any here that question God's judgment on a sinner? Behold! Behold a dreadful witness of it!"

With a convulsive motion he tore away the ministerial band from before his breast. It was revealed![7] But it were irreverent to describe that revelation. For an instant the gaze of the horror-stricken multitude was concentrated on the ghastly miracle; while the minister stood with a flush of triumph in his face, as one who, in the crisis of acutest pain, had won a victory. Then, down he sank upon the scaffold! Hester partly raised him, and supported his head against her bosom. Old Roger Chillingworth knelt down beside him, with a blank, dull countenance, out of which the life seemed to have departed.

"Thou hast escaped me!" he repeated more than once. "Thou hast escaped me!"

"May God forgive thee!" said the minister. "Thou, too, hast deeply sinned!"

He withdrew his dying eyes from the old man, and fixed them on the woman and the child.

"My little Pearl," said he feebly, — and there was a sweet and gentle smile over his face, as of a spirit sinking into deep repose; nay, now that the burden was removed, it seemed almost as if he would be sportive with the child, — "dear little Pearl, wilt thou kiss me now? Thou wouldst not yonder, in the forest! But now thou wilt?"

Pearl kissed his lips. A spell was broken. The great scene of grief, in which the wild infant bore a part, had developed all her sympathies; and as her tears fell upon her father's cheek, they were the pledge that she would grow up amid human joy and sorrow, nor for ever do battle with the world, but be a woman in it. Towards her mother, too, Pearl's errand as a messenger of anguish was all fulfilled.

"Hester," said the clergyman, "farewell!"

"Shall we not meet again?" whispered she, bending her face down close to his. "Shall we not spend our immortal life together? Surely, surely, we have ransomed one another, with all this woe! Thou lookest far into eternity, with those bright dying eyes! Then tell me what thou seest?"

"Hush, Hester, hush!" said he, with tremulous solemnity. "The law we broke! — the sin here so awfully revealed! — let these alone be in thy thoughts! I fear! I fear! It may be, that, when we forgot our God, — when we violated our reverence each for the other's soul, — it was thenceforth vain to hope that we could meet hereafter, in an everlasting and pure reunion. God knows; and He is merciful! He hath proved his mercy, most of all, in my afflictions. By giving me this burning torture to bear upon my breast! By sending yonder dark and terrible old man, to keep the torture always at red-heat! By bringing me hither, to die this death of triumphant ignominy before the people! Had either of these agonies been wanting, I had been lost for ever! Praised be his name! His will be done! Farewell!"

That final word came forth with the minister's expiring breath. The multitude, silent till then, broke out in a strange, deep voice of awe and wonder, which could not as yet find utterance, save in this murmur that rolled so heavily after the departed spirit.

Notes

1. **the eloquent voice**: refers to Dimmesdale's passionate sermon.
2. **the old prophets of Israel**: refers to Israelite prophets in Old Testament, such as Isaiah, Jeremiah, Ezekiel. They predicted that the Israelite would be punished by God for not being faithful, the city of Jerusalem would perish from the earth, people would die.
3. **denounced**: (archaic) pronounce publicly and formally, or solemnly.
4. **Him**: God.
5. **what we dreamed of in the forest**: In previous chapters, Hester met Dimmesdale in the forest and asked him to escape with her and their daughter to Europe to seek their happiness.
6. **the bar of Eternal Justice**: court of Eternal Justice. The bar is the court, the place where the accused stand before the judge. In this case, it would be the Last Judgment, but here Dimmesdale is dying, so he will plead guilty before God, who will judge him correspondingly in the last time.
7. **It was revealed**: Under the torture of Chillingworth and himself, Dmmesdale decided

to reveal his sin and relieve the burden on his mind. But Hawthorne didn't directly say what is revealed, which is to arouse the reader's imagination.

Study Questions

1. Who empowers Dimmesdale to stand on the scaffold?
2. Why does Dimmesdale want to reveal?
3. How do the townspeople interpret this final revelation?
4. Why does Chillingworth try desperately to stop Dimmesdale from confessing his sins on the scaffold?

Essay Topics

1. Explain the significance of the three scaffold scenes.
2. This novel makes extensive use of symbols. How do they help develop the themes and characters in the novel?

3.7 Herman Melville

3.7.1 About the Author

Herman Melville (1819-1891) was born into an established merchant family in New York City. In 1832, his father became bankrupt, which caused a severe financial trouble in the family. Soon his father died and Melville had to leave school at the age of 15. He worked as a bank clerk, a salesman, a farmer and a school teacher, and when all these failed to offer him a decent livelihood, he went to sea at about 20. The early sailing experiences were rewarding, for they gave him a love of the sea, and aroused his desire for adventure. In 1841, Melville went to the South Seas on a whaling ship, where he gained the first-hand information about whaling. Working as a sailor, he had experienced the most brutalizing life in his time for a man, yet years of adventures also furnished him with abundant raw materials for most of his major fictions and his imaginative visions of life.

Melville's writing career, much of which was inspired by his sea voyages, began with the publication of *Typee* in 1846, which was shortly followed by *Omoo* (1847). His first two novels sold well because the public was interested in travel literature. In 1847 Melville married Elisabeth Shaw, daughter of the chief justice of Massachusetts. To support his family, Melville wrote three more novels, *Mardi* (1849), *Redburn* (1849), and *White-Jacket* (1850). In 1850, Melville moved to a farm in Massachusetts, where he had Nathaniel Hawthorne as his neighbor. They became very good friends, exchanging visits, writing to one another, and discussing each other's works. Inspired by the achievement of Hawthorne, Melville wrote his masterpiece, *Moby-Dick* (1851). The story is about Ahab on board his ship *Pequod* in the chase of a big whale. The dramatic description of the hazards of whaling makes the book a very exciting sea narrative and builds a literary monument to an era of whaling industry in the nineteenth century. But *Moby-Dick* is not merely a whaling tale or sea adventure. It turns out to be a symbolic voyage of the mind in quest of the truth and knowledge of the universe, a spiritual exploration into man's deep reality and psychology. The novel is also concerned with many of the issues that dominated nineteenth-century thought in America. The relationship between the land and the sea echoes the conflict between adventure and domesticity, between frontiersman and city-dweller. Captain Ahab's obsessive tragic pursuit of the whale is an indirect commentary on the feelings of disillusionment in mid-nineteenth-century America. Then in 1857, Melville published another novel, *The Confidence Man* (1857), which was a harsh satire of American life set on a Mississippi River steamboat. In his later years, Melville gradually turned to poetry writing. Several of his Civil War poems are among the best American poems of this period. In 1866, Melville took a full-time position as Inspector of Customs at the Port of New York, a position he held for the next nineteen years. Toward the end of his life he turned again to prose fiction and wrote what is probably his second famous work, *Billy Budd*, not published, however, until 1924.

Melville's life is characterized by a search for self on personal, national, and professional levels, and his writing career represents the long search for a new and better vision. His fame today rests mainly on his great narrative power, his ability to create absorbing characters, and his penetrating, tragic vision of life.

3.7.2 An Excerpt from Chapter 41 of *Moby-Dick*

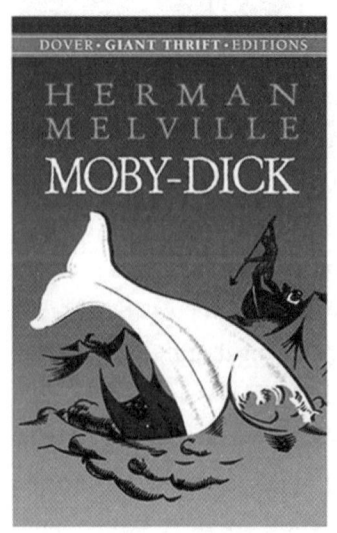

I, Ishmael,[1] was one of that crew; my shouts had gone up with the rest; my oath had been welded with theirs; and stronger I shouted, and more did I hammer and clinch my oath, because of the dread in my soul. A wild, mystical, sympathetical feeling was in me; Ahab's quenchless feud seemed mine. With greedy ears I learned the history of that murderous monster against whom I and all the others had taken our oaths of violence and revenge.

For some time past, though at intervals only, the unaccompanied, secluded White Whale had haunted those uncivilized seas mostly frequented by the Sperm Whale[2] fishermen. But not all of them knew of his existence; only a few of them, comparatively, had knowingly seen him;

while the number who as yet had actually and knowingly given battle to him, was small indeed. For, owing to the large number of whale-cruisers; the disorderly way they were sprinkled over the entire watery circumference, many of them adventurously pushing their quest along solitary latitudes, so as seldom or never for a whole twelvemonth or more on a stretch, to encounter a single news-telling sail[3] of any sort; the inordinate length of each separate voyage; the irregularity of the times of sailing from home; all these, with other circumstances, direct and indirect, long obstructed he spread through the whole world-wide whaling-fleet of the special individualizing tidings concerning Moby Dick. It was hardly to be doubted, that several vessels reported to have encountered, at such or such a time, or on such or such a meridian, a Sperm Whale of uncommon magnitude and malignity, which whale, after doing great mischief to his assailants, had completely escaped them; to some minds it was not an unfair presumption, I say, that the whale in question must have been no other than Moby Dick. Yet as of late the Sperm Whale fishery had been marked by various and not unfrequent instances of great ferocity, cunning, and malice in the monster attacked; therefore it was, that those who by accident ignorantly gave battle to Moby Dick; such hunters, perhaps, for the most part, were content to ascribe the peculiar terror he bred, more, as it were, to the perils of the Sperm Whale fishery at large, than to the individual cause. In that way, mostly, the disastrous encounter between Ahab and the whale had hitherto been popularly regarded.

And as for those who, previously hearing of the White Whale, by chance caught sight of him; in the beginning of the thing they had every one of them, almost, as boldly and fearlessly lowered for him, as for any other whale of that species. But at length, such calamities did ensue in these assaults — not restricted to sprained wrists and ankles, broken limbs, or devouring amputations — but fatal to the last degree of fatality; those repeated disastrous repulses, all accumulating and piling their terrors upon Moby Dick; those things had gone far to shake the fortitude of many brave hunters, to whom the story of the White Whale had eventually come.

Nor did wild rumors of all sorts fail to exaggerate, and still the more horrify the true histories of these deadly encounters. For not only do fabulous rumors naturally grow out of the very body of all surprising terrible events, — as the smitten tree gives birth to its fungi; but, in maritime life, far more than in that of terra firma,[4] wild rumors abound, wherever there is any adequate reality for them to cling to. And as the sea surpasses the land in this matter, so the whale fishery surpasses every other sort of maritime life, in the wonderfulness and fearfulness of the rumors which sometimes circulate there. For not only are whalemen as a body unexempt from that ignorance and superstitiousness hereditary to all sailors; but of all sailors, they are by all odds the most directly brought into contact with whatever is appallingly astonishing in the sea; face to face they not only eye its greatest marvels, but, hand to jaw, give battle to them. Alone, in such remotest waters, that though you sailed a thousand miles, and passed a thousand shores, you would not come to any chiselled hearthstone,[5] or aught hospitable beneath that part of the sun; in such latitudes and longitudes, pursuing too such a calling as he does, the whaleman is wrapped by influences all tending to make his fancy pregnant with many a mighty birth.[6]

No wonder, then, that ever gathering volume from the mere transit over the widest watery spaces, the outblown rumors of the White Whale did in the end incorporate with themselves all manner of morbid hints, and half-formed foetal suggestions of supernatural agencies, which eventually invested Moby Dick with new terrors unborrowed from anything that visibly appears. So that in many cases such a panic did he finally strike, that few who by those rumors, at least, had heard of the White Whale, few of those hunters were willing to encounter the perils of his jaw.

But there were still other and more vital practical influences at work. Not even at the present day has the original prestige of the Sperm Whale, as fearfully distinguished from all other species of the leviathan,[7] died out of the minds of the whalemen as a body. There are those this day among them, who, though intelligent and courageous enough in offering battle to the Greenland or Right Whale,[8] would perhaps — either from professional inexperience, or incompetency, or timidity, decline a contest with the Sperm Whale; at any rate, there are plenty of whalemen, especially among those whaling nations not sailing under the American flag, who have never hostilely encountered the Sperm Whale, but whose sole knowledge of the leviathan is restricted to the ignoble monster primitively pursued in the North; seated on their hatches, these men will hearken with a childish fire-side interest and awe, to the wild, strange tales of Southern whaling. Nor is the pre-eminent tremendousness of the great Sperm Whale anywhere more feelingly comprehended, than on board of those prows which stem him.

And as if the now tested reality of his might had in former legendary times thrown its shadow before it; we find some book naturalists — Olassen and Povelson[9] — declaring the Sperm Whale not only to be a consternation to every other creature in the sea, but also to be so incredibly ferocious as continually to be athirst for human blood. Nor even down to so late a time as Cuvier's,[10] were these or almost similar impressions effaced. For in his Natural History, the Baron himself affirms that at sight of the Sperm Whale, all fish (sharks included) are "struck with the most lively terrors", and "often in the precipitancy of their flight dash themselves against the rocks with such violence as to cause instantaneous death". And however the general experiences in the fishery may amend such reports as these; yet in their full terribleness, even to the bloodthirsty item of Povelson, the superstitious belief in them is, in some vicissitudes of their vocation, revived in the minds of the hunters.

So that overawed by the rumors and portents concerning him, not a few of the fishermen recalled, in reference to Moby Dick, the earlier days of the Sperm Whale fishery, when it was oftentimes hard to induce long practised Right whalemen to embark

Chapter 3 The Literature of the Romantic Period

in the perils of this new and daring warfare; such men protesting that although other leviathans might be hopefully pursued, yet to chase and point lance at such an apparition as the Sperm Whale was not for mortal man. That to attempt it, would be inevitably to be torn into a quick eternity.[11] on this head, there are some remarkable documents that may be consulted.

Nevertheless, some there were, who even in the face of these things were ready to give chase to Moby Dick; and a still greater number who, chancing only to hear of him distantly and vaguely, without the specific details of any certain calamity, and without superstitious accompaniments, were sufficiently hardy not to flee from the battle if offered.

One of the wild suggestings referred to, as at last coming to be linked with the White Whale in the minds of the superstitiously inclined, was the unearthly conceit that Moby Dick was ubiquitous; that he had actually been encountered in opposite latitudes at one and the same instant of time.

Nor, credulous as such minds must have been, was this conceit altogether without some faint show of superstitious probability. For as the secrets of the currents in the seas have never yet been divulged, even to the most erudite research; so the hidden ways of the Sperm Whale when beneath the surface remain, in great part, unaccountable to his pursuers; and from time to time have originated the most curious and contradictory speculations regarding them, especially concerning the mystic modes whereby, after sounding to a great depth, he transports himself with such vast swiftness to the most widely distant points.

It is a thing well known to both American and English whale-ships, and as well a thing placed upon authoritative record years ago by Scoresby,[12] that some whales have been captured far north in the Pacific, in whose bodies have been found the barbs of harpoons darted in the Greenland seas. Nor is it to be gainsaid, that in some of these instances it has been declared that the interval of time between the two assaults could not have exceeded very many days. Hence, by inference, it has been believed by some whalemen, that the nor' west passage,[13] so long a problem to man, was never a problem to the whale. So that here, in the real living experience of living men, the prodigies related in old times of the inland Strello mountain in Portugal (near whose top there was said to be a lake in which the wrecks of ships floated up to the surface); and that still more wonderful story of the Arethusa fountain near Syracuse[14] (whose waters were believed to have come from the Holy Land by an underground passage); these fabulous narrations are almost fully equalled by the realities of the whaleman.

Forced into familiarity, then, with such prodigies as these; and knowing that after repeated, intrepid assaults, the White Whale had escaped alive; it cannot be much matter of surprise that some whalemen should go still further in their superstitions; declaring Moby Dick not only ubiquitous, but immortal (for immortality is but ubiquity in time); that though groves of spears should be planted in his flanks, he would still swim away unharmed; or if indeed he should ever be made to spout thick blood, such a sight would be but a ghastly deception; for again in unensanguined billows hundreds of leagues away, his unsullied jet would once more be seen.

But even stripped of these supernatural surmisings, there was enough in the earthly make and incontestable character of the monster to strike the imagination with unwonted power. For, it was not so much his uncommon bulk that so much distinguished him from other Sperm Whales, but, as was elsewhere thrown out — a peculiar snow-white wrinkled forehead, and a high, pyramidical white hump. These were his prominent features; the tokens whereby, even in the limitless, uncharted seas, he revealed his identity, at a long distance, to those who knew him.

The rest of his body was so streaked, and spotted, and marbled with the same shrouded hue, that, in the end, he had gained his distinctive appellation of the White Whale; a name, indeed, literally justified by his vivid aspect, when seen gliding at high noon through a dark blue sea, leaving a milky-way wake of creamy foam, all spangled with golden gleamings.

Nor was it his unwonted magnitude, nor his remarkable hue, nor yet his deformed lower jaw, that so much invested the whale with natural terror, as that unexampled, intelligent malignity which, according to specific accounts, he had over and over again evinced in his assaults. More than all, his treacherous retreats struck more of dismay than perhaps aught else. For, when swimming before his exulting pursuers, with every apparent symptom of alarm, he had several times been known to turn around suddenly, and, bearing down upon them, either stave their boats to splinters, or drive them back in consternation to their ship.

Already several fatalities had attended his chase. But though similar disasters, however little bruited ashore, were by no means unusual in the fishery; yet, in most instances, such seemed the White Whale's infernal aforethought of ferocity, that every dismembering or death that he caused, was not wholly regarded as having been inflicted by an unintelligent agent.

Judge, then, to what pitches of inflamed, distracted fury the minds of his more desperate hunters were impelled, when amid the chips of chewed boats, and the sinking limbs of torn comrades, they swam out of the white curds of the whale's direful wrath into the serene, exasperating sunlight, that smiled on, as if at a birth or a bridal.

His three boats stove around him, and oars and men both whirling in the eddies; one captain, seizing the line-knife from his broken prow, had dashed at the whale, as an Arkansas duellist at his foe, blindly seeking with a six inch blade to reach the fathom-deep life of the whale. That captain was Ahab. And then it was, that suddenly sweeping his sickle-shaped lower jaw beneath him, Moby Dick had reaped away Ahab's leg, as a mower a blade of grass in the field. No turbaned Turk, no hired Venetian or Malay, could have smote him with more seeming malice. Small reason was there to doubt, then, that ever since that almost fatal encounter, Ahab had cherished a wild vindictiveness against the whale, all the more fell for that in his frantic morbidness he at last came to identify with him, not only all his bodily woes, but all his intellectual and spiritual exasperations. The White Whale swam before him as the monomaniac incarnation of all those malicious agencies which some deep men feel eating in them, till they are left living on with half a heart and half a lung. That intangible malignity which has been from the beginning; to whose dominion even the modern Christians ascribe one-half of the worlds; which the ancient Ophites[15] of the east reverenced in their statue devil; — Ahab did not fall down and worship it like them; but deliriously transferring its idea to the abhorred White Whale, he pitted himself, all mutilated, against it. All that most maddens and torments; all that stirs up the lees of things; all truth with malice in it; all that cracks the sinews and cakes the brain; all the subtle demonisms of life and thought; all evil, to crazy Ahab, were visibly personified, and made practically assailable in Moby Dick. He piled upon the whale's white hump the sum of all the general rage and hate felt by his whole race from Adam down; and then, as if his chest had been a mortar, he burst his hot heart's shell upon it.

...

Notes

1. **Ishmael**: the narrator of the story in the book. The name is from the Bible. In the Old Testament, Ishmael is the son of Abraham who was cast out after the birth of Isaac.
2. **the Sperm Whale**: any of several large, toothed whales of the family Physeteridae, whose massive head has a cavity containing sperm oil.
3. **news-telling sail**: ship that pass messages.
4. **terra firma**: (Latin) solid ground.
5. **chiselled hearthstone**: here implying the warm home.
6. **all tending to make his fancy pregnant with many a mighty birth**: all this contribute to the thinking of many feats in his mind.
7. **leviathan**: a monstrous sea creature mentioned in the Old Testament.
8. **Greenland or Right Whale**: any of several whales of the family Balaenidae, characterized by a large head, whalebone plates in the mouth, and absence of a dorsal fin.
9. **Olassen and Povelson**: Olassen (1726-1768) a biologist of Iceland. He ever traveled nationwide and wrote travelog.
10. **Cuvier**: (1769-1832) a French naturalist who set up the subject of anatomy and put forward zootaxy system.
11. **torn into a quick eternity**: torn into pieces and died immediately.
12. **Scoresby**: William Scoresby, Jr. British explorer in the North Pole. He is the author

of *An Account of the Arctic Region*.
13. **the nor' west passage**: the passage that connects the Atlantic Ocean and the Pacific Ocean.
14. **the Arethusa fountain near Syracuse**: Arethusa, a wood nymph in Greek myths, who was chased by Achelous. To escape, she was changed into a fountain by Artemis and flowed underground from the south of Greece, Sicanian and appeared on the ground in Syracuse. However, Achelous dived into the underground and kept chasing. The two finally had a happy union.
15. **the ancient Ophites**: people who worshiped snake.

Study Questions

1. Why does Ahab want to kill the White Whale?
2. What is Ishmael's interpretation of the terror that Moby-Dick inspires?
3. Describe Ishmael's method of narration. Is he reliable or unreliable as a narrator?

Essay Topics

1. Explain some of the Biblical references in *Moby-Dick*. How does Melville use the Bible as a literary model and as a source for thematic material?
2. Comment on the author's style in his use of symbols and imagery in *Moby-Dick*.

3.8 Abraham Lincoln

3.8.1 About the author

Abraham Lincoln (1809-1865) was born in a log cabin near Hodgenville, Kentucky. His father was a farmer. To help support the family, Abraham spent his youth working on a farm. As his pioneering family made repeated fresh starts in the West, Young Lincoln received little formal schooling and was largely self-taught. In 1831, Lincoln moved to New Salem, Illinois, near Springfield. He held various jobs there, including storekeeper and mill operator. He worked as a farmhand, grocery clerk, and rail splitter. He also worked as a deckhand on a flatboat that floated down the Ohio and Mississippi rivers to New Orleans.

It was in Illinois that Lincoln became interested in politics. In 1832 he ran for the Illinois state legislature, but failed. However, he continued to pursue a political career. Steadily he moved into public view. His debate with Stephen Douglas, his opponent in the Illinois Senate race made him nationally known as a brilliant, compelling speaker.

From 1834 to 1842, Lincoln served four terms in the state legislature and in 1846 was elected to Congress, representing the Whig Party for a term. During the 1834 campaign, he was encouraged to study law. In March of 1837, he was enrolled as an attorney. Back in Springfield, he gradually began to prosper as a lawyer, often representing business interests, but his eloquently stated if moderate anti-slavery views gained him increasing attention. In 1842, he married Mary Todd, the daughter of a socially prominent Lexington family. In 1846, Lincoln was elected to U. S. House of Representatives and served one term. In 1856 he joined the new Republican Party and in 1860 the Republican Party chose Abraham Lincoln as their candidate for president. The elections were held in the fall of 1860 and Lincoln won.

As President, he built the Republican Party into a strong national organization. Further, he rallied most of the northern Democrats to the Union cause. In the years of civil war that followed, the inexperienced Lincoln proved to be one of the most extraordinary leaders, both political and moral. Lincoln defined the Civil War as a struggle to save the Union, but in January 1863 he issued the Emancipation Proclamation, which freed all slaves in areas still under Confederate control. This was an important symbolic gesture that identified the Union's struggle as a war to end slavery. With his immortal Gettysburg Address (Nov. 1863), he further defined the war as the struggle for preservation of the democratic idea which he called "government of the people, by the people, for the people". In 1864, Lincoln stood for re-election and won. In his second inaugural address, he was conciliatory towards the southern states. Having seen the victory of the Union forces, he was beginning to plan a generous reconstruction policy. On April 14, 1865, Lincoln had been attending a play at Ford's Theater in Washington, D. C. and was shot by John Wilkes Booth. Lincoln died the next morning. He was the first US president ever assassinated.

3.8.2 Lincoln's Gettysburg Address (1863)

[*On Nov. 19, 1863, a part of the battlefield of Gettysburg was set aside as a cemetery, where monuments to the soldiers who fell there might be set up. The main oration[1] was delivered by Edward Everett, at the conclusion of which Lincoln dedicated the field in this most pregnant[2] and eloquent of his utterances.*]

Fourscore and seven years ago[3] our fathers brought forth on this continent a new nation, conceived[4] in liberty, and dedicated to the proposition[5] that all men are created equal.

Now we are engaged in a great civil war, testing whether that nation, or any nation so conceived and so dedicated, can long endure. We are met on a great battlefield of that war. We have come to dedicate a portion of that field as a final resting-place for those who here gave their lives that the nation might live. It is altogether fitting[6] and proper that we should do this. But, in a larger sense, we cannot dedicate, we cannot

consecrate,[7] we cannot hallow,[8] this ground. The brave men, living and dead, who struggled here have consecrated it, far above our poor power to add or detract.[9] The world will little note, nor long remember, what we say here, but it can never forget what they did here. It is for us the living, rather, to be dedicated here to the unfinished work[10] which they who fought here have thus far so nobly advanced. It is rather for us to be here dedicated to the great task remaining before us — that from these honored dead we take increased devotion to that cause for which they gave the last full measure of devotion — that we here highly resolve that these dead shall not have died in vain — that this nation, under God, shall have a new birth of freedom and that government of the people, by the people, for the people,[11] shall not perish[12] from the earth.

Notes

1. **oration**: a formal speech, especially one given on a ceremonial occasion.
2. **pregnant**: weighty or significant; full of meaning.
3. **fourscore and seven years ago**: eight-seven years ago. It was in 1863 that Abraham Lincoln gave the address at the site of the battle at Gettysburg, Pennsylvania. Eighty-seven years before had been 1776, the year when the United States of America declared independence.
4. **conceive**: to form or develop in the mind; devise.
5. **proposition**: a plan suggested for acceptance; a proposal. Here the proposition refers to in the Declaration of Independence : "We hold these truths to be self-evident, that all men are created equal, that they are endowed by their Creator with certain unalienable Rights, that among these are Life, Liberty and the pursuit of Happiness."
6. **fitting**: appropriate.
7. **consecrate**: to dedicate solemnly to a service or goal.
8. **hallow**: to respect or honor greatly; revere.
9. **detract**: to draw or take away; divert.
10. **unfinished work** : a creative work that has not been completed. Its creator might have chosen never to finish it, or have been prevented by circumstances outside of his or her control (including death).
11. **government of the people, by the people, for the people**: people own the government, run the government and the government is for the benefit of the people.
12. **perish**: to pass from existence; disappear gradually.

Study Questions

1. According to Lincoln, what was the fighting of the American Civil War "testing"?
2. Why does Lincoln refer to the Civil War as "unfinished work"?
3. What cause did Lincoln mean when he said, "that cause for which they gave the last full measure of devotion"?
4. What did Lincoln mean by the speech's most famous phrase, "government of the people, by the people, for the people"?

Essay Topics

1. Analyze Lincoln's devices for creating coherence in the Gettysburg Address.
2. Comment on the diction and style of Lincoln's Gettysburg Address.

3.9 Henry Wadsworth Longfellow

3.9.1 About the Author

Henry Wadsworth Longfellow (1807-1882) was born in Portland, Maine. As a child, he was fond of reading. He also loved to write stories and poems. He received his education first at Portland Academy and then at Bowdoin College. He was an excellent student whose skill in languages led the trustees at Bowdoin to offer the young graduate a professorship of modern languages. To prepare for the position, Longfellow was required to travel to Europe for further study. During his three-year tour, Longfellow immersed himself in the literature of Europe, and in mastering half a dozen languages. Upon arrival back in America he settled at Bowdoin to teach modern languages including French and Italian from 1829 — 1835.

In 1834 Longfellow accepted a professorship at Harvard University. He did not start his new job until 1837, after he had completed a tour of European and Scandinavian countries. On this trip he fell under the influence of German Romanticism. While working at Harvard, he wrote many of his poems. In 1839, Longfellow published his first book of poems, *Voices of the Night*, which received wide public recognition. In 1854 Longfellow resigned his Harvard professorship to devote himself to his writing career. One of his next most famous works, *The Song of Hiawatha*, showed him at the height of his career. Longfellow continued to write poetry, collected under such titles as *Tales of a Wayside Inn* (1863), *Household Poems* (1865), and *Flower-de-Luce* (1867). He wrote on a wide range of subjects, both contemporary and historical, and he tried many different poetic forms and meters with great technical skills. Longfellow was married twice — after the death of his first wife he married again in 1843 Frances Appleton, who also died tragically in 1861. Despite the loss, Longfellow continued his prolific poetic career, which, in 1868, earned him a private audience with Queen Victoria and honorary degrees at both Oxford and Cambridge.

Longfellow's lyric and narrative poetry has made lasting contributions to the American literary tradition. The best-known shorter poems are "The Village Blacksmith," "The Children's Hour," "Paul Revere's Ride," "The Wreck of the Hesperus," and "Excelsior." His famous longer works include *Evangeline*, *The Song of Hiawatha*, and *The Courtship of Miles Standish*. Today Longfellow remains one of the most popular American poets, mainly for his simplicity of style and for his technical expertise. His poetic work is characterized by familiar themes, easily grasped ideas, and clear, simple, melodious language.

3.9.2 "A Psalm of Life"

WHAT THE HEART OF THE YOUNG MAN SAID TO THE PSALMIST[1]

Tell me not, in mournful numbers,[2]
Life is but an empty dream! —
For the soul is dead that slumbers,
And things are not what they seem.

Life is real! Life is earnest!
And the grave is not its goal;
Dust thou art, to dust returnest,
Was not spoken of the soul.

Not enjoyment, and not sorrow,
Is our destined end or way;
But to act, that each tomorrow
Find us farther than today.

Art is long, and Time is fleeting,
And our hearts, though stout and brave,
Still, like muffled[3] drums, are beating
Funeral marches to the grave.

In the world's broad field of battle,
In the bivouac[4] of Life,

Chapter 3 The Literature of the Romantic Period

Be not like dumb, driven cattle!
Be a hero in the strife!

Trust no Future, howe'er pleasant!
Let the dead Past bury its dead!
Act, — act in the living Present!
Heart within, and God o'erhead!

Lives of great men all remind us
We can make our lives sublime,
And, departing, leave behind us
Footprints on the sands of time;[5]

Footprints, that perhaps another,
Sailing o'er life's solemn main,[6]
A forlorn[7] and shipwrecked brother,
Seeing, shall take heart again.

Let us, then, be up and doing,
With a heart for any fate;
Still achieving, still pursuing,
Learn to labor and to wait.

Notes
1. **psalmist**: a writer or composer of a sacred song or hymn.
2. **numbers**: metrical feet; verses.
3. **muffle**: to wrap or pad in order to deaden the sound.
4. **bivouac**: a temporary camp.
5. **the sands of time**: time, as measured by the sand in an hourglass.
6. **main**: ocean.
7. **forlorn**: wretched or pitiful in appearance or condition.

Study Questions
1. What is the author's attitude towards life and death?
2. Do you feel inspired by the poem? If so, tell how it moves you.
3. Do you agree with the philosophy of life presented in the poem? Why?
4. What do we learn from the lives of the great?

Essay Topics

1. Do you think people's attitudes are different at different times in their lives? Why?
2. Try to summarize the speaker's advice for living.

3.9.3 "The Tide Rises, the Tide Falls"

> The tide rises, the tide falls,
> The twilight darkens, the curlew[1] calls;
> Along the sea-sands damp and brown
> The traveler hastens toward the town,
> And the tide rises, the tide falls.
>
> Darkness settles on roofs and walls,
> But the sea, the sea in darkness calls;
> The little waves, with their soft, white hands
> Efface[2] the footprints in the sands,
> And the tide rises, the tide falls.
>
> The morning breaks; the steeds[3] in their stalls
> Stamp[4] and neigh,[5] as the hostler[6] calls;
> The day returns, but nevermore
> Returns the traveler to the shore.
> And the tide rises, the tide falls.

Notes

1. **curlew**: large wading bird whose call is associated with evening.
2. **efface**: to rub or wipe out; erase.
3. **steed**: a horse, especially a spirited one.
4. **stamp**: to bring down (the foot) forcibly.
5. **neigh**: the long, high-pitched sound made by a horse.
6. **hostler**: one who is employed to tend horses, especially at an inn.

Study Questions

1. According to stanza 1, what is the setting (time and space) of the poem?
2. According to stanza 2, what evidence does the traveler leave behind? What happens to this evidence?

Essay Topics

1. H. W. Longfellow is regarded as a "master technician". Using any poem as an example, explain as fully as possible why he deserves this definition, taking into

consideration the use of appropriate imagery, figurative language, alliteration, etc.
2. Longfellow wrote "A Psalm of Life" when he was young and "The Tide Rises, the Tide Falls" when he was old. How do you think the first poem represents the visions and ideals of a young person? What elements in the second poem indicate the view of a mature and experienced person looking back and assessing life?

3.10 Walt Whitman

3.10.1 About the Author

Walt Whitman (1819-1892) was born on Long Island, New York, the son of a Quaker carpenter. His family soon moved to Brooklyn, where he attended school for a few years. Young Whitman took to reading at an early age, and became acquainted with Homer, Dante, Shakespeare and Scott. By 1830 his formal education was over, and he began to learn the printing trade. Then, he taught school on Long Island for a few years; during this time he also founded the weekly newspaper *Long-Islander*. In New York Whitman witnessed the rapid growth of the city and wanted to write a new kind of poetry in tune with mankind's new faith, hopeful expectations and energy of his days. In 1848 he traveled south and worked for the *New Orleans Crescent*. The sheer physical beauty of the new nation made a vivid impression on him, and he was to draw on this experience in his later poetry.

For the next few years Whitman edited several newspapers and contributed to others. The first edition of *Leaves of Grass* appeared in July 1855 at Whitman's own expense. It was widely ignored. But the third edition published in 1860 was greeted with warm appreciation. At the outset of the Civil War, Whitman volunteered as a nurse in army hospitals; he also wrote dispatches as a correspondent for *The New York Times*. The war inspired a great deal of poetry, which was published in 1865 as *Drum Taps*. Following the Civil War and the publication of the fourth edition of *Leaves of Grass*, Whitman's poetry became increasingly preoccupied with themes relating to the soul, death, and immortality.

Within the span of some dozen years, Whitman was entering the final phase of his career. The poet of the body had given way to the poet of internationalism and the cosmic. Such poems as "Whispers of Heavenly Death," "Darest Thou Now O Soul," "The Last Invocation," and "A Noiseless Patient Spider," with their emphasis on the spiritual, paved the way for "Passage to India" (1871), Whitman's most important poem of the post – Civil War period. Whitman's health had been shaky after he suffered a paralytic stroke in 1873. But he kept on working. By 1891 it was clear that he was dying.

He therefore prepared his so-called "Deathbed" edition of *Leaves of Grass*, which contained 383 titled poems.

Whitman is a poet with a strong sense of mission, having devoted all his life to the creation of the "single" work, *Leaves of Grass*. In this giant book, openness, freedom, and above all, individualism are all that concerned him. His aim was nothing less than to express some new poetical feelings and to initiate a poetic tradition in which difference should be recognized. Whitman maintained that a poet's style should be simple and natural, without orthodox meter or rhyme. His poetry is thus written with fresh use of the language and great variety in rhythm and tonal volume. Thematically, his poetry is centered on ideas of democracy, equality, and brotherhood. Though he was attacked in his lifetime for his offensive subject matter of sexuality and for his unconventional style, Whitman has proved a great figure in the literary history of the United States because he embodies a new ideal, a new world and a new life style. His influence over the following generations is significant and incredible.

3.10.2 Excerpts from "Song of Myself [1]"

1

I celebrate myself, and sing myself,
And what I assume you shall assume,
For every atom belonging to me as good belongs to you.

I loafe and invite my soul,[2]
I lean and loafe at my ease observing a spear of summer grass[3].
My tongue, every atom of my blood, formed from this soil, this air,
Born here of parents born here from parents the same, and their
parents the same,
I, now thirty-seven years old in perfect health begin,
Hoping to cease not till death.

Creeds and schools in abeyance,[4]
Retiring back a while sufficed at what they are, but never forgotten,
I harbor for good or bad, I permit to speak at every hazard,
Nature without check with original energy.

6

A child said *What is the grass?* fetching it to me with full hands;
How could I answer the child? I do not know what it is any more than he.
I guess it must be the flag of my disposition, out of hopeful green stuff woven.

Or I guess it is the handkerchief of the Lord,
A scented gift and remembrancer[5] designedly dropped,
Bearing the owner's name someway in the corners, that we may see
and remark, and say *Whose?*

...

What do you think has become of the young and old men?
And what do you think has become of the women and children?

They are alive and well somewhere,
The smallest sprout shows there is really no death,
And if ever there was it led forward life, and does not wait at the end to arrest it,
And ceased the moment life appeared.

All goes onward and outward, nothing collapses,
And to die is different from what any one supposed, and luckier.

17

These are really the thoughts of all men in all ages and lands, they are not original with me,
If they are not yours as much as mine they are nothing, or next to nothing,
If they are not the riddle and the untying of the riddle they are nothing,
If they are not just as close as they are distant they are nothing.
This is the grass that grows wherever the land is and the water is,
This the common air that bathes the globe.

51

The past and present wilt[6]— I have filled them, emptied them.
And proceed to fill my next fold of the future.

Listener up there! what have you to confide to me?
Look in my face while I snuff the sidle of evening,[7]
(Talk honestly, no one else hears you, and I stay only a minute longer.)
Do I contradict myself?
Very well then I contradict myself,
(I am large, I contain multitudes.)

I concentrate toward them that are nigh,[8] I wait on the door-slab.
Who has done his day's work? who will soonest be through with his supper?
Who wishes to walk with me?
Will you speak before I am gone? will you prove already too late?

52

The spotted hawk swoops by and accuses me, he complains of my gab and my loitering.[9]

I too am not a bit tamed, I too am untranslatable,
I sound my barbaric yawp[10] over the roofs of the world.

The last scud[11] of day holds back for me,
It flings my likeness after the rest and true as any on the shadowed wilds,
It coaxes me to the vapor and the dusk.

I depart as air, I shake my white locks at the runaway sun,
I effuse[12] my flesh in eddies, and drift it in lacy jabs.[13]

Chapter 3 The Literature of the Romantic Period

I bequeath myself to the dirt to grow from the grass I love,
If you want me again look for me under your boot soles.

You will hardly know who I am or what I mean,
But I shall be good health to you nevertheless,
And filter and fiber your blood.

Failing to fetch me at first keep encouraged,
Missing me one place search another,
I stop somewhere waiting for you.

Notes

1. **"Song of Myself"**: This is the longest poem in *Leaves of Grass*. "Myself," which refers to an individual, is the central and principal image in this poem.
2. **I loafe and invite my soul**: This line indicates a separation of the body and the soul, the physical and the spiritual. The union of the body and the soul will not be achieved unless the self is awakened.
3. **a spear of summer grass**: "Grass" is a symbol of hope and youth, "spear" is a symbol of male energy, and "summer" is the hot season. All the three images put together form an energetic and hopeful picture, which indicates Whitman's optimism and experience.
4. **abeyance**: The condition of being temporarily set aside; suspension.
5. **remembrancer**: a thing given or kept in memory of somebody or something.
6. **wilt**: become weak.
7. **snuff the sidle of evening**: put out the light of day, which is moving sideways across the sky.
8. **nigh**: near.
9. **loitering**: to stand idly about; linger aimlessly.
10. **yawp**: loud or coarse talk or utterance.
11. **scud**: low, dark, wind-driven clouds.
12. **effuse**: pour forth.
13. **jab**: to poke or thrust abruptly, especially with something sharp.

Study Questions

1. What is Whitman's attitude toward nature?
2. Consider the image of grass in this poem. What does the grass have to do with life and death?
3. Describe Whitman's diction. What kind of language does he use?

Essay Topics

1. What are the ideals that are celebrated in "Song of Myself"?
2. Discuss Whitman's contribution to American poetry.

3.10.3 "I Hear America Singing"

I hear America singing, the varied carols[1] I hear;

Those of mechanics, each one singing his, as it should be, blithe[2] and strong;

The carpenter singing his, as he measures his plank[3] or beam,

The mason[4] singing his, as he makes ready for work, or leaves off[5] work;

The boatman singing what belongs to him in his boat, the deckhand[6] singing on the steamboat deck;

The shoemaker singing as he sits on his bench, the hatter[7] singing as he stands;

The woodcutter's song, the ploughboy's, on his way in the morning, or at the noon intermission[8], or at sundown;

The delicious singing of the mother, or of the young wife at work, or of the girl sewing or washing;

Each singing what belongs to her, and to none else;

The day what belongs to the day — at night, the party of young fellows, robust[9], friendly,

Singing with open mouths, their strong melodious songs.

Notes

1. **carols**: joyful songs.
2. **blithe**: carefree and lighthearted.
3. **plank**: a piece of lumber cut thicker than a board.
4. **mason**: one who builds or works with stone or brick.
5. **leaves off**: stop; cease.
6. **deckhand**: sailor.
7. **hatter**: one whose occupation is the manufacture, selling, or repair of hats.
8. **intermission**: the period between work.
9. **robust**: full of health and strength; vigorous.

Study Questions

1. Does the poet use any conventional poetic symbols in this poem?
2. Name eight of the people that Whitman hears, according to lines 2-8.
3. What is the tone of the poem?

Chapter 3　The Literature of the Romantic Period

3.11　Emily Dickinson

3.11.1　About the Author

Emily Dickinson (1830-1886) was born in Amherst, Massachusetts. As a young child, she attended a local grammar school and, for about a year, Mount Holyoke Female Seminary in South Hadley. She showed a sharp intelligence, and was able to create many original writings of rhyming stories, delighting her fellow classmates. After 1862, affected by an unhappy love affair, Emily gradually reduced her social contacts, going out less and less into society. By her late twenties, this had led to an almost complete seclusion. However, her private life was pretty much in order. Within the confines of the family home,  the garden, and her circle of friends, she felt with her whole heart, thought with intensity, and imagined with ardor, and she maintained written contact with a variety of thought provoking people. Living a life of simplicity and seclusion, Emily read intensively by herself. Her favorite writers were Keats, the Brontës, the Brownings, and George Eliot; classic myths, the Bible, and Shakespeare were what Emily drew commonly on for allusions and references in her poetry and letters.

It was said that around 1850 she started to compose poems seriously. In fact, she kept on writing all her life, and she wrote altogether 1 775 poems. But only seven of her poems were published during her lifetime. After her death in 1886, her sister discovered her notebooks and published the contents, thus, presenting America with a tremendous poetic legacy that appeared fully formed and without any warning.

As a poet, Dickinson is simply unlike any other one; her compact, forceful language, characterized formally by long disruptive dashes, heavy iambic meters, and angular, imprecise rhymes, is one of the singular literary achievements of the nineteenth century. In her writing, she followed her own feelings and wrote about things she cared about from her life. Her lyric poems capture impressions of particular moments, scenes, or moods, and she characteristically focuses upon topics such as nature, love, immorality, death, faith, doubt, pain, and the self.

Technically, Dickinson's poetry is also unique and unconventional in its own way. Her poems have no titles, hence are always quoted by their first lines. In her poetry there is a particular stress pattern, in which dashes are used as a musical device to create cadence and capital letters as a means of emphasis. The form of her poetry is more or less like that of the hymns in community churches, familiar, communal, and sometimes, irregular. However, her poetic idiom is noted for its directness and plainness. Her poems are usually short, rarely more than twenty lines, and many of them are centered on a single image or symbol and focused on one subject matter. Her poetry, despite its ostensible formal simplicity, is remarkable for its variety, subtlety and richness; and her limited private world has never confined the limitless power of her creativity and imagination.

3.11.2 "I'm Nobody! Who Are You?[1]"

I'm nobody! Who are you?
Are you nobody, too?
Then there's a pair of us — don't tell!
They'd banish us, you know.

How dreary to be somebody!
How public, like a frog
To tell your name the livelong day
To an admiring bog![2]

Notes

1. This poem might indicate Dickinson's attitude towards fame and explain why she preferred reclusion. The poet adopts the persona of an open, naive, and innocent child who seemed to enjoy being nobody.
2. **bog**: an area of wet muddy ground.

Study Questions

1. What is the tone of the poem? Is there any satire in the poem?
2. Why does the speaker choose frog as the representative of a public creature?

3.11.3 "Success Is Counted Sweetest"

Success is counted sweetest
By those who ne'er succeed.
To comprehend a nectar
Requires sorest[1] need.
Not one of all the purple host[2]
Who took the flag[3] today
Can tell the definition,
So clear, of victory!

As he, defeated, dying,
On whose forbidden ear
The distant strains of triumph[4]
Burst agonized and clear!

Chapter 3   The Literature of the Romantic Period

Notes

1. **sorest**: here it is used with the older meaning of greatest.
2. **the purple host**: people of very high rank like kings would wear robes with purple color in ancient times.
3. **took the flag**: won the victory.
4. **strains of triumph**: music of victory.

Study Questions

1. Why does the poet say that "success is counted sweetest by those who ne'er succeed"?
2. Whom should your respect and sympathy go, to the winner or the loser?

3.11.4 "This Is My Letter to the World"

This is my letter to the World
That never wrote to Me —
The simple News that Nature told —
With tender Majesty[1]

Her Message is committed[2]
To Hands I cannot see —
For love of Her — sweet — countrymen —
Judge tenderly — of Me

Notes

1. **majesty**: supreme authority or power.
2. **commit**: to put in trust or charge.

Study Questions

1. According to stanza 1, to whom is the poet's letter addressed? What "News" does it contain?
2. In stanza 2, what does the poet ask her "countrymen" to do?

3.11.5 "Because I Could Not Stop for Death"

Because I could not stop for Death —
He kindly stopped for me —
The Carriage held but just Ourselves —
And Immortality.[1]

79

We slowly drove — He knew no haste,
And I had put away
My labor, and my leisure too,
For His Civility.[2]

We passed the school where children strove
At Recess[3]— in the Ring;
We passed the Fields of Gazing Grain,
We passed the Setting Sun.

Or rather — He passes Us —
The Dews drew quivering and chill —
For only Gossamer,[4] my Gown —
My Tippet[5]— only Tulle[6]—

We paused before a House that seemed
A Swelling of the Ground;
The Roof was scarcely visible —
The Cornice[7]— in the Ground —

Since then — 'tis Centuries — and yet
Feels shorter than the Day
I first surmised[8] the Horses' Heads
Were toward Eternity —

Notes

1. **immortality**: the state of living forever.
2. **civility**: politeness.
3. **recess**: the break between school classes.
4. **gossamer**: a very light, soft fabric.
5. **tippet**: scarf for the neck and shoulders.
6. **tulle**: thin, soft silk material used for scarves and veils.
7. **cornice**: wood that runs along the top edge of a wall used for decoration.
8. **surmised**: guess something.

Study Questions

1. What figures of speech does the poet use to depict Death?
2. What images are used to describe the speaker's journey with Death?
3. Why does the day described seem so long to the speaker?

Chapter 3　The Literature of the Romantic Period

Essay Topics
1. How death and life are logically related with each other in this poem?
2. What makes Dickinson's poems memorable despite their thematic simplicity?

Chapter 4 The Literature of the Realistic Period

4.1 An Introduction

Realism as a movement in American literature ranged from 1865 to 1914, and was a partial reaction to much of the earlier romantic and sentimental tradition. At its basic level, American Realism was grounded in the faithful reporting of all facets of everyday American life, free from subjective prejudice, idealism, or romantic color. Influenced in many ways by the work of French writers such as Balzac and Flaubert, American realists were chiefly concerned with the commonplaces of middle-class life.

The fifty years between the end of the Civil War and the outbreak of the First World War had witnessed great changes in America. First of all, the Civil War brought a more realistic treatment of the American people, who, that is, the common people, were seen as heroes. The war effort, however, also unleashed forces of industry: mass production, technological innovation, and huge profits, thus ushering in a new period of economic boom. The intercontinental rail system, inaugurated in 1869, and the transcontinental telegraph, which began operating in 1861, gave industry access to materials, markets, and communications. Various kinds of mineral wealth were discovered and extracted to help improve the national economy. The constant influx of immigrants provided a seemingly endless supply of inexpensive labor as well. As a result, capital invested in manufacturing industries more than quadrupled; factory employment nearly doubled; industrial output grew at a geometric rate; and agricultural productivity increased dramatically. The burgeoning economy and industry also stepped up urbanization. Just before the breaking of the First World War, the United States had been transformed from a small, young, agricultural ex-colony to a huge, modern, industrial nation.

However, the changes were not all for the good. With rapid economic development, there was an increasing level of class division and labor unrest. On one side, the rampant industrialization and urbanization benefited only a group of powerful capitalists and entrepreneurs, who went down in history as the "robber barons" and made ruthless exploitation of the majority poor to accumulate their original capital. On the other side, under the workings of monopolistic economic practices, large numbers of farmers were pushed off their lands and became city job-seekers. Together with the newly-arrived poor immigrants, they herded themselves into harsh conditioned factories and overcrowded ghettos. With such an oversupply of labor, the workers were reduced to the level of commodities, valued only according to the fluctuating demand for their labor. Women and children were treated no differently in this respect from the men. Therefore, polarization of the well-being started to show up, with the poor poorer and the rich richer. As power and wealth were concentrated into the hands of a few capitalists,

Chapter 4 The Literature of the Realistic Period

political, economic and religious life in the American society became very corrupt. Under such conditions, labor unions grew, and strikes brought the plight of working people to national awareness.

The literary scene after the Civil War proved to be quite different a picture. The industrialism, with its positive and negative effects gave a whole new body of material for the writers to report and interpret. The new concepts of science which included the idea of evolution as progress, the view of nature as ruthless struggle for survival, the philosophy of scientific materialism, and a mechanistic interpretation of life all contributed to a changed understanding of the meaning of life. The rapid growth of education and the rise of the mass-circulation magazine created a mass audience for writers, and the passage in 1891 of the International Copyright Act protected foreign authors from piracy in America and by the same token protected the native literary product from being undercut by pirated editions of foreign works. All these provided a great impetus to the rise of American Realism.

Guided by the principle of adhering to the truthful presentation of life, the realistic writers touched upon various contemporary social and political issues of the American society. They built their plots and characters around people's ordinary, everyday lives. Additionally, their works contained regional dialects and extensive dialogue which connected well with the public. The major spokesman of the American Realism was William Dean Howells, who believed that Realism should concentrate on common life experiences which could instruct and inform readers rather than on the gross, immoral subject matter and pessimistic tone of European Realist literature. Howells endeavored to present the truth of the American society, focusing his discussion on the rising middle class and the way they lived. Mark Twain seemed to share a lot with Howells in literary presentation, but he preferred to have his own region and its people at the forefront of his stories. This particular concern about the local character of a region came about as Regionalism, a unique variation of American literary realism. Writers of this group captured the local color of a region through the accurate description of the characters' activities and realistic use of dialect. Henry James laid a greater emphasis on the inner world of man. He came to believe that the literary artist should not simply hold a mirror to the surface of social life in particular times and places. In addition, the writer should use language to probe the deepest reaches of the psychological and moral nature of human beings. Other writers who are usually considered realists were Rebecca Harding Davis, Harriet Beecher Stowe, Sarah Orne Jewett, and Kate Chopin.

Meanwhile another important literary tendency began to develop out of the realistic movement: the school of naturalism. The two most important impacts were Darwin's evolutionary theory and the French novelist Emile Zola's idea about fiction writing. Their ideas like "the survival of the fittest" and "the human beast" became catchwords and standards of moral reference in an amoral world. How is the naturalism different from nineteenth century realism? First, it differs in subject matter. It took ugly and unpleasant stories and people as subjects. Second, it threw out anything peculiarly human or religious, denying that man had any moral freedom of choice and asserting that his whole life was determined by heredity and environment. Often it is completely pessimistic, taking the gloomiest view of life. Famous naturalist writers were Theodore Dreiser, Jack London, Stephen Crane and Frank Norris.

4.2 Mark Twain

4.2.1 About the Author

Samuel Langhorne Clemens (Mark Twain) (1835-1910) was born in Florida, Missouri and grew up in nearby Hannibal, on the Mississippi River. In his youth, Clemens was a mischievous boy. Though he was plagued by poor health in his early years, by age nine he had already learned to smoke, led a small band of pranksters, and had developed an aversion to school. In 1847 when he was twelve, his father died. Clemens had to leave school and made a living by trying various trades. Successively he was a printer's apprentice, a silver miner, a steamboat pilot on the Mississippi and a journalist. In 1861, with the beginning of the Civil War, Clemens spent a few inglorious weeks as a volunteer in the Confederate army, but he soon deserted for the west. In 1863 he began signing his name with the pseudonym "Mark Twain," a river term meaning "two fathoms deep". In 1865, he published his frontier tale "The Celebrated Jumping Frog of Calaveras County," which brought him recognition from a wider public. But his full literary career began to blossom in 1869 with a travel book *Innocents Abroad*, an account of American tourists in Europe which poked fun at the pretentious, decadent and undemocratic Old World in a satirical tone.

Clemens's major works were produced when he was in the prime of his life. Two of the best books during this period are *The Adventures of Tom Sawyer* (1876) and *Adventures of Huckleberry Finn* (1884). The former is usually regarded as a classic book written for boys about their particular horrors and joys, while the latter, being a boy's book specially written for the adults, is Twain's most representative work, describing a journey down the Mississippi undertaken by two fugitives, Huck and Jim. Clemens set both of these novels in his native Missouri and drew heavily on his boyhood memories of growing up in Hannibal. He examined American culture on the edge of the frontier and dealt seriously with such issues as slavery, poverty, and class differences. Clemens's natural wit and keen observations of human nature found full expression in his fiction.

Clemens had a very miserable life in his later years. His son and two daughters died in heartbreaking circumstances; the publishing house in which he was a partner collapsed; he had invested his money and it turned out to be disastrous. For whatever the reason, the high spirits of optimism in his works started to coexist with a caustic and increasingly bleak view of human nature. By the turn of the century, the change in Clemens from an optimist to an almost despairing pessimist could be felt and his cynicism and disillusionment became obvious.

Clemens is known as a local colorist, who preferred to present social life through portraits of the local characters of his regions, including people living in that area, the landscape, and other peculiarities like the customs, dialects, costumes and so on. Consequently, the rich material of his boyhood experience became the endless resources for his fiction, and the Mississippi valley and the West became his major theme. Unlike James and Howells, Clemens wrote about the lower-class people, because they were the people he knew well and their life was the one he himself had lived. Moreover he successfully used local color and historical settings to illustrate and shed light on the contemporary society. Another fact that made Clemens unique is his magic power with language, his use of vernacular. His words are colloquial, concrete and direct in effect, and his sentence structures are simple, even ungrammatical, which is typical of the spoken language.

4.2.2 An Excerpt from Chapter 19 of *Adventures of Huckleberry Finn*

Two or three days and nights went by; I reckon I might say they swum by, they slid along so quiet and smooth and lovely. Here is the way we put in the time. It was a monstrous big river[1] down there — sometimes a mile and a half wide; we[2] run nights, and laid up and hid daytimes; soon as night was most gone we stopped navigating and tied up — nearly always in the dead water under a towhead; and then cut young cottonwoods and willows, and hid the raft with them. Then we set out the lines. Next we slid into the river and had a swim, so as to freshen up and cool off; then we set down on the sandy bottom where the water was about knee-deep,

and watched the daylight come. Not a sound anywheres — perfectly still — just like the whole world was asleep, only sometimes the bullfrogs a-cluttering, maybe. The first thing to see, looking away over the water, was a kind of dull line — that was the woods on t'other side; you couldn't make nothing else out; then a pale place in the sky; then more paleness spreading around; then the river softened up away off, and warn't[3] black any more, but gray; you could see little dark spots drifting along ever so far away — trading scows, and such things; and long black streaks — rafts; sometimes you could hear a sweep screaking; or jumbled up voices, it was so still, and sounds come so far; and by and by you could see a streak on the water which you know by the look of the streak that there's a snag there in a swift current which breaks on it and makes that streak look that way; and you see the mist curl up off of the water, and the east reddens up, and the river, and you make out a log-cabin in the edge of the woods, away on the bank on t' other side of the river, being a woodyard, likely, and piled by them cheats so you can throw a dog through it anywheres; then the nice breeze springs up, and comes fanning you from over there, so cool and fresh and sweet to smell on account of the woods and the flowers; but sometimes not that way, because they've left dead fish laying around, gars and such, and they do get pretty rank; and next you've got the full day, and everything smiling in the sun, and the song-birds just going it!

...

One of these fellows was about seventy or upwards, and had a bald head and very gray whiskers. He had an old battered-up slouch hat on, and a greasy blue woollen shirt, and ragged old blue jeans britches stuffed into his boot-tops, and home-knit galluses — no, he only had one. He had an old long-tailed blue jeans coat with slick brass buttons flung over his arm, and both of them had big, fat, ratty-looking carpet-bags.

The other fellow was about thirty, and dressed about as ornery. After breakfast we all laid off and talked, and the first thing that come out was that these chaps didn't know one another.

"What got you into trouble?" says the baldhead to t' other chap.

"Well, I'd been selling an article to take the tartar off the teeth — and it does take it off, too, and generly[4] the enamel along with it — but I stayed about one night longer than I ought to, and was just in the act of sliding out when I ran across you on the trail this side of town, and you told me they were coming, and begged me to help you to get off. So I told you I was expecting trouble myself, and would scatter out with you. That's the whole yarn — what's yourn?"[5]

"Well, I'd ben a-runnin' a little temperance revival thar[6] 'bout a week, and was the pet of the women folks, big and little, for I was makin' it mighty warm for the rummies, I tell you, and takin' as much as five or six dollars a night — ten cents a head, children and niggers free — and business a-growin' all the time, when somehow or another a little report got around last night that I had a way of puttin' in my time with a private jug on the sly. A nigger rousted me out this mornin', and told me the people was getherin' on the quiet with their dogs and horses, and they'd be along pretty soon and give me 'bout half an hour's start, and then run me down if they could; and if they got me they'd tar and feather me and ride me on a rail, sure. I didn't wait for no breakfast — I warn't hungry."

"Old man," said the young one, "I reckon we might double-team it together; what do you think?"

Chapter 4 The Literature of the Realistic Period

"I ain't undisposed. What's your line — mainly?"

"Jour printer[7] by trade; do a little in patent medicines; theater-actor — tragedy, you know; take a turn to mesmerism and phrenology when there's a chance; teach singing-geography school for a change; sling a lecture sometimes — oh, I do lots of things — most anything that comes handy, so it ain't work. What's your lay?"

"I've done considerble in the doctoring way in my time. Layin' on o' hands is my best holt[8]— for cancer and paralysis, and sich[9] things; and I k'n[10] tell a fortune pretty good when I've got somebody along to find out the facts for me. Preachin's my line, too, and workin' camp-meetin's, and missionaryin' around."

Nobody never said anything for a while; then the young man hove a sigh and says:

"Alas!"

"What 're you alassin' about?" says the baldhead.

"To think I should have lived to be leading such a life, and be degraded down into such company." And he begun to wipe the corner of his eye with a rag.

"Dern your skin, ain't the company good enough for you?" says the baldhead, pretty pert and uppish.

"Yes, it is good enough for me; it's as good as I deserve; for who fetched me so low when I was so high? I did myself. I don't blame you, gentlemen — far from it; I don't blame anybody. I deserve it all. Let the cold world do its worst; one thing I know — there's a grave somewhere for me. The world may go on just as it's always done, and take everything from me — loved ones, property, everything; but it can't take that. Some day I'll lie down in it and forget it all, and my poor broken heart will be at rest."

He went on a-wiping.

"Drot your pore broken heart," says the baldhead; "what are you heaving your pore broken heart at us f'r? We hain't done nothing."

"No, I know you haven't. I ain't blaming you, gentlemen. I brought myself down— yes, I did it myself. It's right I should suffer — perfectly right — I don't make any moan."

"Brought you down from whar? Whar was you brought down from?"

"Ah, you would not believe me; the world never believes — let it pass — 'tis no matter. The secret of my birth —"

"The secret of your birth! Do you mean to say —"

"Gentlemen," says the young man, very solemn, "I will reveal it to you, for I feel I may have confidence in you. By rights I am a duke!"

Jim's eyes bugged out when he heard that; and I reckon mine did, too. Then the baldhead says: "No! you can't mean it?"

"Yes. My great-grandfather, eldest son of the Duke of Bridgewater, fled to this country about the end of the last century, to breathe the pure air of freedom; married here, and died, leaving a son, his own father dying about the same time. The second son of the late duke seized the titles and estates — the infant real duke was ignored. I am the lineal descendant of that infant — I am the rightful Duke of Bridgewater; and here am I, forlorn, torn from my high estate, hunted of men, despised by the cold world, ragged, worn, heartbroken, and degraded to the companionship of felons on a raft!"

Jim pitied him ever so much, and so did I. We tried to comfort him, but he said it warn't much use, he couldn't be much comforted; said if we was a mind to acknowledge him, that would do him more good than most anything else; so we said we would, if he would tell us how. He said we ought to bow when we spoke to him, and say "Your Grace," or "My Lord," or "Your Lordship" — and he wouldn't mind it if we called him plain "Bridgewater," which, he said, was a title anyway, and not a name; and one of us ought to wait on him at dinner, and do any little thing for him he wanted done.

Well, that was all easy, so we done it. All through dinner Jim stood around and waited on him, and says, "Will yo' Grace have some o' dis or some o' dat?"[11] and so on, and a body could see it was mighty pleasing to him.

But the old man got pretty silent by and by — didn't have much to say, and didn't look pretty comfortable over all that petting that was going on around that duke. He seemed to have something on his mind. So, along in the afternoon, he says:

"Looky here, Bilgewater,[12]" he says, "I'm nation sorry for you, but you ain't the only person that's had troubles like that."

"No?"

"No you ain't. You ain't the only person that's ben snaked down wrongfully out'n a high place."

"Alas!"

"No, you ain't the only person that's had a secret of his birth." And, by jings,[13] he begins to cry.

"Hold! What do you mean?"

"Bilgewater, kin I trust you?" says the old man, still sort of sobbing.

"To the bitter death!" He took the old man by the hand and squeezed it, and says, "That secret of your being: speak!"

"Bilgewater, I am the late Dauphin!"

You bet you, Jim and me stared this time. Then the duke says:

"You are what?"

"Yes, my friend, it is too true — your eyes is lookin' at this very moment on the pore disappeared Dauphin, Looy[14] the Seventeen, son of Looy the Sixteen and Marry Antonette."

"You! At your age! No! You mean you're the late Charlemagne;[15] you must be six or seven hundred years old, at the very least."

"Trouble has done it, Bilgewater, trouble has done it; trouble has brung these gray

Chapter 4 The Literature of the Realistic Period

hairs and this premature balditude. Yes, gentlemen, you see before you, in blue jeans and misery, the wanderin', exiled, trampled on, and sufferin' rightful King of France."

Well, he cried and took on so that me and Jim didn't know hardly what to do, we was so sorry — and so glad and proud we'd got him with us, too. So we set in, like we done before with the duke, and tried to comfort him. But he said it warn't no use, nothing but to be dead and done with it all could do him any good; though he said it often made him feel easier and better for a while if people treated him according to his rights, and got down on one knee to speak to him, and always called him "Your Majesty," and waited on him first at meals, and didn't set down in his presence till he asked them. So Jim and me set to majestying him, and doing this and that and t'other for him, and standing up till he told us we might set down. This done him heaps of good, and so he got cheerful and comfortable. But the duke kind of soured on him, and didn't look a bit satisfied with the way things was going; still, the king acted real friendly towards him, and said the duke's great-grandfather and all the other Dukes of Bilgewater was a good deal thought of by his father, and was allowed to come to the palace considerable; but the duke stayed huffy a good while, till by and by the king says:

"Like as not we got to be together a blamed long time on this h-yer[16] raft, Bilgewater, and so what's the use o' your bein' sour? It 'll only make things oncomfortable.[17] It ain't my fault I warn't born a duke, it ain't your fault you warn't born a king — so what's the use to worry? Make the best o' things the way you find 'em, says I — that's my motto. This ain't no bad thing that we've struck here — plenty grub and an easy life — come, give us your hand, duke, and le's[18] all be friends."

The duke done it, and Jim and me was pretty glad to see it. It took away all the uncomfortableness and we felt mighty good over it, because it would a been a miserable business to have any unfriendliness on the raft; for what you want, above all things, on a raft, is for everybody to be satisfied, and feel right and kind towards the others.

It didn't take me long to make up my mind that these liars warn' no kings nor dukes at all, but just low-down humbugs and frauds. But I never said nothing, never let on; kept it to myself; it's the best way; then you don't have no quarrels, and don't get into no trouble. If they wanted us to call them kings and dukes, I hadn't no objections, 'long as[19] it would keep peace in the family; and it warn't no use to tell Jim, so I didn't tell him. If I never learnt nothing else out of pap, I learnt that the best way to get along with his kind of people is to let them have their own way.

Notes
1. **a monstrous big river**: the Mississippi River.
2. **we**: Huckleberry Finn and the black slave Jim.
3. **warn't**: weren't.
4. **generly**: (colloq.) generally.

5. **yourn**: (colloq.) yours.
6. **thar**: (colloq.) there.
7. **jour printer**: journeyman printer.
8. **holt**: (colloq.) hold.
9. **sich**: (colloq.) such.
10. **k'n**: (colloq.) can.
11. **Will yo' Grace have some o' dis or some o' dat**: Will your grace have some of this or some of that?
12. **Bilgewater**: mispronunciation of "Bridgewater".
13. **by jings**: (colloq.) by jinx.
14. **Looy**: mispronunciation of "Louis".
15. **Charlemagne**: Emperor Charlemagne (742-814), founder of the Holy Roman Empire.
16. **h-yer**: here.
17. **oncomfortable**: uncomfortable.
18. **le's**: let's.
19. **'long as**: so long as.

Study Questions

1. How do the King and Duke make Huck and Jim believe them?
2. Why does Huck think the duke and the king are after him when they first meet?
3. How does Jim feel when he sees Huck again? What does he think has happened to him?

Essay Topics

1. Why does Mark Twain use a child as the center of consciousness in this novel?
2. Discuss Twain's use of dialects in the novel. What effect does this usage have on the reader?

4.3 O. Henry

4.3.1 About the Author

O. Henry (1862-1910) was the pen name of the American short story writer William Sydney Porter, who was born in Greensboro, North Carolina. When he was three, his mother died, and he was raised by his grandmother and an aunt. When young, Porter was an avid reader. He studied at his aunt's elementary school and then enrolled at the Linsey Street High School. At the age of fifteen he left school and went to work in an uncle's drugstore. For reasons of unsatisfactory health and unfavorable home conditions, he left for Texas in 1882. During the following years, he worked as amateur ranchman, land-office clerk, editor, and bank teller. In 1887 he married Athol Estes Roach; they had one daughter.

In 1894 cash was found to have gone missing from the First National Bank in Austin, where Porter had worked as a bank teller. Shortly thereafter, he was arrested for embezzlement and was put to prison for five years. While in prison, Porter started to write short stories to earn money to support his daughter Margaret. The stories of adventure set in the Southwest and in Central America gained an immediate success among readers. After doing three out of the five years sentence, Porter was released from the prison in 1901 and changed his name to O. Henry.

With confidence in himself as a writer, he arrived in New York during the spring of 1902. His chief quest was to obtain first-hand material of the city for his short stories. The first collection of his stories, *Cabbages and Kings*, appeared in 1904 and became an immediate success. With the publication of his second book, *The Four Million* (1906), he was hailed as the discoverer of romance in the streets of New York. Other collections followed, including: *The Trimmed Lamp* (1907), *The Heart of the West* (1907), *Whirligigs* (1910), *Sixes and Sevens* (1911), *Rolling Stones* (1912), and *Waifs and Strays* (1917). He died of tuberculosis, complicated by alcoholism and diabetes, in 1910.

O. Henry wrote with realistic details based on his first hand experiences both in Texas and in New York City. Fundamentally a product of his time, O. Henry's work provides one of the best English examples of catching the entire flavor of an age. Whether roaming the cattle-lands of Texas, exploring the art of the "gentle grifter," or investigating the tensions of class and wealth in the early twentieth-century New York, O. Henry had an inimitable hand for isolating some element of society and describing it with an incredible economy and grace of language. His stories were seen as straightforward and simple, written in the plain vernacular language and humorous style. They may rely on a sameness of plot, but the sharp, unexpected twist at the end is still his distinctive trademark today.

4.3.2 "The Cop and the Anthem"

On his bench in Madison Square Soapy moved uneasily. When wild geese honk high of nights, and when women without sealskin coats grow kind to their husbands, and when Soapy moves uneasily on his bench in the park, you may know that winter is near at hand.

A dead leaf fell in Soapy's lap. That was Jack Frost's card. Jack is kind to the regular denizens[1] of Madison Square, and gives fair warning of his annual call. At the corners of four streets he hands his pasteboard to the North Wind, footman of the

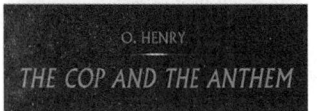

mansion of All Outdoors, so that the inhabitants thereof may make ready.

Soapy's mind became cognisant of the fact that the time had come for him to resolve himself into a singular Committee of Ways and Means to provide against the coming rigour, and therefore he moved uneasily on his bench.

The hibernatorial ambitions of Soapy were not of the highest. In them there were no considerations of Mediterranean cruises, of soporific Southern skies drifting in the Vesuvian Bay. Three months on the Island[2] was what his soul craved. Three months of assured board and bed and congenial company, safe from Boreas[3] and bluecoats,[4] seemed to Soapy the essence of things desirable.

For years the hospitable Blackwell's had been his winter quarters. Just as his more fortunate fellow New Yorkers had bought their tickets to Palm Beach and the Riviera each winter, so Soapy had made his humble arrangements for his annual hegira[5] to the Island. And now the time was come. On the previous night three Sabbath newspapers, distributed beneath his coat, about his ankles and over his lap, had failed to repulse the cold as he slept on his bench near the spurting fountain in the ancient square. So the Island loomed big and timely in Soapy's mind. He scorned the provisions made in the name of charity for the city's dependents. In Soapy's opinion the Law was more benign than Philanthropy. There was an endless round of institutions, municipal and eleemosynary,[6] on which he might set out and receive lodging and food accordant with the simple life. But to one of Soapy's proud spirit the gifts of charity are encumbered. If not in coin you must pay in humiliation of spirit for every benefit received at the hands of philanthropy. As Caesar had his Brutus, every bed of charity must have its toll of a bath, every loaf of bread its compensation of a private and personal inquisition. Wherefore it is better to be a guest of the law, which though conducted by rules, does not meddle unduly with a gentleman's private affairs.

Soapy, having decided to go to the Island, at once set about accomplishing his desire. There were many easy ways of doing this. The pleasantest was to dine luxuriously at some expensive restaurant; and then, after declaring insolvency, be handed over quietly and without uproar to a policeman. An accommodating magistrate would do the rest.

Soapy left his bench and strolled out of the square and across the level sea of asphalt, where Broadway and Fifth Avenue flow together. Up Broadway he turned, and halted at a glittering cafe, where are gathered together nightly the choicest products of the grape, the silkworm and the protoplasm.[7]

Soapy had confidence in himself from the lowest button of his vest upward. He was shaven, and his coat was decent and his neat black, ready-tied four-in-hand had been presented to him by a lady missionary on Thanksgiving Day. If he could reach a table in the restaurant unsuspected success would be his. The portion of him that would show above the table would raise no doubt in the waiter's mind. A roasted mallard duck, thought Soapy, would be about the thing — with a bottle of Chablis,[8] and then Camembert,[9] a demi-tasse[10] and a cigar. One dollar for the cigar would be enough. The total would not be so high as to call forth any supreme manifestation of revenge from the cafe management; and yet the meat would leave him filled and happy for the journey to his winter refuge.

But as Soapy set foot inside the restaurant door the head waiter's eye fell upon his frayed trousers and decadent shoes. Strong and ready hands turned him about and conveyed him in silence and haste to the sidewalk and averted the ignoble fate of the menaced mallard.

Soapy turned off Broadway. It seemed that his route to the coveted island was not to be an epicurean one. Some other way of entering limbo must be thought of.

At a corner of Sixth Avenue electric lights and cunningly displayed wares behind plate-glass made a shop window conspicuous. Soapy took a cobblestone and dashed it through the glass. People came running around the corner, a policeman in the lead. Soapy stood still, with his hands in his pockets, and smiled at the sight of brass buttons.

"Where's the man that done that?" inquired the officer excitedly.

"Don't you figure out that I might have had something to do with it?" said Soapy, not without sarcasm, but friendly, as one greets good fortune.

The policeman's mind refused to accept Soapy even as a clue. Men who smash windows do not remain to parley with the law's minions. They take to their heels. The policeman saw a man half way down the block running to catch a car. With drawn club he joined in the pursuit. Soapy, with disgust in his heart, loafed along, twice unsuccessful.

On the opposite side of the street was a restaurant of no great pretensions. It catered to large appetites and modest purses. Its crockery and atmosphere were thick; its soup and napery thin. Into this place Soapy took his accusive[11] shoes and telltale trousers without challenge. At a table he sat and consumed beefsteak, flapjacks, doughnuts and pie. And then to the waiter be betrayed the fact that the minutest coin and himself were strangers.

"Now, get busy and call a cop," said Soapy. "And don't keep a gentleman waiting."

"No cop for youse," said the waiter, with a voice like butter cakes and an eye like the cherry in a Manhattan cocktail. "Hey, Con!"

Neatly upon his left ear on the callous pavement two waiters pitched Soapy. He arose, joint by joint, as a carpenter's rule opens, and beat the dust from his clothes.

Arrest seemed but a rosy dream. The Island seemed very far away. A policeman who stood before a drug store two doors away laughed and walked down the street.

Five blocks Soapy travelled before his courage permitted him to woo capture again. This time the opportunity presented what he fatuously termed to himself a "cinch." A young woman of a modest and pleasing guise was standing before a show window gazing with sprightly interest at its display of shaving mugs and inkstands, and two yards from the window a large policeman of severe demeanour leaned against a water plug.

It was Soapy's design to assume the role of the despicable and execrated "masher." The refined and elegant appearance of his victim and the contiguity of the conscientious cop encouraged him to believe that he would soon feel the pleasant official clutch upon his arm that would insure his winter quarters on the right little, tight little isle.

Soapy straightened the lady missionary's readymade tie, dragged his shrinking cuffs into the open, set his hat at a killing cant and sidled toward the young woman. He made eyes at her, was taken with sudden coughs and "hems," smiled, smirked and went brazenly through the impudent and contemptible litany of the "masher." With half an eye Soapy saw that the policeman was watching him fixedly. The young woman moved away a few steps, and again bestowed her absorbed attention upon the shaving mugs. Soapy followed, boldly stepping to her side, raised his hat and said:

"Ah there, Bedelia! Don't you want to come and play in my yard?"

The policeman was still looking. The persecuted young woman had but to beckon a finger and Soapy would be practically *en route* [12] for his insular haven. [13] Already he imagined he could feel the cozy warmth of the station-house. The young woman faced him and, stretching out a hand, caught Soapy's coat sleeve.

"Sure, Mike," she said joyfully, "if you'll blow me[14] to a pail of suds.[15] I'd have spoke to you sooner, but the cop was watching."

With the young woman playing the clinging ivy to his oak Soapy walked past the policeman overcome with gloom. He seemed doomed to liberty.

At the next corner he shook off his companion and ran. He halted in the district where by night are found the lightest streets, hearts, vows and librettos.

Women in furs and men in greatcoats moved gaily in the wintry air. A sudden fear seized Soapy that some dreadful enchantment had rendered him immune to arrest. The thought brought a little of panic upon it, and when he came upon another policeman lounging grandly in front of a transplendent[16] theatre he caught at the immediate straw of "disorderly conduct."

On the sidewalk Soapy began to yell drunken gibberish at the top of his harsh voice. He danced, howled, raved and otherwise disturbed the welkin.[17]

The policeman twirled his club, turned his back to Soapy and remarked to a citizen.

"'Tis one of them Yale lads celebratin' the goose egg they give to the Hartford College. Noisy; but no harm. We've instructions to lave them be."

Disconsolate, Soapy ceased his unavailing racket. Would never a policeman lay hands on him? In his fancy the Island seemed an unattainable Arcadia.[18] He buttoned his thin coat against the chilling wind.

In a cigar store he saw a well-dressed man lighting a cigar at a swinging light. His silk umbrella he had set by the door on entering. Soapy stepped inside, secured the umbrella and sauntered off with it slowly. The man at the cigar light followed hastily.

"My umbrella," he said, sternly.

"Oh, is it?" sneered Soapy, adding insult to petit larceny. "Well, why don't you call a policeman? I took it. Your umbrella! Why don't you call a cop? There stands one on the corner."

The umbrella owner slowed his steps. Soapy did likewise, with a presentiment that luck would again run against him. The policeman looked at the two curiously.

"Of course," said the umbrella man — "that is — well, you know how these mistakes occur — I — if it's your umbrella I hope you'll excuse me — I picked it up this morning in a restaurant — If you recognise it as yours, why — I hope you'll — "

"Of course it's mine," said Soapy, viciously.

The ex-umbrella man retreated. The policeman hurried to assist a tall blonde in an opera cloak across the street in front of a street car that was approaching two blocks away.

Soapy walked eastward through a street damaged by improvements. He hurled the umbrella wrathfully into an excavation. He muttered against the men who wear helmets and carry clubs. Because he wanted to fall into their clutches, they seemed to regard him as a king who could do no wrong.

At length Soapy reached one of the avenues to the east where the glitter and turmoil was but faint. He set his face down this toward Madison Square, for the homing instinct survives even when the home is a park bench.

But on an unusually quiet corner Soapy came to a standstill. Here was an old church, quaint and rambling and gabled. Through one violet-stained window a soft light glowed, where, no doubt, the organist loitered over the keys, making sure of his mastery of the coming Sabbath anthem. For there drifted out to Soapy's ears sweet music that caught and held him transfixed against the convolutions of the iron fence.

The moon was above, lustrous and serene; vehicles and pedestrians were few; sparrows twittered sleepily in the eaves — for a little while the scene might have been a country churchyard. And the anthem that the organist played cemented Soapy to the iron fence, for he had known it well in the days when his life contained such things as mothers and roses and ambitions and friends and immaculate thoughts and collars.

The conjunction of Soapy's receptive state of mind and the influences about the old church wrought a sudden and wonderful change in his soul. He viewed with swift horror the pit into which he had tumbled, the degraded days, unworthy desires, dead hopes, wrecked faculties and base motives that made up his existence.

And also in a moment his heart responded thrillingly to this novel mood. An instantaneous and strong impulse moved him to battle with his desperate fate. He would pull himself out of the mire; he would make a man of himself again; he would conquer the evil that had taken possession of him. There was time; he was comparatively young yet; he would resurrect his old eager ambitions and pursue them without faltering. Those solemn but sweet organ notes had set up a revolution in him. To-morrow he would go into the roaring downtown district and find work. A fur importer had once offered him a place as driver. He would find him to-morrow and ask for the position. He would be somebody in the world. He would —

Soapy felt a hand laid on his arm. He looked quickly around into the broad face of a policeman.

"What are you doin' here?" asked the officer.

"Nothin'," said Soapy.

"Then come along," said the policeman.

"Three months on the Island," said the Magistrate in the Police Court the next morning.

Notes
1. **denizens**: inhabitants.
2. **the Island**: Blackwell's island in the East River, it is called Welfare Island.
3. **Boreas**: (Greek Myth.) the god personifying the north wind.
4. **bluecoat**: referring to a policeman who wears a blue uniform.
5. **hegira**: the flight of Mohammed from Mecca to Medina in A. D. 622. It figuratively means a flight to escape danger.
6. **eleemosynary**: contributed as an act of charity; gratuitous.
7. **protoplasm**: flesh and blood.
8. **Chablis**: a white French wine.
9. **Camembert**: a soft cheese originally made in France.
10. **demi-tasse**: a small cup of coffee.
11. **accusive**: tending to accuse. This is a coinage of the author.
12. *en route*: on the way.
13. **haven**: a place of refuge or rest; a sanctuary.
14. **blow me**: damned.
15. **a pail of suds**: (slang) some beer.
16. **transplendent**: brilliantly luxurious; another coinage of the author.
17. **the welkin**: sky; air.
18. **Arcadia**: an imaginary ideal place.

Chapter 4 The Literature of the Realistic Period

Study Questions

1. How does the author establish the tone of the story in the opening paragraph?
2. What words and sentence structures does the author choose to form his unique style?
3. How does the author make the "surprising ending" effective?

4.4 Henry James

4.4.1 About the Author

Henry James (1843-1916) was born into a wealthy family in New York City. During his early years, he was taken back and forth between America and Europe. As a result of this extensive traveling, James received a kind of irregular education in which he attended a variety of day schools and was taught by private tutors in England, France and Switzerland. At the age of nineteen he briefly attended Harvard Law School, but was more interested in literature than law studying. He read intensively the classics of English, American, French and German literatures, and Russian classics in translation. In 1864, James published his first story, "A Tragedy of Error," in the *Continental Monthly*. During the decade after the Civil War, James published a number of short stories and book reviews in prominent American periodicals.

While he was in Europe, James met some famous writers such as Flaubert, Maupassant, Zola and Turgenev, who exerted a great influence over him. James lived and wrote in England for the majority of his adult life. James was a proliferate writer. All together he wrote twenty novels and more than one hundred short stories, as well as literary criticism, plays, travelogues, and reviews. His models were Dickens, Balzac, and Hawthorne. In his early period of literary career, he wrote *The American* (1877), *Europeans* (1878), *Daisy Miller* (1879), and his first acknowledged masterpiece *The Portrait of a Lady* (1881), which established his reputation as a major literary figure. In his later period, James published *The Wings of the Dove* (1902), *The Ambassadors* (1903) and *The Golden Bowl* (1904). In addition to writing fiction, he continued with his critical essays, publishing *French Poets and Novelist* in 1878 and *Hawthorne* in 1879.

James's own personal life remained enigmatic in several respects. Highly social, he was nevertheless extremely private and reserved. Repeatedly encouraged to marry by members of his family, he steadfastly refused. His intimate relationships are still shrouded in mystery. In 1876, James finally settled down in London and in 1915 he became a naturalized British citizen, largely in protest against America's failure to join England in the First World War. The following year he died in London shortly after receiving the Order of Merit from King George V for his services to the British nation.

James's fame generally rests upon his novels and stories with the international theme. These novels are always set against a larger international background, usually between Europe and America, and centered on the confrontation of the two different cultures. The typical pattern of the conflict between the two cultures would be that of a young American man or woman who goes to Europe and affronts his or her destiny. The unsophisticated American would be beguiled, betrayed, cruelly wronged at the hands of Europeans who pretend to stand for the highest possible civilization. Marriage and love are used by James as the focal point of the confrontation between the two value systems, and the protagonist usually goes through a painful process of a spiritual growth, gaining knowledge of good and evil from the conflict.

The Portrait of a Lady is a typical example of the international theme. It concerns a young American woman, Isabel Archer, who goes to England to stay with her aunt and uncle. Isabel inherits money and forms a friendship with Madame Merle, who introduces her to Gilbert Osmond, a middle-aged snobbish widower with a young daughter, Pansy. Isabel believes Osmond to be a man of perfect taste and marries him. But later she learns that Osmond and Merle have been lovers and have plotted her marriage to get hold of her fortune. However, Isabel would not accept her failure. After experiencing disappointment and loss, she gradually became mature. And her final choice, to return to her marriage, signifies her triumph.

Moreover, James's realism is characterized by his psychological approach to his subject matter. His fictional world is concerned more with the inner life of human beings than with overt human actions. This emphasis on psychology and on the human consciousness proves to be a big breakthrough in novel writing and has great influence over the coming generations. That is why James is generally regarded as the forerunner of the 20th-century "stream-of-consciousness" novels and the founder of psychological realism. As to his language, James is often refined and elegant. With a large vocabulary, he is always accurate in word selection, trying to find the best expression for his literary imagination. Therefore Henry James is not only one of the most important realists of the period before the First World War, but also the most expert stylist of his time.

4.4.2　An Excerpt from Chapter 1 of *The Portrait of a Lady*

Under certain circumstances there are few hours in life more agreeable than the hour dedicated to the ceremony known as afternoon tea. There are circumstances in which, whether you partake of the tea or not — some people of course never do — the situation is in itself delightful. Those that I have in mind in beginning to unfold this simple history offered an admirable setting to an innocent pastime. The implements of the little feast had been disposed[1] upon the lawn of an old English country-house, in what I should call the perfect middle of a splendid summer afternoon. Part of the afternoon had waned, but much of it was left, and what was left was of the finest and rarest quality. Real dusk would not arrive for many hours; but the flood of summer light[2] had begun to ebb, the air had grown mellow, the shadows were long upon the smooth, dense turf. They lengthened slowly, however, and the scene expressed that sense of leisure still to come which is perhaps the chief source of one's enjoyment of such a scene at such an hour. From five o'clock to eight is on certain occasions a little eternity; but on such an occasion as this the interval could be only an eternity of pleasure. The persons concerned in it were taking their pleasure quietly, and they were not of

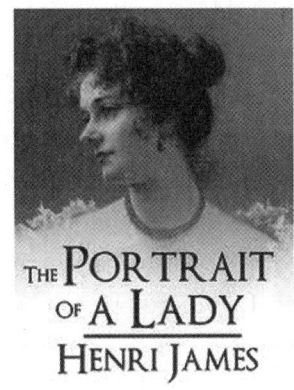

the sex which is supposed to furnish the regular votaries[3] of the ceremony I have mentioned. The shadows on the perfect lawn were straight and angular; they were the shadows of an old man sitting in a deep wicker-chair near the low table on which the tea had been served, and of two younger men strolling to and fro, in desultory[4] talk, in front of him. The old man had his cup in his hand; it was an unusually large cup, of a different pattern from the rest of the set and painted in brilliant colors. He disposed of its contents with much circumspection, holding it for a long time close to his chin, with his face turned to the house. His companions had either finished their tea or were indifferent to their privilege; they smoked cigarettes as they continued to stroll. One of them, from time to time, as he passed, looked with a certain attention at the elder man, who, unconscious of observation, rested his eyes upon the rich red[5] front of his dwelling. The house that rose beyond the lawn was a structure to repay such consideration and was the most characteristic object in the peculiarly English picture I have attempted to sketch.

It stood upon a low hill, above the river — the river being the Thames at some forty miles from London. A long gabled front of red brick, with the complexion of which time and the weather had played all sorts of pictorial tricks, only, however, to improve and refine it, presented to the lawn its patches of ivy, its clustered chimneys, its windows smothered in creepers. The house had a name and a history;[6] the old gentleman taking his tea would have been delighted to tell you these things: how it had been built under Edward the Sixth,[7] had offered a night's hospitality to the great Elizabeth[8] (whose august person had extended itself upon a huge, magnificent, and terribly angular bed which still formed the principal honor of the sleeping apartments), had been a good deal bruised and defaced in Cromwell's wars,[9] and then, under the Restoration, repaired and much enlarged; and how, finally, after having been remodeled and disfigured in the eighteenth century, it had passed into the careful keeping of a shrewd American banker, who had bought it originally because (owing to circumstances too complicated to set forth) it was offered at a great bargain: bought it with much grumbling at its ugliness, its antiquity, its incommodity, and who now, at the end of twenty years, had become conscious of a real aesthetic passion for it, so that he knew all its points and would tell you just where to stand to see them in combination and just the hour when the shadows of its various protuberances[10]— which fell so softly upon the warm, weary brickwork — were of the right measure. Besides this, as I have said, he could have counted off most of the successive owners and occupants, several of whom were known to general fame; doing so, however, with an undemonstrative conviction that the latest phase of its destiny was not the least honorable. The front of the house overlooking that portion of the lawn with which we are concerned was not the entrance-front; this was in quite another quarter. Privacy here reigned supreme, and the wide carpet of turf that covered the level hilltop seemed but the extension of a luxurious interior. The great still oaks and beeches flung down a shade as dense as that of velvet curtains; and the place was furnished, like a room, with cushioned seats, with rich-colored rugs, with the books and papers that lay upon the grass. The river was at some distance; where the ground began to slope, the lawn, properly speaking, ceased. But it was none the less a charming walk down to the water.

The old gentleman at the tea-table, who had come from America thirty years before, had brought with him, at the top of his baggage, his American physiognomy;[11] and he had not only brought it with him, but he had kept it in the best order, so that, if necessary, he might have taken it back to his own country with perfect confidence. At present, obviously, nevertheless, he was not likely to displace himself; his journeys were over, and he was taking the rest that precedes the great rest. He had a narrow, clean-shaven face, with features evenly distributed and an expression of placid acuteness. It was evidently a face in which the range of representation was not large, so that the air of contented shrewdness was all the more of a merit. It seemed to tell that he had been successful in life, yet it seemed to tell also that his success had not been exclusive and invidious, but had had much of the inoffensiveness of failure. He had certainly had a great experience of men, but there was an almost rustic simplicity[12] in the faint smile that played upon his lean, spacious cheek and lighted up his humorous eye as he at last slowly and carefully deposited his big tea-cup upon the table. He was neatly dressed, in well-brushed black; but a shawl was folded upon his knees, and his feet were encased in thick, embroidered slippers. A beautiful collie dog lay upon the grass near his chair, watching the master's face almost as tenderly as the master took in the still more magisterial physiognomy of the house; and a little bristling, bustling terrier bestowed a desultory attendance upon the other gentlemen.

One of these was a remarkably well-made man of five-and-thirty, with a face as English as that of the old gentleman I have just sketched was something else; a noticeably handsome face, fresh-colored, fair and frank, with firm, straight features, a lively grey eye and the rich adornment of a chestnut beard. This person had a certain fortunate, brilliant exceptional look — the air of a happy temperament fertilized by a high civilization — which would have made almost any observer envy him at a venture. He was booted and spurred, as if he had dismounted from a long ride; he wore a white hat, which looked too large for him; he held his two hands behind him, and in one of them — a large, white, well-shaped fist — was crumpled a pair of soiled dog-skin gloves.

His companion, measuring the length of the lawn beside him, was a person of quite a different pattern, who, although he might have excited grave curiosity, would not, like the other, have provoked you to wish yourself, almost blindly, in his place. Tall, lean, loosely and feebly put together, he had an ugly, sickly, witty, charming face, furnished, but by no means decorated, with a straggling[13] moustache and whisker. He looked clever and ill — a combination by no means felicitous; and he wore a brown velvet jacket. He carried his hands in his pockets, and there was something in the way he did it that showed the habit was inveterate. His gait had a shambling, wandering quality; he was not very firm on his legs. As I have said, whenever he passed the old man in the chair he rested his eyes upon him; and at this moment, with their faces brought into relation, you would easily have seen they were father and son. The father caught his son's eye at last and gave him a mild, responsive smile.

"I'm getting on very well," he said.

"Have you drunk your tea?" asked the son.

"Yes, and enjoyed it."

"Shall I give you some more?"

The old man considered, placidly. "Well, I guess I'll wait and see." He had, in speaking, the American tone.

"Are you cold?" the son enquired.

The father slowly rubbed his legs. "Well, I don't know. I can't tell till I feel."

"Perhaps some one might feel for you," said the younger man, laughing.

"Oh, I hope some one will always feel for me! Don't you feel for me, Lord Warburton?"

"Oh yes, immensely," said the gentleman addressed as Lord Warburton, promptly. "I'm bound to say you look wonderfully comfortable."

"Well, I suppose I am, in most respects." And the old man looked down at his green shawl and smoothed it over his knees. "The fact is I've been comfortable so many years that I suppose I've got so used to it I don't know it."

"Yes, that's the bore of comfort," said Lord Warburton. "We only know when we're uncomfortable."

...

"I haven't the honor of knowing your niece," Lord Warburton said. "I think it's the first time I've heard of her."

"She's a niece of my wife's; Mrs. Touchett brings her to England."

Then young Mr. Touchett explained. "My mother, you know, has been spending the winter in America, and we're expecting her back. She writes that she has discovered a niece and that she has invited her to come out with her."

"I see — very kind of her," said Lord Warburton. "Is the young lady interesting?"

"We hardly know more about her than you; my mother has not gone into details. She chiefly communicates with us by means of telegrams, and her telegrams are rather inscrutable. They say women don't know how to write them, but my mother has thoroughly mastered the art of condensation. 'Tired America, hot weather awful, return England with niece, first steamer decent cabin.' That's the sort of message we get from her — that was the last that came. But there had been another before, which I think contained the first mention of the niece. 'Changed hotel, very bad, impudent clerk, address here. Taken sister's girl, died last year, go to Europe, two sisters, quite independent.' Over that my father and I have scarcely stopped puzzling; it seems to admit of so many interpretations."

"There's one thing very clear in it," said the old man; "she has given the hotel-clerk a dressing."

"I'm not sure even of that, since he has driven her from the field. We thought at first that the sister mentioned might be the sister of the clerk; but the subsequent mention of a niece seems to prove that the allusion is to one of my aunts. Then there was a question as to whose the two other sisters were; they are probably two of my late aunt's daughters. But who's 'quite independent,' and in what sense is the term used? — that point's not yet settled. Does the expression apply more particularly to the young lady my mother has adopted, or does it characterise her sisters equally? — and is it used in a moral or in a financial sense? Does it mean that they've been left well off, or that they wish to be under no obligations? or does it simply mean that they're fond of their own way?"

"Whatever else it means, it's pretty sure to mean that," Mr. Touchett remarked.

"You'll see for yourself," said Lord Warburton. "When does Mrs. Touchett arrive?"

"We're quite in the dark; as soon as she can find a decent cabin. She may be waiting for it yet; on the other hand she may already have disembarked in England."

"In that case she would probably have telegraphed to you."

"She never telegraphs when you would expect it — only when you don't," said the old man. "She likes to drop in on me suddenly; she thinks she'll find me doing something wrong. She has never done so yet, but she's not discouraged."

"It's her share in the family trait, the independence she speaks of." Her son's appreciation of the matter was more favorable. "Whatever the high spirit of those young ladies may be, her own is a match for it. She likes to do everything for herself and has no belief in any one's power to help her. She thinks me of no more use than a postage-stamp without gum, and she would never forgive me if I should presume to go to Liverpool to meet her."

Chapter 4 The Literature of the Realistic Period

"Will you at least let me know when your cousin arrives?" Lord Warburton asked.

"Only on the condition I've mentioned — that you don't fall in love with her!" Mr. Touchett replied.

"That strikes me as hard. Don't you think me good enough?"

"I think you too good — because I shouldn't like her to marry you. She hasn't come here to look for a husband, I hope; so many young ladies are doing that, as if there were no good ones at home. Then she's probably engaged; American girls are usually engaged, I believe. Moreover I'm not sure, after all, that you'd be a remarkable husband."

"Very likely she's engaged; I've known a good many American girls, and they always were; but I could never see that it made any difference, upon my word! As for my being a good husband," Mr. Touchett's visitor pursued, "I'm not sure of that either. One can but try!"

"Try as much as you please, but don't try on my niece," smiled the old man, whose opposition to the idea was broadly humorous.

"Ah, well," said Lord Warburton with a humor broader still, "perhaps after all, she's not worth trying on!"

Notes

1. **disposed**: having inclination to.
2. **the flood of summer light**: the shining of summer light.
3. **votaries**: a person who is fervently devoted, as to a leader or an ideal; a faithful follower.
4. **desultory**: moving or jumping from one thing to another; disconnected.
5. **the rich red**: warm and strong in the color of red.
6. **The house had a name and a history**: the house had great reputation and a glorious history.
7. **Edward the Sixth**: (1537-1553) King of Britain, crowned at the age of nine.
8. **the great Elizabeth**: (1533-1603) Elizabeth I, Queen of Britain, was also called The Virgin Queen.
9. **Cromwell's wars**: the English Civil War (1642-1649) in which Cromwell, a military figure led the Parliamentary side to victory. After that, he, as lord protector, ruled England from 1653 to 1658.
10. **protuberances**: being swelling outward.
11. **physiognomy**: facial features, especially when regarded as revealing character.
12. **rustic simplicity**: lack of sophistication or elegance.
13. **straggling**: being left behind.

Study Questions

1. Why does Henry James open his novel this way?
2. What do you think is the function of the environmental description?
3. What do you understand about the three male characters?
4. Why does Isabel Archer not appear in the opening chapter?

Essay Topics

1. How does the first chapter prepare for the whole novel's thematic development?
2. Why does the author arrange the three male characters to be engaged in the stereotypically feminine activities of sipping tea and gossiping at the beginning of the novel?

4.5 Theodore Dreiser

4.5.1 About the Author

Theodore Dreiser (1871-1945) was born into a large family in Terre Haute, Indiana. In 1869, his father's woolen mill was destroyed by fire and the family was forced to move numerous times out of financial necessity. Dreiser was educated at various public schools in Indiana. When he was 16, he left home. During the following years, he worked as a driver for a laundry, in a real estate office, and as a collector for a furniture store. With the help from a sympathetic high school teacher, Dreiser attended the University of Indiana. However, he only remained in college for one year, from 1889 to 1890. After that he became a newspaper reporter in 1892. Dreiser was a voracious reader. He read Shakespeare, Bunyan, Fielding, Dickens, Thackeray, Thoreau, Emerson, and Twain, but his true literary influences were from Balzac, Charles Darwin and Herbert Spencer.

Dreiser longed to become a writer, and his career as a novelist began in 1900 with *Sister Carrie*, which tells the story of a small-town girl who moves to Chicago and eventually becomes a Broadway star in New York City. After the first success, Dreiser wrote quite a number of long and short fictions. In *The Financier* (1912) and *The Titan* (1914), he drew harsh portraits of a type of ruthless businessman. In *The "Genius"* (1915), he presented a study of the artistic temperament in a mercenary society. In *The Financier* (1912), he turned his attention more specifically to American social and economic institutions. Real fame, however, did not come to Dreiser until 1925, when his *An American Tragedy* had great popular success. The novel, based on an actual murder case and concerned with the efforts of a weak young man to rise from pious poverty into glamorous society, was dramatized.

Dreiser's personal experiences enabled him to capture precisely the desire to escape poverty and to possess wealth in a society that was experiencing transformation — the tide of migration from country to city; the impersonal nature of the urban setting of factories, tenements, and department stores; the contrast of poverty and wealth; and the new culture of conspicuous consumption were all at the center of Dreiser's work. In his later life Dreiser became interested in socialism, visiting the former Soviet Union as a guest of the government and writing his perceptions: *Dreiser Looks at Russia* (1928) and *Tragic America* (1931).

A pioneer of naturalism in American literature, Dreiser wrote novels reflecting his mechanistic view of life, a concept that held humanity as the victim of such ungovernable forces as economics, biology, society, and even chance. It is not surprising to find in Dreiser's fiction a world of jungle, where "kill or to be killed" was the law. Dreiser's naturalism found expression in almost every book he wrote. In *Sister Carrie* Dreiser expressed his naturalistic pursuit by expounding the purposelessness of life and attacking the conventional moral standards. After a series of incidents and coincidents, Carrie obtains fame and comfort while Hurstwood loses his wealth, social position, pride and eventually his life. In his "Trilogy of Desire," Dreiser's focus shifted from the pathos of the helpless protagonists at the bottom of the society to the power of the American financial tycoons in the late 19th century. In *An American Tragedy* Dreiser intended to tell us that it is the social pressure that makes Clyde's downfall inevitable. Clyde's tragedy is one that depends upon the American social system which encouraged people to pursue the dream of success at all costs. However, Dreiser never forgot to imply that these human desires in life could hardly be defined. They are there like a powerful "magnetism" governing human existence and reducing human beings to nothing. So like all naturalists he was restrained from finding a solution to the social problems that appeared in his novels and accordingly almost all his works have tragic endings.

Dreiser's significance in American literary history has been generally acknowledged because of his fearlessness, his honesty, his determination to have done with conventional posturings and evasions. He broke away from the genteel tradition of literature and dramatized the life in a very realistic way. There is no comment, no judgment but facts of life in the stories. His style is not polished but very serious and well-calculated to achieve the thematic ends he sought.

4.5.2　An Excerpt from Chapter 47 of *Sister Carrie*

...

Hurstwood put his hands, red from cold, down in his pockets. Tears came into his eyes.

"That's right," he said; "I'm no good now. I was all right. I had money. I'm

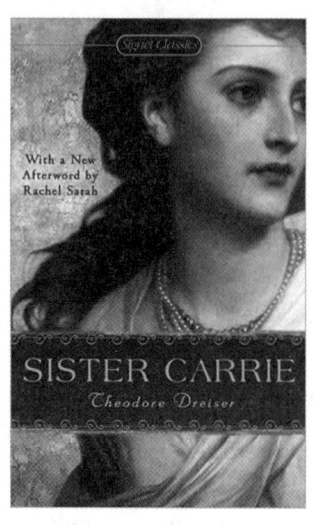

going to quit this," and, with death in his heart, he started down toward the Bowery. People had turned on the gas before and died; why shouldn't he? He remembered a lodging-house where there were little, close rooms, with gas-jets[1] in them, almost pre-arranged, he thought, for what he wanted to do, which rented for fifteen cents. Then he remembered that he had no fifteen cents.

On the way he met a comfortable-looking gentleman, coming, clean-shaven, out of a fine barber shop.

"Would you mind giving me a little something?" he asked this man boldly.

The gentleman looked him over and fished for a dime. Nothing but quarters were in his pocket.

"Here," he said, handing him one, to be rid of him. "Be off, now."

Hurstwood moved on, wondering. The sight of the large, bright coin pleased him a little. He remembered that he was hungry and that he could get a bed for ten cents. With this, the idea of death passed, for the time being, out of his mind. It was only when he could get nothing but insults that death seemed worth while.

One day, in the middle of the winter, the sharpest spell of the season set in. It broke grey and cold in the first day, and on the second snowed. Poor luck pursuing him, he had secured but ten cents by nightfall, and this he bad spent for food. At evening he found himself at the Boulevard and Sixty-seventh Street, where he finally turned his face Bowery-ward. Especially fatigued because of the wandering propensity which had seized him in the morning, he now half dragged his wet feet, shuffling the soles upon the sidewalk. An old, thin coat was turned up about his red ears-his cracked derby hat[2] was pulled down until it turned them outward. His hands were in his pockets.

"I'll just go down Broadway," he said to himself.

When he reached Forty-second Street, the fire signs were already blazing brightly. Crowds were hastening to dine. Through bright windows, at every corner, might be seen gay companies in luxuriant restaurants. There were coaches and crowded cable cars.

In his weary and hungry state, he should never have come here. The contrast was too sharp. Even he was recalled keenly to better things.

"What's the use?" he thought. "It's all up with me. I'll quit this."

People turned to look after him, so uncouth was his shambling figure. Several officers followed him with their eyes, to see that he did not beg of anybody.

Once he paused in an aimless, incoherent sort of way and looked through the windows of an imposing restaurant, before which blazed a fire sign, and through the large, plate windows of which could be seen the red and gold decorations, the palms, the white napery, and shining glassware, and, above all, the comfortable crowd. Weak as his mind had become, his hunger was sharp enough to show the importance of this. He stopped stock still, his frayed trousers soaking in the slush, and peered foolishly in.

"Eat," he mumbled. "That's right, eat. Nobody else wants any."

Then his voice dropped even lower, and his mind half lost the fancy it had.

"It's mighty cold," he said. "Awful cold."

At Broadway and Thirty-ninth Street was blazing, in incandescent fire, Carrie's name. "Carrie Madenda," it read, "and the Casino Company." All the wet, snowy sidewalk was bright with this radiated fire. It was so bright that it attracted Hurstwood's gaze. He looked up, and then at a large, gilt-framed poster-board, on which was a fine lithograph of Carrie, life-size.

Hurstwood gazed at it a moment, snuffling and hunching one shoulder, as if something were scratching him. He was so run down, however, that his mind was not exactly clear.

"That's you," he said at last, addressing her. "Wasn't good enough for you, was I? Huh!"

He lingered, trying to think logically. This was no longer possible with him.

"She's got it," he said, incoherently, thinking of money. "Let her give me some."

He started around to the side door. Then he forgot what he was going for and paused, pushing his hands deeper to warm the wrists. Suddenly it returned. The stage door! That was it.

He approached that entrance and went in.

"Well?" said the attendant, staring at him. Seeing him pause, he went over and shoved him. "Get out of here," he said.

"I want to see Miss Madenda," he said.

"You do, eh?" the other said, almost tickled at the spectacle. "Get out of here," and he shoved him again. Hurstwood had no strength to resist.

"I want to see Miss Madenda," he tried to explain, even as he was being hustled away. "I'm all right. I —"

The man gave him a last push and closed the door. As he did so, Hurstwood slipped and fell in the snow. It hurt him, and some vague sense of shame returned. He began to cry and swear foolishly.

"God damned dog!" he said. "Damned old cur," wiping the slush from his worthless coat. "I — I hired such people as you once."

Now a fierce feeling against Carrie welled up — just one fierce, angry thought before the whole thing slipped out of his mind.

"She owes me something to eat," he said. "She owes it to me."

Hopelessly he turned back into Broadway again and slopped onward and away, begging, crying, losing track of his thoughts, one after another, as a mind decayed and disjointed is wont to do.

It was truly a wintry evening, a few days later, when his one distinct mental decision was reached. Already, at four o'clock, the somber hue of night was thickening the air. A heavy snow was falling — a fine picking, whipping snow, borne forward by a swift wind in long, thin lines. The streets were bedded with it — six inches of cold, soft carpet, churned to a dirty brown by the crush of teams and the feet of men. Along Broadway men picked their way in ulsters and umbrellas. Along the Bowery, men slouched through it with collars and hats pulled over their ears. In the former thoroughfare business men and travelers were making for comfortable hotels. In the latter, crowds on cold errands shifted past dingy stores, in the deep recesses of which lights were already gleaming. There were early lights in the cable cars, whose usual clatter was reduced by the mantle about the wheels. The whole city was muffled by this fast-thickening mantle.

In her comfortable chambers at the Waldorf,[3] Carrie was reading at this time Pere Goriot,[4] which Ames had recommended to her. It was so strong, and Ames's mere recommendation had so aroused her interest, that she caught nearly the full sympathetic significance of it. For the first time, it was being borne in upon her how silly and worthless had been her earlier reading, as a whole. Becoming wearied, however, she yawned and came to the window, looking out upon the old winding procession of carriages rolling up Fifth Avenue.

"Isn't it bad?" she observed to Lola.

"Terrible!" said that little lady, joining her. "I hope it snows enough to go sleigh riding."

"Oh, dear," said Carrie, with whom the sufferings of Father Goriot were still keen. "That's all you think of. Aren't you sorry for the people who haven't anything to-night?"

"Of course I am," said Lola; "but what can I do? I haven't anything."

Carrie smiled.

"You wouldn't care, if you had," she returned.

"I would, too," said Lola. "But people never gave me anything when I was hard up."

"Isn't it just awful?" said Carrie, studying the winter's storm.

"Look at that man over there," laughed Lola, who had caught sight of some one falling down. "How sheepish men look when they fall, don't they?"

"We'll have to take a coach to-night," answered Carrie, absently.

In the lobby of the Imperial, Mr. Charles Drouet was just arriving, shaking the snow from a very handsome ulster. Bad weather had driven him home early and stirred his desire for those pleasures which shut out the snow and gloom of life. A good dinner, the company of a young woman, and an evening at the theatre were the chief things for him.

"Why, hello, Harry!" he said, addressing a lounger in one of the comfortable lobby

Chapter 4   The Literature of the Realistic Period

chairs. "How are you?"

"Oh, about six and six," said the other.

"Rotten weather, isn't it?"

"Well, I should say," said the other. "I've been just sitting here thinking where I'd go to-night."

"Come along with me," said Drouet. "I can introduce you to something dead swell."

"Who is it?" said the other.

"Oh, a couple of girls over here in Fortieth Street. We could have a dandy time. I was just looking for you."

"Supposing we get 'em and take 'em out to dinner?"

"Sure," said Drouet. "Wait'll I go upstairs and change my clothes."

"Well, I'll be in the barber shop," said the other. "I want to get a shave."

"All right," said Drouet, creaking off in his good shoes toward the elevator. The old butterfly was as light on the wing as ever.

On an incoming vestibuled Pullman,[5] speeding at forty miles an hour through the snow of the evening, were three others, all related.

"First call for dinner in the dining-car," a Pullman servitor was announcing, as he hastened through the aisle in snow-white apron and jacket.

"I don't believe I want to play any more," said the youngest, a black-haired beauty, turned supercilious by fortune, as she pushed a euchre hand away from her.

"Shall we go into dinner?" inquired her husband, who was all that fine raiment[6] can make.

"Oh, not yet," she answered. "I don't want to play any more, though."

"Jessica," said her mother, who was also a study in what good clothing can do for age, "push that pin down in your tie — it's coming up."

Jessica obeyed, incidentally touching at her lovely hair and looking at a little jewel-faced watch. Her husband studied her, for beauty, even cold, is fascinating from one point of view.

"Well, we won't have much more of this weather," he said. "It only takes two weeks to get to Rome."

Mrs. Hurstwood nestled comfortably in her corner and smiled. It was so nice to be the mother-in-law of a rich young man — one whose financial state had borne her personal inspection.

"Do you suppose the boat will sail promptly?" asked Jessica, "if it keeps up like this?"

"Oh, yes," answered her husband. "This won't make any difference."

Passing down the aisle came a very fair-haired banker's son, also of Chicago, who had long eyed this supercilious beauty. Even now he did not hesitate to glance at her, and she was conscious of it. With a specially conjured show of indifference, she turned her pretty face wholly away. It was not wifely modesty at all. By so much was her pride satisfied.

At this moment Hurstwood stood before a dirty four-story building in a side street quite near the Bowery, whose one-time coat of buff had been changed by soot and rain. He mingled with a crowd of men — a crowd which had been, and was still, gathering by degrees.

It began with the approach of two or three, who hung about the closed wooden doors and beat their feet to keep them warm. They had on faded derby hats with dents in them. Their misfit coats were heavy with melted snow and turned up at the collars. Their trousers were mere bags, frayed at the bottom and wobbling over big, soppy shoes, torn at the sides and worn almost to shreds. They made no effort to go in, but shifted ruefully about, digging their hands deep in their pockets and leering at the crowd and the increasing lamps. With the minutes, increased the number. Three were old men with grizzled beards and sunken eyes, men who were comparatively young but shrunken by diseases, men who were middle-aged. None were fat. There was a face in the thick of the collection which was as white as drained veal. There was another red as brick. Some came with thin, rounded shoulders, others with wooden legs, still others with frames so lean that clothes only flapped about them. There were great ears, swollen noses, thick lips, and, above all, red, blood-shot eyes. Not a normal, healthy face in the whole mass; not a straight figure; not a straightforward, steady glance.

In the drive of the wind and sleet they pushed in on one another. There were wrists, unprotected by coat or pocket, which were red with cold. There were ears, half covered by every conceivable semblance of a hat, which still looked stiff and bitten. In the snow they shifted, now one foot, now another, almost rocking in unison.

With the growth of the crowd about the door came a murmur. It was not conversation, but a running comment directed at any one in general. It contained oaths and slang phrases.

"By damn, I wish they'd hurry up."

"Look at the copper watchin'."[7]

"Maybe it ain't winter, nuther!"

"I wisht I was in Sing Sing."[8]

Now a sharper lash of wind cut down and they huddled closer. It was an edging, shifting, pushing throng. There was no anger, no pleading, no threatening words. It was all sullen endurance, unlightened by either wit or good fellowship.

A carriage went jingling by with some reclining figure in it. One of the men nearest the door saw it.

"Look at the bloke[9] ridin'."

"He ain't so cold."

Chapter 4 The Literature of the Realistic Period

"Eh, eh, eh!" yelled another, the carriage having long since passed out of hearing.

Little by little the night crept on. Along the walk a crowd turned out on its way home. Men and shop-girls went by with quick steps. The cross-town cars began to be crowded. The gas lamps were blazing, and every window bloomed ruddy with a steady flame. Still the crowd hung about the door, unwavering.

"Ain't they ever goin' to open up?" queried a hoarse voice, suggestively.

This seemed to renew the general interest in the closed door, and many gazed in that direction. They looked at it as dumb brutes look, as dogs paw and whine and study the knob. They shifted and blinked and muttered, now a curse, now a comment. Still they waited and still the snow whirled and cut them with biting flakes. On the old hats and peaked shoulders it was piling. It gathered in little heaps and curves and no one brushed it off. In the centre of the crowd the warmth and steam melted it, and water trickled off hat rims and down noses, which the owners could not reach to scratch. On the outer rim the piles remained unmelted. Hurstwood, who could not get in the centre, stood with head lowered to the weather and bent his form.

A light appeared through the transom overhead. It sent a thrill of possibility through the watchers. There was a murmur of recognition. At last the bars grated inside and the crowd pricked up its ears. Footsteps shuffled within and it murmured again. Some one called: "Slow up there, now," and then the door opened. It was push and jam for a minute, with grim, beast silence to prove its quality, and then it melted inward, like logs floating, and disappeared. There were wet hats and wet shoulders, a cold, shrunken, disgruntled mass, pouring in between bleak walls. It was just six o'clock and there was supper in every hurrying pedestrian's face. And yet no supper was provided here — nothing but beds.

Hurstwood laid down his fifteen cents and crept off with weary steps to his allotted room. It was a dingy affair — wooden, dusty, hard. A small gas-jet furnished sufficient light for so rueful a corner.

"Hm!" he said, clearing his throat and locking the door.

Now he began leisurely to take off his clothes, but stopped first with his coat, and tucked it along the crack under the door. His vest he arranged in the same place. His old wet, cracked hat he laid softly upon the table. Then he pulled off his shoes and lay down.

It seemed as if he thought a while, for now he arose and turned the gas out, standing calmly in the blackness, hidden from view. After a few moments, in which he reviewed nothing, but merely hesitated, he turned the gas on again, but applied no match. Even then he stood there, hidden wholly in that kindness which is night, while the uprising fumes filled the room. When the odour reached his nostrils, he quit his attitude and fumbled for the bed.

"What's the use?" he said weakly, as he stretched himself to rest.

And now Carrie had attained that which in the beginning seemed life's object, or at least, such fraction of it as human beings ever attain of their original desires. She could look about on her gowns and carriage, her furniture and bank account. Friends there were, as the world takes it — those who would bow and smile in acknowledgment of her success. For these she had once craved. Applause there was, and publicity — once far off, essential things, but now grown trivial and indifferent. Beauty also — her type of loveliness — and yet she was lonely. In her rocking-chair she sat, when not otherwise engaged — singing and dreaming.

Thus in life there is ever the intellectual and the emotional nature — the mind that reasons, and the mind that feels. Of one come the men of action — generals and statesmen; of the other, the poets and dreamers — artists all.

As harps in the wind, the latter respond to every breath of fancy, voicing in their moods all the ebb and flow of the ideal.

Man has not yet comprehended the dreamer any more than he has the ideal. For him the laws and morals of the world are unduly severe. Ever hearkening to the sound of beauty, straining for the flash of its distant wings, he watches to follow, wearying his feet in travelling. So watched Carrie, so followed, rocking and singing.

And it must be remembered that reason had little part in this. Chicago dawning, she saw the city offering more of loveliness than she had ever known, and instinctively, by force of her moods alone, clung to it. In fine raiment and elegant surroundings, men seemed to be contented. Hence, she drew near these things. Chicago, New York; Drouet, Hurstwood; the world of fashion and the world of stage — these were but incidents. Not them, but that which they represented, she longed for. Time proved the representation false.

Oh, the tangle of human life! How dimly as yet we see. Here was Carrie, in the beginning poor, unsophisticated, emotional; responding with desire to everything most lovely in life, yet finding herself turned as by a wall. Laws to say: "Be allured, if you will, by everything lovely, but draw not nigh unless by righteousness." Convention to say: "You shall not better your situation save by honest labor." If honest labor be unremunerative and difficult to endure; if it be the long, long road which never reaches beauty, but wearies the feet and the heart; if the drag to follow beauty be such that one abandons the admired way, taking rather the despised path leading to her dreams quickly, who shall cast the first stone?[10] Not evil, but longing for that which is better, more often directs the steps of the erring. Not evil, but goodness more often allures the feeling mind unused to reason.

Amid the tinsel and shine of her state walked Carrie, unhappy. As when Drouet took her, she had thought: "Now am I lifted into that which is best"; as when Hurstwood seemingly offered her the better way: "Now am I happy." But since the world goes its way past all who will not partake of its folly, she now found herself alone. Her purse was open to him whose need was greatest. In her walks on Broadway, she no longer thought of the elegance of the creatures who passed her. Had they more of that peace and beauty which glimmered afar off, then were they to be envied.

Drouet abandoned his claim and was seen no more. Of Hurstwood's death she was not even aware. A slow, black boat setting out from the pier at Twenty-seventh Street upon its weekly errand bore, with many others, his nameless body to the Potter's Field.[11]

Thus passed all that was of interest concerning these twain in their relation to her. Their influence upon her life is explicable alone by the nature of her longings. Time was when both represented for her all that was most potent in earthly success. They were the personal representatives of a state most blessed to attain — the titled ambassadors of comfort and peace, aglow with their credentials. It is but natural that when the world which they represented no longer allured her, its ambassadors should be discredited. Even had Hurstwood returned in his original beauty and glory, he could not now have allured her. She had learned that in his world, as in her own present state, was not happiness.

Sitting alone, she was now an illustration of the devious ways by which one who feels, rather than reasons, may be led in the pursuit of beauty. Though often disillusioned, she was still waiting for that halcyon day when she should be led forth among dreams become real. Ames had pointed out a farther step, but on and on beyond that, if accomplished, would lie others for her. It was forever to be the pursuit of that radiance of delight which tints the distant hilltops of the world.

Oh, Carrie, Carrie! Oh, blind strivings of the human heart! Onward, onward, it saith, and where beauty leads, there it follows. Whether it be the tinkle of a lone sheep bell o'er some quiet landscape, or the glimmer of beauty in sylvan[12] places, or the show of soul in some passing eye, the heart knows and makes answer, following. It is when the feet weary and hope seems vain that the heartaches and the longings arise. Know, then, that for you is neither surfeit nor content. In your rocking-chair, by your window dreaming, shall you long, alone. In your rocking-chair, by your window, shall you dream such happiness as you may never feel.

Notes
1. **gas-jets**: an outlet of gas.
2. **derby hat**: a stiff felt hat with a round crown and a narrow, curved brim.
3. **Waldorf**: a luxuriant hotel in New York.
4. ***Pere Goriot***: *Father Goriot*, the famous novel of Balzac, a French writer.
5. **Pullman**: a sleeper car invented by George Mortimer Pullman (1831-1897).
6. **raiment**: (archaic or poetic) clothing; garments.
7. **Look at the copper watchin'**: look at the police man watching.
8. **Sing Sing**: name of one prison in the state of New York.
9. **bloke**: (slang) fellow.

10. **who shall cast the first stone**: see New Testament John 8 "They say unto him, Master, this woman was taken in adultery, in the very act. Now Moses in the law commanded us, that such should be stoned: but what sayest thou?" Jesus bent over and wrote on the ground with his finger as if he didn't hear what they said. As they stood there and continued asking him questions, he straight up and said, "He that is without sin among you, let him first cast a stone at her." Then he bent over again and wrote on the ground. When they heard this, they all left, one by one with the older ones first.
11. **the Potter's Field**: the public cemetery in the outskirt of New York. Poor or unknown men are buried there.
12. **sylvan**: abounding in trees; wooded.

Study Questions

1. Why does Hurstwood fail? Why does Carrie succeed? Can any moral lessons be drawn from either of their fates? Why?
2. Why does Carrie still suffer from unsatisfied desires after she became successful?

Essay Topics

1. How is Carrie's identity developed over the course of the novel?
2. How do you see Dreiser's naturalism influencing his work in *Sister Carrie*?

4.6 Robert Frost

4.6.1 About the Author

Robert Frost (1874-1963) was born in San Francisco, California. When he was 11 years old, his father died and his mother moved the family east to Lawrence, Massachusetts, where Frost's paternal grandfather was living. To support the family, his mother resumed her career as a schoolteacher. Frost attended high school in Lawrence, where he became interested in reading and poetry writing. In 1892, Frost attended Darthmouth College for a few months. Then he drifted through a string of occupations, working as a teacher, cobbler, and editor of the Lawrence *Sentinel*. In 1895, Frost married Elinor Miriam White, who became a major inspiration in his poetry. From 1897 to 1899 he attended Harvard College as a special student but left without a degree. Over the next ten years he wrote poems, operated a farm in Derry, New Hampshire, and supplemented his income by teaching at Derry's Pinkerton Academy.

In 1912, Frost moved his family to England, where he found companionship among the post-Georgian poets and was admired by such critics and poets as Ezra Pound, Amy Lowell, and Ford Madox Ford. He also succeeded in publishing two collections of *poetry*, *A Boy's Will* (1913) and *North of Boston* (1914), which contained some of his best-known poems: "Mending Wall," "The Death of the Hired Man," "Home Burial," "A Servant to Servants," "After Apple-Picking," and "The Wood-Pile." In 1915, Frost returned to the United States, settling on a farm near Franconia, New Hampshire. Besides farming, he also taught and lectured at several universities, including Amherst, Harvard, and the University of Michigan. He continued his poetry writing all these years and published quite a number of poetic works. Frost received four Pulitzer Prizes for poetry and was accepted into the American Academy of Arts and Letters in 1930.

Frost's poems show deep appreciation of natural world. Many of his poems are fragrant with natural quality. Images and metaphors in his poems are drawn from the simple country life and the pastoral landscape that can be easily understood — mowing, scything, wind's rustling in the grass, bird's singing, as well as ponds, roads, the cycle of the seasons, and the alternation of night and day. The careful local observations and homely details of his poems often have deep symbolic, even metaphysical, significance.

By using simple spoken language and conversational rhythms, Frost achieved an effortless grace in his style. He combined traditional verse forms — the sonnet, rhyming couplets, blank verse — with a clear American local speech rhythm, the speech of New England farmers with its idiosyncratic diction and syntax. In verse form he was assorted; he wrote in both the metrical forms and the free verse, and sometimes he wrote in a form that borrows freely from the merits of both, in a form that might be called semi-free or semi-conventional.

Although his verse forms are traditional, Frost is a quintessentially modern poet. His poems are concerned with human tragedies and fears, his reaction to the complexities of human life, and his ultimate acceptance of human burdens. He is also a pioneer in the interplay of rhythm and meter and in the poetic use of the vocabulary and inflections of everyday speech. His poetry is thus both traditional and experimental, regional and universal.

4.6.2 "Fire and Ice"

Some say the world will end in fire,
Some say in ice.
From what I've tasted of desire
I hold with those who favor fire.

But if it had to perish twice,
I think I know enough of hate
To say that for destruction ice
Is also great
And would suffice.

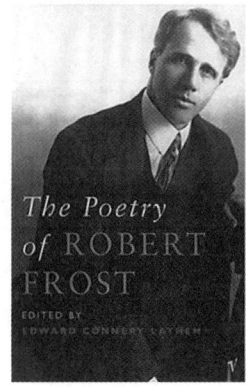

Study Questions

1. What are the symbolical meanings of the two images: fire and ice?
2. Why does the speaker hold with those who favor fire?
3. What is the theme of this poem?

4.6.3 "Nothing Gold Can Stay"

> Nature's first green is gold,
> Her hardest hue to hold.
> Her early leaf's a flower;
> But only so an hour.
> Then leaf subsides to leaf.
> So Eden sank to grief,
> So dawn goes down to day
> Nothing gold can stay.

Study Questions

1. What does the image "gold" mean to you?
2. How does grief in Eden relate to the passing of seasons?
3. What does the poet mean by concluding that "Nothing gold can stay"?

4.6.4 "The Road Not Taken"

> Two roads diverged in a yellow wood,
> And sorry I could not travel both
> And be one traveler, long I stood
> And looked down one as far as I could
> To where it bent in the undergrowth.
>
> Then took the other, as just as fair,
> And having perhaps the better claim,[1]
> Because it was grassy and wanted wear;[2]
> Though as for that the passing there
> Had worn them really about the same.
>
> And both that morning equally lay
> In leaves no step had trodden black.
> Oh, I kept the first for another day!
> Yet knowing how way leads on to way,[3]
> I doubted if I should ever come back.

I shall be telling this with a sigh
Somewhere ages and ages hence:
Two roads diverged in a wood, and I —
I took the one less traveled by,
And that has made all the difference.

Notes

1. **better claim**: better reason.
2. **wanted wear**: lacked wear; not much traveled by.
3. **way leads on to way**: roads that are often linked to other roads.

Study Questions

1. What motivates the speaker when he makes his choice?
2. Why does the choice of roads make so much difference to the speaker years later?
3. What might the two roads symbolically represent?

Essay Topics

Discuss the anticipation or remorse of the speaker in making his choice.

4.6.5 "Stopping by Woods on a Snowy Evening"

Whose woods these are I think I know.
His house is in the village though;
He will not see me stopping here
To watch his woods fill up with snow.

My little horse must think it queer
To stop without a farmhouse near
Between the woods and frozen lake
The darkest evening of the year.

He gives his harness bells a shake
To ask if there is some mistake.
The only other sound's the sweep
Of easy wind and downy flake.

The woods are lovely, dark and deep.
But I have promises to keep,
And miles to go before I sleep,
And miles to go before I sleep.

Study Questions

1. What do you know about the speaker?
2. What might the woods and snow and dark symbolize?
3. Why does Frost end the poem repeating the same line?

4.6.6 "Mending Wall"

Something there is that doesn't love a wall,
That sends the frozen-ground-swell¹ under it,
And spills² the upper boulders³ in the sun,
And makes gaps even two can pass abreast. ⁴
The work of hunters is another thing:
I have come after them and made repair
Where they have left not one stone on a stone,
But they would have the rabbit out of hiding,
To please the yelping⁵ dogs. The gaps I mean,
No one has seen them made or heard them made,
But at spring mending-time we find them there.
I let my neighbor know beyond the hill;
And on a day we meet to walk the line⁶
And set the wall between us once again.
We keep the wall between us as we go.
To each the boulders that have fallen to each.
And some are loaves⁷ and some so nearly balls
We have to use a spell⁸ to make them balance:
"Stay where you⁹ are until our backs are turned!"
We wear our fingers rough¹⁰ with handling them.
Oh, just another kind of out-door game,
One on a side. It comes to little more:
There where it is we do not need the wall:
He is all pine and I am apple orchard.
My apple trees will never get across
And eat the cones¹¹ under his pines, I tell him.
He only says, "Good fences make good neighbors". ¹²
Spring is the mischief in me, and I wonder
If I could put a notion in his head:
"Why do they make good neighbors? Isn't it
Where there are cows?
But here there are no cows.

Before I built a wall I'd ask to know
What I was walling in or walling out,[13]
And to whom I was like to give offence.
Something there is that doesn't love a wall,
That wants it down."I could say "Elves"[14] to him,
But it's not elves exactly, and I'd rather
He said it for himself. I see him there
Bringing a stone grasped firmly by the top
In each hand, like an old-stone[15] savage armed.
He moves in darkness as it seems to me
Not of woods only and the shade of trees.
He will not go behind his father's saying,
And he likes having thought of it so well
He says again,"Good fences make good neighbors."

Notes

1. **swell**: rise.
2. **spills**: cause to appear.
3. **boulders**: a large rounded mass of rock lying on the surface of the ground or embedded in the soil.
4. **abreast**: side by side.
5. **yelping**: a short, sharp cry or bark.
6. **walk the line**: to set the border or boundary.
7. **loaves**: pl of loaf.
8. **spell**: shift.
9. **you**: here refers the boulders.
10. **wear our fingers rough**: make our fingers coarse.
11. **cones**: fruit of pine.
12. **Good fences make good neighbors**: an English saying, the literal meaning of it is good relationships between neighbors can be helped to be established if there is a well-built fence between them.
13. **walling in or walling out**: include or exclude.
14. **Elves**: *pl* of elf, a kind of fairy, mischievous little creature.
15. **old-stone**: here means the old Stone Age.

Study Questions

1. According to lines 1-9, what happens because "Something there is that doesn't love a wall"? What other kind of destruction to the wall, described in lines 5-9, is not as significant to the speaker?

2. Describe how the speaker and his neighbor go about fixing the wall at spring time (lines 12-22).

3. According to the speaker in lines 24-36, why do he and his neighbor not need a wall? What does the neighbor say?

Essay Topics

1. Describe the character of the neighbor as seen by the speaker.
2. Does the speaker definitely want the wall torn down? How do you know?
3. What is the effect of simple language in "Mending Wall"?

4.7 Willa Cather

4.7.1 About the author

Willa Cather (1873-1947) was born into a Baptist family in Back Creek Valley, Virginia. When she was nine years old, her family moved to a farm near Red Cloud, in the Nebraska frontier. There she grew up among the immigrants from France, Germany, Scandinavia, Bohemia, and Russia and enjoyed the simple pleasures of the prairie landscape. Fascinating her most were the immigrant cultures in the area, the weather, and the gripping extraordinary environment the plains were capable of producing, which would feature so strongly in her writings.

Cather received her early education first at home and then at Red Cloud High School. She attended the University of Nebraska in 1891, receiving her BA in 1895. She moved to Pittsburgh, Pennsylvania after graduation. Here, she held a variety of jobs, such as an editor of a Pittsburgh newspaper, a drama critic, a book critic, a telegraph editor of *The Daily Leader* and a high-school teacher.

In 1905, she published *The Troll Garden*, a collection of short stories. Then she moved to New York to work as *McClure's magazine* editor. *McClure's Magazine* serialized her first novel, *Alexander's Bridge*, a work heavily influenced by her admiration for the style of Henry James. Cather resigned in 1912 from *McClure's Magazine* in order to devote all her time to writing. She wrote 12 novels, the most popular of which include *My Ántonia* (1918), *O Pioneers*! (1913), *The Song of the Lark* (1915), and *Death Comes for the Archbishop* (1927). In 1923 she was awarded the Pulitzer Prize for *One of Ours*, published in 1922. This work had been inspired by reading her cousin G. P. Cather's wartime letters home to his mother. Cather never married but in later life in New York she found a lifelong companion, Edith Lewis.

Willa Cather was noted for her books about immigrants struggling to make a living in

Chapter 4 The Literature of the Realistic Period

the Midwest during the late 1800s. Her work is mixed with the story of people and their development in history including their opinions of personal life, the drama of the immigrant arriving in a new world and the views of personal passion in art. She speaks of nature, but she also writes the most intimate pictures of the inner setting — the heart, the soul, and the home. In her works she creates strong female characters, who have the courage and vision to face all obstacles in their difficult lives. Her novels vibrate not only with the spoken language of ordinary people but also with the visual images that help a reader truly to see a place. It is precisely her allegiance to her subject, her thoroughly realistic picture of the lives of Nebraska homesteaders that makes her a pioneer in American fiction.

4.7.2 "Neighbor Rosicky"

I

When Doctor Burleigh told neighbour Rosicky he had a bad heart, Rosicky protested.

"So? No, I guess my heart was always pretty good. I got a little asthma, maybe. Just a awful short breath when I was pitchin' hay last summer, dat's all."

"Well now, Rosicky, if you know more about it than I do, what did you come to me for? It's your heart that makes you short of breath, I tell you. You're sixty-five years old, and you've always worked hard, and your heart's tired. You've got to be careful from now on, and you can't do heavy work any more. You've got five boys at home to do it for you."

The old farmer looked up at the Doctor with a gleam of amusement in his queer triangular-shaped eyes. His eyes were large and lively, but the lids were caught up in the middle in a curious way, so that they formed a triangle. He did not look like a sick man. His brown face was creased but not wrinkled, he had a ruddy colour in his smooth-shaven cheeks and in his lips, under his long brown moustache. His hair was thin and ragged around his ears, but very little grey. His forehead, naturally high and crossed by deep parallel lines, now ran all the way up to his pointed crown. Rosicky's face had the habit of looking interested, — suggested a contented disposition and a reflective quality that was gay rather than grave. This gave him a certain detachment, the easy manner of an onlooker and observer.

"Well, I guess you ain't got no pills fur a bad heart, Doctor Ed. I guess the only thing is fur me to git me a new one."

Doctor Burleigh swung round in his desk-chair and frowned at the old farmer. "I think if I were you I'd take a little care of the old one, Rosicky."

Rosicky shrugged. "Maybe I don't know how. I expect you mean fur me not to drink my coffee no more."

"I wouldn't, in your place. But you'll do as you choose about that. I've never yet been able to separate a Bohemian[1] from his coffee or his pipe. I've quit trying. But the sure thing is you've got to cut out farm work. You can feed the stock and do chores about the barn, but you can't do anything in the fields that makes you short of breath."

"How about shelling corn?"

"Of course not!"

Rosicky considered with puckered brows.

"I can't make my heart go no longer'n it wants to, can I, Doctor Ed?"

"I think it's good for five or six years yet, maybe more, if you'll take the strain off it. Sit around the house and help Mary. If I had a good wife like yours, I'd want to stay around the house."

His patient chuckled. "It ain't no place fur a man. I don't like no old man hanging round the kitchen too much. An' my wife, she's a awful hard worker her own self."

"That's it; you can help her a little. My Lord, Rosicky, you are one of the few men I know who has a family he can get some comfort out of; happy dispositions, never quarrel among themselves, and they treat you right. I want to see you live a few years and enjoy them."

"Oh, they're good kids, all right," Rosicky assented.

The Doctor wrote him a prescription and asked him how his oldest son, Rudolph, who had married in the spring, was getting on. Rudolph had struck out for himself, on rented land. "And how's Polly? I was afraid Mary mightn't like an American daughter-in-law, but it seems to be working out all right."

"Yes, she's a fine girl. Dat widder[2] woman bring her daughters up very nice. Polly got lots of spunk, an' she got some style, too. Da's nice, for young folks to have some style." Rosicky inclined his head gallantly. His voice and his twinkly smile were an affectionate compliment to his daughter-in-law.

"It looks like a storm, and you'd better be getting home before it comes. In town in the car?" Doctor Burleigh rose.

"No, I'm in de wagon. When you got five boys, you ain't got much chance to ride round in de Ford. I ain't much for cars, noway."

"Well, it's a good road out to your place; but I don't want you bumping around in a wagon much. And never again on a hay-rake, remember!"

Rosicky placed the Doctor's fee delicately behind the desk-telephone, looking the other way, as if this were an absent-minded gesture. He put on his plush cap and his corduroy jacket with a sheepskin collar, and went out.

The Doctor picked up his stethoscope and frowned at it as if he were seriously annoyed with the instrument. He wished it had been telling tales about some other man's heart, some old man who didn't look the Doctor in the eye so knowingly, or hold out such a warm brown hand when he said good-bye. Doctor Burleigh had been a poor boy in the country before he went away to medical school; he had known Rosicky almost ever since he could remember, and he had a deep affection for Mrs. Rosicky.

Only last winter he had had such a good breakfast at Rosicky's, and that when he needed it. He had been out all night on a long, hard confinement[3] case at Tom Marshall's, — a big rich farm where there was plenty of stock and plenty of feed and a great deal of expensive farm machinery of the newest model, and no comfort whatever. The woman had too many children and too much work, and she was no manager. When the baby was born at last, and handed over to the assisting neighbour woman, and the mother was properly attended to, Burleigh refused any breakfast in that slovenly house, and drove his buggy— the snow was too deep for a car— eight miles to Anton Rosicky's place. He didn't know another farm-house where a man could get such a warm welcome, and such good strong coffee with rich cream. No wonder the old chap didn't want to give up his coffee!

He had driven in just when the boys had come back from the barn and were washing up for breakfast. The long table, covered with a bright oilcloth, was set out with dishes waiting for them, and the warm kitchen was full of the smell of coffee and hot biscuit and sausage. Five big handsome boys, running from twenty to twelve, all with what Burleigh called natural good manners, — they hadn't a bit of the painful self-consciousness he himself had to struggle with when he was a lad. One ran to put his horse away, another helped him off with his fur coat and hung it up, and Josephine, the youngest child and the only daughter, quickly set another place under her mother's direction.

With Mary, to feed creatures was the natural expression of affection, — her chickens, the calves, her big hungry boys. It was a rare pleasure to feed a young man whom she seldom saw and of whom she was as proud as if he belonged to her. Some country housekeepers would have stopped to spread a white cloth over the oilcloth, to change the thick cups and plates for their best china, and the wooden-handled knives for plated ones. But not Mary.

"You must take us as you find us, Doctor Ed. I'd be glad to put out my good things for you if you was expected, but I'm glad to get you any way at all."

He knew she was glad, — she threw back her head and spoke out as if she were announcing him to the whole prairie. Rosicky hadn't said anything at all; he merely smiled his twinkling smile, put some more coal on the fire, and went into his own room to pour the Doctor a little drink in a medicine glass. When they were all seated, he watched his wife's face from his end of the table and spoke to her in Czech. Then, with the instinct of politeness which seldom failed him, he turned to the Doctor and said slyly: "I was just tellin' her not to ask you no questions about Mrs. Marshall till you eat some breakfast. My wife, she's terrible fur to ask questions."

The boys laughed, and so did Mary. She watched the Doctor devour her biscuit and sausage, too much excited to eat anything herself. She drank her coffee and sat taking in everything about her visitor. She had known him when he was a poor country boy, and was boastfully proud of his success, always saying: "What do people go to Omaha for, to see a doctor, when we got the best one in the State right here?" If Mary liked people at all, she felt physical pleasure in the sight of them, personal exultation in any good fortune that came to them. Burleigh didn't know many women like that, but he knew she was like that.

When his hunger was satisfied, he did, of course, have to tell them about Mrs. Marshall, and he noticed what a friendly interest the boys took in the matter.

Rudolph, the oldest one (he was still living at home then), said: "The last time I was over there, she was lifting them big heavy milk-cans, and I knew she oughtn't to be doing it."

"Yes, Rudolph told me about that when he come home, and I said it wasn't right," Mary put in warmly. "It was all right for me to do them things up to the last, for I was terrible strong, but that woman's weakly. And do you think she'll be able to nurse it, Ed?" She sometimes forgot to give him the title she was so proud of. "And to think of your being up all night and then not able to get a decent breakfast! I don't know what's the matter with such people."

"Why, Mother," said one of the boys, "if Doctor Ed had got breakfast there, we wouldn't have him here. So you ought to be glad."

"He knows I'm glad to have him, John, any time. But I'm sorry for that poor woman, how bad she'll feel the Doctor had to go away in the cold without his breakfast."

"I wish I'd been in practice when these were getting born." The doctor looked down the row of close-clipped heads. "I missed some good breakfasts by not being."

The boys began to laugh at their mother because she flushed so red, but she stood her ground and threw up her head. "I don't care, you wouldn't have got away from this house without breakfast. No doctor ever did. I'd have had something ready fixed that Anton could warm up for you."

The boys laughed harder than ever, and exclaimed at her: "I'll bet you would!" "She would, that!"

"Father, did you get breakfast for the doctor when we were born?"

"Yes, and he used to bring me my breakfast, too, mighty nice. I was always awful hungry!" Mary admitted with a guilty laugh.

While the boys were getting the Doctor's horse, he went to the window to examine the house plants. "What do you do to your geraniums to keep them blooming all winter, Mary? I never pass this house that from the road I don't see your windows full of flowers."

She snapped off a dark red one, and a ruffled new green leaf, and put them in his buttonhole. "There, that looks better. You look too solemn for a young man, Ed. Why don't you git married? I'm worried about you. Settin' at breakfast, I looked at you real hard, and I seen you've got some grey hairs already."

"Oh, yes! They're coming. Maybe they'd come faster if I married."

"Don't talk so. You'll ruin your health eating at the hotel. I could send your wife a nice loaf of nut bread, if you only had one. I don't like to see a young man getting grey. I'll tell you something, Ed; you make some strong black tea and keep it handy in a bowl, and every morning just brush it into your hair, an' it'll keep the grey from showin' much. That's the way I do!"

Sometimes the Doctor heard the gossipers in the drug-store wondering why Rosicky didn't get on faster. He was industrious, and so were his boys, but they were rather free and easy, weren't pushers, and they didn't always show good judgment. They were comfortable, they were out of debt, but they didn't get much ahead. Maybe, Doctor Burleigh reflected, people as generous and warm-hearted and affectionate as the Rosickys never got ahead much; maybe you couldn't enjoy your life and put it into the bank, too.

II

When Rosicky left Doctor Burleigh's office he went into the farm-implement store to light his pipe and put on his glasses and read over the list Mary had given him. Then he went into the general merchandise place next door and stood about until the pretty girl with the plucked eyebrows, who always waited on him, was free. Those eyebrows, two thin India-ink strokes, amused him, because he remembered how they used to be. Rosicky always prolonged his shopping by a little joking; the girl knew the old fellow admired her, and she liked to chaff[4] with him.

"Seems to me about every other week you buy ticking, Mr. Rosicky, and always the best quality," she remarked as she measured off the heavy bolt[5] with red stripes.

"You see, my wife is always makin' goose-fedder pillows, an' de thin stuff don't hold in dem little down-fedders."

"You must have lots of pillows at your house."

"Sure. She makes quilts of dem, too. We sleeps easy. Now she's makin' a fedder quilt for my son's wife. You know Polly, that married my Rudolph. How much my bill, Miss Pearl?"

"Eight eighty-five."

"Chust make it nine, and put in some candy fur de women."

"As usual. I never did see a man buy so much candy for his wife. First thing you know, she'll be getting too fat."

"I'd like dat. I ain't much fur all dem slim women like what de style is now."

"That's one for me, I suppose, Mr. Bohunk!" Pearl sniffed and elevated her India-ink strokes.

When Rosicky went out to his wagon, it was beginning to snow, — the first snow of the season, and he was glad to see it. He rattled out of town and along the highway through a wonderfully rich stretch of country, the finest farms in the county. He admired this High Prairie, as it was called, and always liked to drive through it. His own place lay in a rougher territory, where there was some clay in the soil and it was not so productive. When he bought his land, he hadn't the money to buy on High Prairie; so he told his boys, when they grumbled, that if their land hadn't some clay in it, they wouldn't own it at all. All the same, he enjoyed looking at these fine farms, as he enjoyed looking at a prize bull.

After he had gone eight miles, he came to the graveyard, which lay just at the edge of his own hay-land. There he stopped his horses and sat still on his wagon seat, looking about at the snowfall. Over yonder on the hill he could see his own house, crouching low, with the clump of orchard behind and the windmill before, and all down the gentle hill-slope the rows of pale gold cornstalks stood out against the white field. The snow was falling over the cornfield and the pasture and the hay-land, steadily, with very little wind, — a nice dry snow. The graveyard had only a light wire fence about it and was all overgrown with long red grass. The fine snow, settling into this red grass and upon the few little evergreens and the headstones, looked very pretty.

It was a nice graveyard, Rosicky reflected, sort of snug and homelike, not cramped or mournful, — a big sweep all round it. A man could lie down in the long grass and see the complete arch of the sky over him, hear the wagons go by; in summer the mowing-machine rattled right up to the wire fence. And it was so near home. Over there across the cornstalks his own roof and windmill looked so good to him that he promised himself to mind the Doctor and take care of himself. He was awful fond of his place, he admitted. He wasn't anxious to leave it. And it was a comfort to think that he would never have to go farther than the edge of his own hayfield. The snow, falling over his barnyard and the graveyard, seemed to draw things together like. And they were all old neighbours in the graveyard, most of them friends; there was nothing to feel awkward or embarrassed about. Embarrassment was the most disagreeable feeling Rosicky knew. He didn't often have it, — only with certain people whom he didn't understand at all.

Well, it was a nice snowstorm; a fine sight to see the snow falling so quietly and graciously over so much open country. On his cap and shoulders, on the horses' backs and manes, light, delicate, mysterious it fell; and with it a dry cool fragrance was

Chapter 4 The Literature of the Realistic Period

released into the air. It meant rest for vegetation and men and beasts, for the ground itself; a season of long nights for sleep, leisurely breakfasts, peace by the fire. This and much more went through Rosicky's mind, but he merely told himself that winter was coming, clucked to his horses, and drove on.

When he reached home, John, the youngest boy, ran out to put away his team for him, and he met Mary coming up from the outside cellar with her apron full of carrots. They went into the house together. On the table, covered with oilcloth figured with clusters of blue grapes, a place was set, and he smelled hot coffee-cake of some kind. Anton never lunched in town; he thought that extravagant, and anyhow he didn't like the food. So Mary always had something ready for him when he got home.

After he was settled in his chair, stirring his coffee in a big cup, Mary took out of the oven a pan of kolache[6] stuffed with apricots, examined them anxiously to see whether they had got too dry, put them beside his plate, and then sat down opposite him.

Rosicky asked her in Czech if she wasn't going to have any coffee.

She replied in English, as being somehow the right language for transacting business: "Now what did Doctor Ed say, Anton? You tell me just what."

"He said I was to tell you some compliments, but I forgot 'em." Rosicky's eyes twinkled.

"About you, I mean. What did he say about your asthma?"

"He says I ain't got no asthma." Rosicky took one of the little rolls in his broad brown fingers. The thickened nail of his right thumb told the story of his past.

"Well, what is the matter? And don't try to put me off."

"He don't say nothing much, only I'm a little older, and my heart ain't so good like it used to be."

Mary started and brushed her hair back from her temples with both hands as if she were a little out of her mind. From the way she glared, she might have been in a rage with him.

"He says there's something the matter with your heart? Doctor Ed says so?"

"Now don't yell at me like I was a hog in de garden, Mary. You know I always did like to hear a woman talk soft. He didn't say anything de matter wid my heart, only it ain't so young like it used to be, an' he tell me not to pitch hay or run de corn-sheller."

Mary wanted to jump up, but she sat still. She admired the way he never under any circumstances raised his voice or spoke roughly. He was city-bred, and she was country-bred; she often said she wanted her boys to have their papa's nice ways.

"You never have no pain there, do you? It's your breathing and your stomach that's been wrong. I wouldn't believe nobody but Doctor Ed about it. I guess I'll go see him myself. Didn't he give you no advice?"

"Chust to take it easy like, an' stay round de house dis winter. I guess you got some carpenter work for me to do. I kin make some new shelves for you, and I want dis long time to build a closet in de boys' room and make dem two little fellers keep dere clo'es hung up."

Rosicky drank his coffee from time to time, while he considered. His moustache was of the soft long variety and came down over his mouth like the teeth of a buggy-rake over a bundle of hay. Each time he put down his cup, he ran his blue handkerchief over his lips. When he took a drink of water, he managed very neatly with the back of his hand.

Mary sat watching him intently, trying to find any change in his face. It is hard to see anyone who has become like your own body to you. Yes, his hair had got thin, and his high forehead had deep lines running from left to right. But his neck, always clean shaved except in the busiest seasons, was not loose or baggy. It was burned a dark reddish brown, and there were deep creases in it, but it looked firm and full of blood. His cheeks had a good colour. On either side of his mouth there was a half-moon down the length of his cheek, not wrinkles, but two lines that had come there from his habitual expression. He was shorter and broader than when she married him; his back had grown broad and curved, a good deal like the shell of an old turtle, and his arms and legs were short.

He was fifteen years older than Mary, but she had hardly ever thought about it before. He was her man, and the kind of man she liked. She was rough, and he was gentle, — city-bred, as she always said. They had been shipmates on a rough voyage and had stood by each other in trying times. Life had gone well with them because, at bottom, they had the same ideas about life. They agreed, without discussion, as to what was most important and what was secondary. They didn't often exchange opinions, even in Czech, — it was as if they had thought the same thought together. A good deal had to be sacrificed and thrown overboard in a hard life like theirs, and they had never disagreed as to the things that could go. It had been a hard life, and a soft life, too. There wasn't anything brutal in the short, broad-backed man with the three-cornered eyes and the forehead that went on to the top of his skull. He was a city man, a gentle man, and though he had married a rough farm girl, he had never touched her without gentleness.

They had been at one accord not to hurry through life, not to be always skimping and saving. They saw their neighbours buy more land and feed more stock than they did, without discontent. Once when the creamery agent came to the Rosickys to persuade them to sell him their cream, he told them how much money the Fasslers, their nearest neighbours, had made on their cream last year.

"Yes," said Mary, "and look at them Fassler children! Pale, pinched little things, they look like skimmed milk. I'd rather put some colour into my children's faces than put money into the bank."

Chapter 4　The Literature of the Realistic Period

The agent shrugged and turned to Anton.

"I guess we'll do like she says, " said Rosicky.

III

Mary very soon got into town to see Doctor Ed, and then she had a talk with her boys and set a guard over Rosicky. Even John, the youngest, had his father on his mind. If Rosicky went to throw hay down from the loft, one of the boys ran up the ladder and took the fork from him. He sometimes complained that though he was getting to be an old man, he wasn't an old woman yet. That winter he stayed in the house in the afternoons and carpentered, or sat in the chair between the window full of plants and the wooden bench where the two pails of drinking-water stood. This spot was called "Father's corner, " though it was not a corner at all. He had a shelf there, where he kept his Bohemian papers and his pipes and tobacco, and his shears and needles and thread and tailor's thimble. Having been a tailor in his youth, he couldn't bear to see a woman patching at his clothes, or at the boys'. He liked tailoring, and always patched all the overalls and jackets and work shirts. Occasionally he made over a pair of pants one of the older boys had outgrown, for the little fellow.

While he sewed, he let his mind run back over his life. He had a good deal to remember, really; life in three countries. The only part of his youth he didn't like to remember was the two years he had spent in London, in Cheapside[7], working for a German tailor who was wretchedly poor.

Those days, when he was nearly always hungry, when his clothes were dropping off him for dirt, and the sound of a strange language kept him in continual bewilderment, had left a sore spot in his mind that wouldn't bear touching.

He was twenty when he landed at Castle Garden[8] in New York, and he had a protector[9] who got him work in a tailor shop in Vesey Street, down near the Washington Market. He looked upon that part of his life as very happy. He became a good workman, he was industrious, and his wages were increased from time to time. He minded his own business and envied nobody's good fortune. He went to night school and learned to read English. He often did overtime work and was well paid for it, but somehow he never saved anything. He couldn't refuse a loan to a friend, and he was self-indulgent. He liked a good dinner, and a little went for beer, a little for tobacco; a good deal went to the girls. He often stood through an opera on Saturday nights; he could get standing-room for a dollar. Those were the great days of opera in New York, and it gave a fellow something to think about for the rest of the week. Rosicky had a quick ear, and a childish love of all the stage splendour; the scenery, the costumes, the ballet. He usually went with a chum, and after the performance they had beer and maybe some oysters somewhere. It was a fine life; for the first five years or so it satisfied him completely. He was never hungry or cold or dirty, and everything amused him: a fire, a dog fight, a parade, a storm, a ferry ride. He thought New York the finest, richest, friendliest city in the world.

Moreover, he had what he called a happy home life. Very near the tailor shop was a small furniture-factory, where an old Austrian, Loeffler, employed a few skilled men and made unusual furniture, most of it to order, for the rich German housewives up-town. The top floor of Loeffler's five-storey factory was a loft, where he kept his choice lumber and stored the odd pieces of furniture left on his hands. One of the young workmen he employed was a Czech, and he and Rosicky became fast friends. They persuaded Loeffler to let them have a sleeping-room in one corner of the loft. They bought good beds and bedding and had their pick of the furniture kept up there. The loft was low-pitched, but light and airy, full of windows, and good-smelling by reason of the fine lumber put up there to season. Old Loeffler used to go down to the docks and buy wood from South America and the East from the sea captains. The young men were as foolish about their house as a bridal pair. Zichec, the young cabinet-maker, devised every sort of convenience, and Rosicky kept their clothes in order. At night and on Sundays, when the quiver of machinery underneath was still, it was the quietest place in the world, and on summer nights all the sea winds blew in. Zichec often practised on his flute in the evening. They were both fond of music and went to the opera together. Rosicky thought he wanted to live like that for ever.

But as the years passed, all alike, he began to get a little restless. When spring came round, he would begin to feel fretted, and he got to drinking. He was likely to drink too much of a Saturday night. On Sunday he was languid and heavy, getting over his spree. On Monday he plunged into work again. So he never had time to figure out what ailed him, though he knew something did. When the grass turned green in Park Place, and the lilac hedge at the back of Trinity churchyard put out its blossoms, he was tormented by a longing to run away. That was why he drank too much; to get a temporary illusion of freedom and wide horizons.

Rosicky, the old Rosicky, could remember as if it were yesterday the day when the young Rosicky found out what was the matter with him. It was on a Fourth of July afternoon, and he was sitting in Park Place in the sun. The lower part of New York was empty. Wall Street, Liberty Street, Broadway, all empty. So much stone and asphalt with nothing going on, so many empty windows. The emptiness was intense, like the stillness in a great factory when the machinery stops and the belts and bands cease running. It was too great a change, it took all the strength out of one. Those blank buildings, without the stream of life pouring through them, were like empty jails. It struck young Rosicky that this was the trouble with big cities; they built you in from the earth itself, cemented you away from any contact with the ground. You lived in an unnatural world, like the fish in an aquarium, who were probably much more comfortable than they ever were in the sea.

On that very day he began to think seriously about the articles he had read in the Bohemian papers, describing prosperous Czech farming communities in the West. He believed he would like to go out there as a farm hand; it was hardly possible that he could ever have land of his own. His people had always been workmen; his father and grandfather had worked in shops. His mother's parents had lived in the country, but they rented their farm and had a hard time to get along. Nobody in his family had ever owned any land, — that belonged to a different station of life altogether. Anton's mother died when he was little, and he was sent into the country to her parents. He stayed with them until he was twelve, and formed those ties with the earth and the farm animals and growing things which are never made at all unless they are made early. After his grandfather died, he went back to live with his father and stepmother, but she was very hard on him, and his father helped him to get passage to London.

After that Fourth of July day in Park Place, the desire to return to the country never left him. To work on another man's farm would be all he asked; to see the sun rise and set and to plant things and watch them grow. He was a very simple man. He was like a tree that has not many roots, but one tap-root that goes down deep. He subscribed for a Bohemian paper printed in Chicago, then for one printed in Omaha. His mind got farther and farther west. He began to save a little money to buy his liberty. When he was thirty-five, there was a great meeting in New York of Bohemian athletic societies, and Rosicky left the tailor shop and went home with the Omaha delegates to try his fortune in another part of the world.

IV

Perhaps the fact that his own youth was well over before he began to have a family was one reason why Rosicky was so fond of his boys. He had almost a grandfather's indulgence for them. He had never had to worry about any of them— except, just now, a little about Rudolph.

On Saturday night the boys always piled into the Ford, took little Josephine, and went to town to the moving-picture show. One Saturday morning they were talking at the breakfast table about starting early that evening, so that they would have an hour or so to see the Christmas things in the stores before the show began. Rosicky looked down the table.

"I hope you boys ain't disappointed, but I want you to let me have de car tonight. Maybe some of you can go in with de neighbours."

Their faces fell. They worked hard all week, and they were still like children. A new jack-knife or a box of candy pleased the older ones as much as the little fellow.

"If you and Mother are going to town," Frank said, "maybe you could take a couple of us along with you, anyway."

"No, I want to take de car down to Rudolph's, and let him an' Polly go in to de show. She don't git into town enough, an' I'm afraid she's gettin' lonesome, an' he can't afford no car yet."

That settled it. The boys were a good deal dashed. Their father took another piece of apple-cake and went on: "Maybe next Saturday night de two little fellers can go along wid dem."

"Oh, is Rudolph going to have the car every Saturday night?"

Rosicky did not reply at once; then he began to speak seriously: "Listen, boys; Polly ain't lookin' so good. I don't like to see nobody lookin' sad. It comes hard fur a town girl to be a farmer's wife. I don't want no trouble to start in Rudolph's family. When it starts, it ain't so easy to stop. An American girl don't git used to our ways all at once. I like to tell Polly she and Rudolph can have the car every Saturday night till after New Year's, if it's all right with you boys."

"Sure it's all right, Papa," Mary cut in. "And it's good you thought about that. Town girls is used to more than country girls. I lay awake nights, scared she'll make Rudolph discontented with the farm."

The boys put as good a face on it as they could. They surely looked forward to their Saturday nights in town. That evening Rosicky drove the car the half-mile down to Rudolph's new, bare little house.

Polly was in a short-sleeved gingham dress, clearing away the supper dishes. She was a trim, slim little thing, with blue eyes and shingled[10] yellow hair, and her eyebrows were reduced to a mere brush-stroke, like Miss Pearl's.

"Good evening, Mr. Rosicky. Rudolph's at the barn, I guess." She never called him father, or Mary mother. She was sensitive about having married a foreigner. She never in the world would have done it if Rudolph hadn't been such a handsome, persuasive fellow and such a gallant lover. He had graduated in her class in the high school in town, and their friendship began in the ninth grade. Rosicky went in, though he wasn't exactly asked. "My boys ain't goin' to town tonight, an' I brought de car over fur you two to go in to de picture show."

Polly, carrying dishes to the sink, looked over her shoulder at him. "Thank you. But I'm late with my work tonight, and pretty tired. Maybe Rudolph would like to go in with you."

"Oh, I don't go to de shows! I'm too old-fashioned. You won't feel so tired after you ride in de air a ways. It's a nice clear night, an' it ain't cold. You go an' fix yourself up, Polly, an' I'll wash de dishes an' leave everything nice fur you."

Polly blushed and tossed her bob[11]. "I couldn't let you do that, Mr. Rosicky. I wouldn't think of it."

Rosicky said nothing. He found a bib apron on a nail behind the kitchen door. He

Chapter 4　The Literature of the Realistic Period

slipped it over his head and then took Polly by her two elbows and pushed her gently toward the door of her own room. "I washed up de kitchen many times for my wife, when de babies was sick or somethin'. You go an' make yourself look nice. I like you to look prettier'n any of dem town girls when you go in. De young folks must have some fun, an' I'm goin' to look out fur you, Polly."

That kind, reassuring grip on her elbows, the old man's funny bright eyes, made Polly want to drop her head on his shoulder for a second. She restrained herself, but she lingered in his grasp at the door of her room, murmuring tearfully: "You always lived in the city when you were young, didn't you? Don't you ever get lonesome out here?"

As she turned round to him, her hand fell naturally into his, and he stood holding it and smiling into her face with his peculiar, knowing, indulgent smile without a shadow of reproach in it. "Dem big cities is all right fur de rich, but dey is terrible hard fur de poor."

"I don't know. Sometimes I think I'd like to take a chance. You lived in New York, didn't you?"

"An' London. Da's bigger still. I learned my trade dere. Here's Rudolph comin', you better hurry."

"Will you tell me about London some time?"

"Maybe. Only I ain't no talker, Polly. Run an' dress yourself up."

The bedroom door closed behind her, and Rudolph came in from the outside, looking anxious. He had seen the car and was sorry any of his family should come just then. Supper hadn't been a very pleasant occasion. Halting in the doorway, he saw his father in a kitchen apron, carrying dishes to the sink. He flushed crimson and something flashed in his eye. Rosicky held up a warning finger.

"I brought de car over fur you an' Polly to go to de picture show, an' I made her let me finish here so you won't be late. You go put on a clean shirt, quick!"

"But don't the boys want the car, Father?"

"Not tonight dey don't." Rosicky fumbled under his apron and found his pants pocket. He took out a silver dollar and said in a hurried whisper: "You go an' buy dat girl some ice cream an' candy tonight, like you was courtin'. She's awful good friends wid me."

Rudolph was very short of cash, but he took the money as if it hurt him. There had been a crop failure all over the county. He had more than once been sorry he'd married this year.

In a few minutes the young people came out, looking clean and a little stiff. Rosicky hurried them off, and then he took his own time with the dishes. He scoured the pots and pans and put away the milk and swept the kitchen. He put some coal in the stove and shut off the draughts, so the place would be warm for them when they got home late at night. Then he sat down and had a pipe and listened to the clock tick.

Generally speaking, marrying an American girl was certainly a risk. A Czech should marry a Czech. It was lucky that Polly was the daughter of a poor widow woman; Rudolph was proud, and if she had a prosperous family to throw up at him, they could never make it go. Polly was one of four sisters, and they all worked; one was book-keeper in the bank, one taught music, and Polly and her younger sister had been clerks, like Miss Pearl. All four of them were musical, had pretty voices, and sang in the Methodist choir, which the eldest sister directed.

Polly missed the sociability of a store position. She missed the choir, and the company of her sisters. She didn't dislike housework, but she disliked so much of it. Rosicky was a little anxious about this pair. He was afraid Polly would grow so discontented that Rudy would quit the farm and take a factory job in Omaha. He had worked for a winter up there, two years ago, to get money to marry on. He had done very well, and they would always take him back at the stockyards. But to Rosicky that meant the end of everything for his son. To be a landless man was to be a wage-earner, a slave, all your life; to have nothing, to be nothing.

Rosicky thought he would come over and do a little carpentering for Polly after the New Year. He guessed she needed jollying. Rudolph was a serious sort of chap, serious in love and serious about his work.

Rosicky shook out his pipe and walked home across the fields. Ahead of him the lamplight shone from his kitchen windows. Suppose he were still in a tailor shop on Vesey Street, with a bunch of pale, narrow-chested sons working on machines, all coming home tired and sullen to eat supper in a kitchen that was a parlour also; with another crowded, angry family quarrelling just across the dumb-waiter[12] shaft, and squeaking pulleys at the windows where dirty washings hung on dirty lines above a court full of old brooms and mops and ash-cans . . .

He stopped by the windmill to look up at the frosty winter stars and draw a long breath before he went inside. That kitchen with the shining windows was dear to him; but the sleeping fields and bright stars and the noble darkness were dearer still.

V

On the day before Christmas the weather set in very cold; no snow, but a bitter, biting wind that whistled and sang over the flat land and lashed one's face like fine wires. There was baking going on in the Rosicky kitchen all day, and Rosicky sat inside, making over a coat that Albert had outgrown into an overcoat for John. Mary had a big red geranium in bloom for Christmas, and a row of Jerusalem cherry trees, full of berries. It was the first year she had ever grown these; Doctor Ed brought her the seeds from Omaha when he went to some medical convention. They reminded Rosicky of plants he had seen in England; and all afternoon, as he stitched, he sat thinking about those two years in London, which his mind usually shrank from even after all this while.

He was a lad of eighteen when he dropped down into London, with no money and no connexions except the address of a cousin who was supposed to be working at a confectioner's. When he went to the pastry shop, however, he found that the cousin had gone to America. Anton tramped the streets for several days, sleeping in doorways and on the Embankment[13], until he was in utter despair. He knew no English, and the sound of the strange language all about him confused him. By chance he met a poor German tailor who had learned his trade in Vienna[14], and could speak a little Czech. This tailor, Lifschnitz, kept a repair shop in a Cheapside basement, underneath a cobbler. He didn't much need an apprentice, but he was sorry for the boy and took him in for no wages but his keep and what he could pick up. The pickings were supposed to be coppers given you when you took work home to a customer. But most of the customers called for their clothes themselves, and the coppers that came Anton's way were very few. He had, however, a place to sleep. The tailor's family lived upstairs in three rooms; a kitchen, a bedroom, where Lifschnitz and his wife and five children slept, and a living-room. Two corners of this living-room were curtained off for lodgers; in one Rosicky slept on an old horsehair sofa, with a feather quilt to wrap himself in. The other corner was rented to a wretched, dirty boy, who was studying the violin. He actually practised there. Rosicky was dirty, too. There was no way to be anything else. Mrs. Lifschnitz got the water she cooked and washed with from a pump in a brick court, four flights down. There were bugs in the place, and multitudes of fleas, though the poor woman did the best she could. Rosicky knew she often went empty to give another potato or a spoonful of dripping to the two hungry, sad-eyed boys who lodged with her. He used to think he would never get out of there, never get a clean shirt to his back again. What would he do, he wondered, when his clothes actually dropped to pieces and the worn cloth wouldn't hold patches any longer?

It was still early when the old farmer put aside his sewing and his recollections. The sky had been a dark grey all day, with not a gleam of sun, and the light failed at four o'clock. He went to shave and change his shirt while the turkey was roasting. Rudolph and Polly were coming over for supper.

After supper they sat round in the kitchen, and the younger boys were saying how sorry they were it hadn't snowed. Everybody was sorry. They wanted a deep snow that would lie long and keep the wheat warm, and leave the ground soaked when it melted.

"Yes, sir!" Rudolph broke out fiercely; "if we have another dry year like last year, there's going to be hard times in this country."

Rosicky filled his pipe. "You boys don't know what hard times is. You don't owe nobody, you got plenty to eat an' keep warm, an' plenty water to keep clean. When you got them, you can't have it very hard."

Rudolph frowned, opened and shut his big right hand, and dropped it clenched upon his knee. "I've got to have a good deal more than that, Father, or I'll quit this farming gamble. I can always make good wages railroading, or at the packing house[15], and be sure of my money."

"Maybe so," his father answered dryly.

Mary, who had just come in from the pantry and was wiping her hands on the roller towel, thought Rudy and his father were getting too serious. She brought her darning-basket and sat down in the middle of the group.

"I ain't much afraid of hard times, Rudy," she said heartily. "We've had a plenty, but we've always come through. Your father wouldn't never take nothing very hard, not even hard times. I got a mind to tell you a story on him. Maybe you boys can't hardly remember the year we had that terrible hot wind, that burned everything up on the Fourth of July? All the corn an' the gardens. An' that was in the days when we didn't have alfalfa yet, — I guess it wasn't invented.

"Well, that very day your father was out cultivatin' corn, and I was here in the kitchen makin' plum preserves. We had bushels of plums that year. I noticed it was terrible hot, but it's always hot in the kitchen when you're preservin', an' I was too busy with my plums to mind. Anton come in from the field about three o'clock, an' I asked him what was the matter.

"'Nothin', he says, 'but it's pretty hot, an' I think I won't work no more today.' He stood round for a few minutes, an' then he says: 'Ain't you near through? I want you should git up a nice supper for us tonight. It's Fourth of July.'

"I told him to git along, that I was right in the middle of preservin', but the plums would taste good on hot biscuit. 'I'm goin' to have fried chicken, too,' he says, and he went off an' killed a couple. You three oldest boys was little fellers, playin' round outside, real hot an' sweaty, an' your father took you to the horse tank down by the windmill an' took off your clothes an' put you in. Them two box-elder trees was little then, but they made shade over the tank. Then he took off all his own clothes, an' got in with you. While he was playin' in the water with you, the Methodist preacher drove into our place to say how all the neighbours was goin' to meet at the schoolhouse that night, to pray for rain. He drove right to the windmill, of course, and there was your father and you three with no clothes on. I was in the kitchen door, an' I had to laugh, for the preacher acted like he ain't never seen a naked man before. He surely was embarrassed, an' your father couldn't git to his clothes; they was all hangin' up on the windmill to let the sweat dry out of 'em. So he laid in the tank where he was, an' put one of you boys on top of him to cover him up a little, an' talked to the preacher.

"When you got through playin' in the water, he put clean clothes on you and a clean shirt on himself, an' by that time I'd begun to get supper. He says: 'It's too hot in here to eat comfortable. Let's have a picnic in the orchard. We'll eat our supper behind the mulberry hedge, under them linden trees.'

Chapter 4　The Literature of the Realistic Period

"So he carried our supper down, an' a bottle of my wild-grape wine, an' everything tasted good, I can tell you. The wind got cooler as the sun was goin' down, and it turned out pleasant, only I noticed how the leaves was curled up on the linden trees. That made me think, an' I asked your father if that hot wind all day hadn't been terrible hard on the gardens an' the corn.

"'Corn,' he says, 'there ain't no corn.'

"'What you talkin' about?' I said. 'Ain't we got forty acres?'

"'We ain't got an ear,' he says, 'nor nobody else ain't got none. All the corn in this country was cooked by three o'clock today, like you'd roasted it in an oven.'

"'You mean you won't get no crop at all?' I asked him. I couldn't believe it, after he'd worked so hard.

"'No crop this year,' he says. 'That's why we're havin' a picnic. We might as well enjoy what we got.'

"An' that's how your father behaved, when all the neighbours was so discouraged they couldn't look you in the face. An' we enjoyed ourselves that year, poor as we was, an' our neighbours wasn't a bit better off for bein' miserable. Some of 'em grieved till they got poor digestions and couldn't relish what they did have."

The younger boys said they thought their father had the best of it. But Rudolf was thinking that, all the same, the neighbours had managed to get ahead more, in the fifteen years since that time.

There must be something wrong about his father's way of doing things. He wished he knew what was going on in the back of Polly's mind. He knew she liked his father, but he knew, too, that she was afraid of something. When his mother sent over coffee-cake or prune tarts or a loaf of fresh bread, Polly seemed to regard them with a certain suspicion. When she observed to him that his brothers had nice manners, her tone implied that it was remarkable they should have. With his mother she was stiff and on her guard. Mary's hearty frankness and gusts of good humour irritated her. Polly was afraid of being unusual or conspicuous in any way, of being "ordinary," as she said!

When Mary had finished her story, Rosicky laid aside his pipe.

"You boys like me to tell you about some of dem hard times I been through in London? Warmly encouraged, he sat rubbing his forehead along the deep creases. It was bothersome to tell a long story in English (he nearly always talked to the boys in Czech), but he wanted Polly to hear this one.

"Well, you know about dat tailor shop I worked in in London? I had one Christmas dere I ain't never forgot. Times was awful bad before Christmas; de boss ain't got much work, an' have it awful hard to pay his rent. It ain't so much fun, bein' poor in a big city like London, I'll say! All de windows is full of good t'ings to eat, an' all de pushcarts in de streets is full, an' you smell 'em all de time, an' you ain't got no money, — not a damn bit. I didn't mind de cold so much, though I didn't have no

137

overcoat, chust a short jacket I'd outgrown so it wouldn't meet on me, an' my hands was chapped raw. But I always had a good appetite, like you all know, an' de sight of dem pork pies in de windows was awful fur me!

"Day before Christmas was terrible foggy dat year, an' dat fog gits into your bones and makes you all damp like. Mrs. Lifschnitz didn't give us nothin' but a little bread an' drippin' for supper, because she was savin' to try for to give us a good dinner on Christmas Day. After supper de boss say I can go an' enjoy myself, so I went into de streets to listen to de Christmas singers. Dey sing old songs an' make very nice music, an' I run round after dem a good ways, till I got awful hungry. I t'ink maybe if I go home, I can sleep till morning an' forgit my belly.

"I went into my corner real quiet, and roll up in my fedder quilt. But I ain't got my head down, till I smell somet'ing good. Seem like it git stronger an' stronger, an' I can't git to sleep noway. I can't understand dat smell. Dere was a gas light in a hall across de court, dat always shine in at my window a little. I got up an' look round. I got a little wooden box in my corner fur a stool, 'cause I ain't got no chair. I picks up dat box, and under it dere is a roast goose on a platter! I can't believe my eyes. I carry it to de window where de light comes in, an' touch it and smell it to find out, an' den I taste it to be sure. I say, I will eat chust one little bite of dat goose, so I can go to sleep, and tomorrow I won't eat none at all. But I tell you, boys, when I stop, one half of dat goose was gone!"

The narrator bowed his head, and the boys shouted. But little Josephine slipped behind his chair and kissed him on the neck beneath his ear.

"Poor little Papa, I don't want him to be hungry!"

"Da's long ago, child. I ain't never been hungry since I had your mudder to cook fur me."

"Go on and tell us the rest, please," said Polly.

"Well, when I come to realize what I done, of course, I felt terrible. I felt better in de stomach, but very bad in de heart. I set on my bed wid dat platter on my knees, an' it all come to me; how hard dat poor woman save to buy dat goose, and how she get some neighbour to cook it dat got more fire, an' how she put it in my corner to keep it away from dem hungry children. Dey was a old carpet hung up to shut my corner off, an' de children wasn't allowed to go in dere. An' I know she put it in my corner because she trust me more'n she did de violin boy. I can't stand it to face her after I spoil de Christmas. So I put on my shoes and go out into de city. I tell myself I better throw myself in de river; but I guess I ain't dat kind of a boy.

"It was after twelve o'clock, an' terrible cold, an' I start out to walk about London all night. I walk along de river awhile, but dey was lots of drunks all along; men, and women too. I chust move along to keep away from de police. I git onto de Strand, an' den over to New Oxford Street, where dere was a big German restaurant on de ground floor, wid big windows all fixed up fine, an' I could see de people havin' parties inside. While I was lookin' in, two men and two ladies come out, laughin' and talkin' and feelin' happy about all dey been eatin' an' drinkin', and dey was speakin' Czech, — not like de Austrians, but like de home folks talk it.

"I guess I went crazy, an' I done what I ain't never done before nor since. I went right up to dem gay people an' begun to beg dem: 'Fellow-countrymen, for God's sake give me money enough to buy a goose!'

"Dey laugh, of course, but de ladies speak awful kind to me, an' dey take me back into de restaurant and give me hot coffee and cakes, an' make me tell all about how I happened to come to London, an' what I was doin' dere. Dey take my name and where I work down on paper, an' both of dem ladies give me ten shillings[16].

"De big market at Covent Garden ain't very far away, an' by dat time it was open. I go dere an' buy a big goose an' some pork pies, an' potatoes and onions, an' cakes an' oranges fur de children, — all I could carry! When I git home, everybody is still asleep. I pile all I bought on de kitchen table, an' go in an' lay down on my bed, an' I ain't waken up till I hear dat woman scream when she come out into her kitchen. My goodness, but she was surprise! She laugh an' cry at de same time, an' hug me and waken all de children. She ain't stop fur no breakfast; she git de Christmas dinner ready dat morning, and we all sit down an' eat all we can hold. I ain't never seen dat violin boy have all he can hold before.

"Two three days after dat, de two men come to hunt me up, an' dey ask my boss, and he give me a good report an' tell dem I was a steady boy all right. One of dem Bohemians was very smart an' run a Bohemian newspaper in New York, an' de odder was a rich man, in de importing business, an' dey been travelling togedder. Dey told me how t'ings was easier in New York, an' offered to pay my passage when dey was goin' home soon on a boat. My boss say to me: 'You go. You ain't got no chance here, an' I like to see you git ahead, fur you always been a good boy to my woman, and fur dat fine Christmas dinner you give us all.' An' da's how I got to New York."

That night when Rudolph and Polly, arm in arm, were running home across the fields with the bitter wind at their backs, his heart leaped for joy when she said she thought they might have his family come over for supper on New Year's Eve. "Let's get up a nice supper, and not let your mother help at all; make her be company for once."

"That would be lovely of you, Polly," he said humbly. He was a very simple, modest boy, and he, too, felt vaguely that Polly and her sisters were more experienced and worldly than his people.

VI

The winter turned out badly for farmers. It was bitterly cold, and after the first light snows before Christmas there was no snow at all, — and no rain. March was as bitter as February. On those days when the wind fairly punished the country, Rosicky sat by his window. In the fall he and the boys had put in a big wheat planting, and now the seed had frozen in the ground. All that land would have to be ploughed up and planted over again, planted in corn. It had happened before, but he was younger then, and he never worried about what had to be. He was sure of himself and of Mary; he knew they could bear what they had to bear, that they would always pull through somehow. But he was not so sure about the young ones, and he felt troubled because Rudolph and Polly were having such a hard start.

Sitting beside his flowering window while the panes rattled and the wind blew in under the door, Rosicky gave himself to reflection as he had not done since those Sundays in the loft of the furniture-factory in New York, long ago. Then he was trying to find what he wanted in life for himself; now he was trying to find what he wanted for his boys, and why it was he so hungered to feel sure they would be here, working this very land, after he was gone.

They would have to work hard on the farm, and probably they would never do much more than make a living. But if he could think of them as staying here on the land, he wouldn't have to fear any great unkindness for them. Hardships, certainly; it was a hardship to have the wheat freeze in the ground when seed was so high; and to have to sell your stock because you had no feed. But there would be other years when everything came along right, and you caught up. And what you had was your own. You didn't have to choose between bosses and strikers, and go wrong either way. You didn't have to do with dishonest and cruel people. They were the only things in his experience he had found terrifying and horrible; the look in the eyes of a dishonest and crafty man, of a scheming and rapacious[17] woman.

In the country, if you had a mean neighbour, you could keep off his land and make him keep off yours. But in the city, all the foulness and misery and brutality of your neighbours was part of your life. The worst things he had come upon in his journey through the world were human, — depraved and poisonous specimens of man. To this day he could recall certain terrible faces in the London streets. There were mean people everywhere, to be sure, even in their own country town here. But they weren't tempered, hardened, sharpened, like the treacherous people in cities who live by grinding or cheating or poisoning their fellow-men. He had helped to bury two of his fellow-workmen in the tailoring trade, and he was distrustful of the organized industries that see one out of the world in big cities. Here, if you were sick, you had Doctor Ed to look after you; and if you died, fat Mr. Haycock, the kindest man in the world, buried you.

It seemed to Rosicky that for good, honest boys like his, the worst they could do on the farm was better than the best they would be likely to do in the city. If he'd had a mean boy, now, one who was crooked and sharp and tried to put anything over on his brothers, then town would be the place for him. But he had no such boy. As for Rudolph, the discontented one, he would give the shirt off his back to anyone who touched his heart. What Rosicky really hoped for his boys was that they could get through the world without ever knowing much about the cruelty of human beings. "Their mother and me ain't prepared them for that, " he sometimes said to himself.

These thoughts brought him back to a grateful consideration of his own case. What an escape he had had, to be sure! He, too, in his time, had had to take money for repair work from the hand of a hungry child who let it go so wistfully; because it was money due his boss. And now, in all these years, he had never had to take a cent from anyone in bitter need, — never had to look at the face of a woman become like a wolf's from struggle and famine. When he thought of these things, Rosicky would put on his cap and jacket and slip down to the barn and give his work-horses a little extra oats, letting them eat it out of his hand in their slobbery fashion. It was his way of expressing what he felt, and made him chuckle with pleasure.

The spring came warm, with blue skies, — but dry, dry as a bone. The boys began ploughing up the wheat-fields to plant them over in corn. Rosicky would stand at the fence corner and watch them, and the earth was so dry it blew up in clouds of brown dust that hid the horses and the sulky plough and the driver. It was a bad outlook.

The big alfalfa-field that lay between the home place and Rudolph's came up green, but Rosicky was worried because during that open windy winter a great many Russian thistle plants had blown in there and lodged. He kept asking the boys to rake them out; he was afraid their seed would root and "take the alfalfa". Rudolph said that was nonsense. The boys were working so hard planting corn, their father felt he couldn't insist about the thistles, but he set great store by that big alfalfa field. It was a feed you could depend on, — and there was some deeper reason, vague, but strong. The peculiar green of that clover woke early memories in old Rosicky, went back to something in his childhood in the old world. When he was a little boy, he had played in fields of that strong blue-green colour.

One morning, when Rudolph had gone to town in the car, leaving a work-team idle in his barn, Rosicky went over to his son's place, put the horses to the buggy-rake, and set about quietly raking up those thistles. He behaved with guilty caution, and rather enjoyed stealing a march on Doctor Ed, who was just then taking his first vacation in seven years of practice and was attending a clinic in Chicago. Rosicky got the thistles raked up, but did not stop to burn them. That would take some time, and his breath was pretty short, so he thought he had better get the horses back to the barn.

He got them into the barn and to their stalls, but the pain had come on so sharp in his chest that he didn't try to take the harness off. He started for the house, bending lower with every step. The cramp in his chest was shutting him up like a jack-knife.

When he reached the windmill, he swayed and caught at the ladder. He saw Polly coming down the hill, running with the swiftness of a slim greyhound. In a flash she had her shoulder under his armpit.

"Lean on me, Father, hard! Don't be afraid. We can get to the house all right."

Somehow they did, though Rosicky became blind with pain; he could keep on his legs, but he couldn't steer his course. The next thing he was conscious of was lying on Polly's bed, and Polly bending over him wringing out bath towels in hot water and putting them on his chest. She stopped only to throw coal into the stove, and she kept the tea-kettle and the black pot going. She put these hot applications on him for nearly an hour, she told him afterwards, and all that time he was drawn up stiff and blue, with the sweat pouring off him.

As the pain gradually loosed its grip, the stiffness went out of his jaws, the black circles round his eyes disappeared, and a little of his natural colour came back. When his daughter-in-law buttoned his shirt over his chest at last, he sighed.

"Da's fine, de way I feel now, Polly. It was a awful bad spell, an' I was so sorry it all come on you like it did."

Polly was flushed and excited. "Is the pain really gone? Can I leave you long enough to telephone over to your place?"

Rosicky's eyelids fluttered. "Don't telephone, Polly. It ain't no use to scare my wife. It's nice and quiet here, an' if I ain't too much trouble to you, just let me lay still till I feel like myself. I ain't got no pain now. It's nice here."

Polly bent over him and wiped the moisture from his face. "Oh, I'm so glad it's over!" she broke out impulsively. "It just broke my heart to see you suffer so, Father."

Rosicky motioned her to sit down on the chair where the tea-kettle had been, and looked up at her with that lively affectionate gleam in his eyes. "You was awful good to me, I won't never forgit dat. I hate it to be sick on you like dis. Down at de barn I say to myself, dat young girl ain't had much experience in sickness, I don't want to scare her, an' maybe she's got a baby comin' or somet'ing."

Polly took his hand. He was looking at her so intently and affectionately and confidingly; his eyes seemed to caress her face, to regard it with pleasure. She frowned with her funny streaks of eyebrows, and then smiled back at him.

"I guess maybe there is something of that kind going to happen. But I haven't told anyone yet, not my mother or Rudolph. You'll be the first to know."

His hand pressed hers. She noticed that it was warm again. The twinkle in his yellow-brown eyes seemed to come nearer.

"I like mighty well to see dat little child, Polly," was all he said. Then he closed his eyes and lay half-smiling. But Polly sat still, thinking hard. She had a sudden feeling that nobody in the world, not her mother, not Rudolph, or anyone, really loved her as much as old Rosicky did. It perplexed her. She sat frowning and trying to puzzle it out.

Chapter 4 The Literature of the Realistic Period

It was as if Rosicky had a special gift for loving people, something that was like an ear for music or an eye for colour. It was quiet, unobtrusive; it was merely there. You saw it in his eyes, — perhaps that was why they were merry. You felt it in his hands, too. After he dropped off to sleep, she sat holding his warm, broad, flexible brown hand. She had never seen another in the least like it. She wondered if it wasn't a kind of gypsy hand, it was so alive and quick and light in its communications, — very strange in a farmer. Nearly all the farmers she knew had huge lumps of fists, like mauls, or they were knotty and bony and uncomfortable-looking, with stiff fingers. But Rosicky's was like quicksilver[18], flexible, muscular, about the colour of a pale cigar, with deep, deep creases across the palm. It wasn't nervous, it wasn't a stupid lump; it was a warm brown human hand, with some cleverness in it, a great deal of generosity, and something else which Polly could only call "gypsy-like", — something nimble and lively and sure, in the way that animals are.

Polly remembered that hour long afterwards; it had been like an awakening to her. It seemed to her that she had never learned so much about life from anything as from old Rosicky's hand. It brought her to herself; it communicated some direct and untranslatable message.

When she heard Rudolph coming in the car, she ran out to meet him.

"Oh, Rudy, your father's been awful sick! He raked up those thistles he's been worrying about, and afterwards he could hardly get to the house. He suffered so I was afraid he was going to die."

Rudolph jumped to the ground. "Where is he now?"

"On the bed. He's asleep. I was terribly scared, because, you know, I'm so fond of your father." She slipped her arm through his and they went into the house. That afternoon they took Rosicky home and put him to bed, though he protested that he was quite well again.

The next morning he got up and dressed and sat down to breakfast with his family. He told Mary that his coffee tasted better than usual to him, and he warned the boys not to bear any tales to Doctor Ed when he got home. After breakfast he sat down by his window to do some patching and asked Mary to thread several needles for him before she went to feed her chickens, — her eyes were better than his, and her hands steadier. He lit his pipe and took up John's overalls. Mary had been watching him anxiously all morning, and as she went out of the door with her bucket of scraps, she saw that he was smiling. He was thinking, indeed, about Polly, and how he might never have known what a tender heart she had if he hadn't got sick over there. Girls nowadays didn't wear their heart on their sleeve. But now he knew Polly would make a fine woman after the foolishness wore off. Either a woman had that sweetness at her heart or she hadn't. You couldn't always tell by the look of them; but if they had that, everything came out right in the end.

After he had taken a few stitches, the cramp began in his chest, like yesterday. He put his pipe cautiously down on the window-sill and bent over to ease the pull. No use, — he had better try to get to his bed if he could. He rose and groped his way across the familiar floor, which was rising and falling like the deck of a ship. At the door he fell. When Mary came in, she found him lying there, and the moment she touched him she knew that he was gone.

Doctor Ed was away when Rosicky died, and for the first few weeks after he got home he was hard driven. Every day he said to himself that he must get out to see that family that had lost their father. One soft, warm moonlight night in early summer he started for the farm. His mind was on other things, and not until his road ran by the graveyard did he realize that Rosicky wasn't over there on the hill where the red lamplight shone, but here, in the moonlight. He stopped his car, shut off the engine, and sat there for a while.

A sudden hush had fallen on his soul. Everything here seemed strangely moving and significant, though signifying what, he did not know. Close by the wire fence stood Rosicky's mowing-machine, where one of the boys had been cutting hay that afternoon; his own workhorses had been going up and down there. The new-cut hay perfumed all the night air. The moonlight silvered the long, billowy grass that grew over the graves and hid the fence; the few little evergreens stood out black in it, like shadows in a pool. The sky was very blue and soft, the stars rather faint because the moon was full.

For the first time it struck Doctor Ed that this was really a beautiful graveyard. He thought of city cemeteries; acres of shrubbery and heavy stone, so arranged and lonely and unlike anything in the living world. Cities of the dead, indeed; cities of the forgotten, of the "put away". But this was open and free, this little square of long grass which the wind for ever stirred. Nothing but the sky overhead, and the many-coloured fields running on until they met that sky. The horses worked here in summer; the neighbours passed on their way to town; and over yonder, in the cornfield, Rosicky's own cattle would be eating fodder as winter came on. Nothing could be more un-deathlike than this place; nothing could be more right for a man who had helped to do the work of great cities and had always longed for the open country and had got to it at last. Rosicky's life seemed to him complete and beautiful.

Notes

1. **Bohemian**: person from Bohemia, a region of western Czechoslovakia.
2. **widder**: Rosicky's pronunciation of widow.
3. **confinement**: childbirth.
4. **chaff**: to tease and joke in a good-natured way.
5. **bolt**: roll of cloth of a specific length.
6. **kolache**: buns made of sweet dough filled with jam or fruit.

7. **Cheapside**: working-class area in the East End of London.
8. **Castle Garden**: chief immigrant station of the United States between 1855 and 1890.
9. **protector**: friend or relative who helps a new immigrant.
10. **shingled**: woman's short haircut in which the hair over the nape of the neck is shaped close to the head.
11. **bob**: short hair.
12. **dumb-waiter**: small elevator used to send food, trash, etc. from one floor to another.
13. **Embankment**: part of the north bank of the Thames River in London.
14. **Vienna**: capital city of Austria, near the Czechoslovakian border.
15. **packing house**: plant where meat is processed and packed.
16. **shillings**: In the British monetary system before 1971, the shilling was a coin worth 1/20 of a pound. Ten shillings would have been a fairly generous gift at the time the story took place.
17. **rapacious**: greedy.
18. **quicksilver**: fluid and moving, like mercury.

Study Questions

1. What would you say is the major theme in this story? What are other possible themes?
2. What qualities distinguish Rosicky? Does he change, grow, evolve over the course of the story?
3. How are Rosicky's flashbacks to his past experiences in London and New York significant?
4. What is the essential source of tension or conflict in the story?

Essay Topics

1. How is Cather's attitude towards rural life different from that of Sherwood Anderson?
2. What attitude does Cather project about city life?

4.8 Sherwood Anderson

4.8.1 About the author

Sherwood Anderson (1876-1941) was born into a poor family in Camden, Ohio. As a boy, Anderson attended school only intermittently, while helping to support his family by working as a newsboy, housepainter, stock handler, and stable groom. At the age of 17 he moved to Chicago where he worked as a warehouse laborer and attended business classes at night. During the Spanish-American war Anderson fought in Cuba and returned after the war to Ohio, for a final year of schooling at Wittenberg College, Springfield.

For the next few years Anderson moved restlessly around Ohio. His life calmed

 down for some time with marriage and with work as a paint manufacturer. Yet following a difficult period of marital and business problems, he suffered a psychological crisis, which led to his leaving this business and his family and returning to Chicago to pursue a writing career.

Anderson's two first novels were *Windy McPherson's Son* (1916) and *Marching Men* (1917), both containing the psychological themes of inner lives of Midwestern villages, the pursuit of success and disillusionment. His third novel, *Winesburg, Ohio*, consisted of twenty-three thematically related sketches and stories. It offers portraits of the town's various inhabitants and their secret losses and dreams. Without lapsing into the tone of melodrama or preachy morality popular in fiction at the time, Anderson deftly shows us the small world of Winesburg, both suffocating and comforting to its residents. This book made Anderson a revolutionary force in both the form and subject matter of the American short story. For a short time, a number of young writers looked up to Anderson, whose age and experience, along with his unconventional lifestyle, served as a model for anyone who sought to critique and rebel against the norms of modern society. He also published *Poor White* (1920), *The Triumph of the Egg* (1921), *A Story Teller's Story* (1924), *Dark Laughter* (1925), *Horses and Men* (1932), *Beyond Desire* (1932), and *Death in the Woods* (1933). Anderson died of peritonitis on his way to visit Panama.

The stories in his books are characterized by a casual development, complexity of motivation, and an interest in psychological process. Written in a simple, realistic language illuminated by a muted lyricism, Anderson has dramatized crucial episodes in the lives of his characters. Many of his contributions to American Literature reflect his own struggles between the material and spiritual worlds as husband, father, author, and businessman and also cover issues as wide-ranging from labor conditions to marriage. Noted for his poetic realism, psychological insight, and sense of the tragic, Anderson has helped to establish a simple, consciously naive short-story style. His choice of subject matter and style has influenced many American writers who followed him, including F. Scott Fitzgerald, Ernest Hemingway, and William Faulkner. He is considered today one of the most important figures in American fiction — one who combined turn-of-the-century realism with an almost poetic introspection into the frailties and uncertainties of modern man.

4.8.2 "The egg"

My father was, I am sure, intended by nature to be a cheerful, kindly man. Until he was thirty-four years old he worked as a farm-hand for a man named Thomas Butterworth whose place lay near the town of Bidwell, Ohio. He had then a horse of his

Chapter 4 The Literature of the Realistic Period

own and on Saturday evenings drove into town to spend a few hours in social intercourse with other farm-hands. In town he drank several glasses of beer and stood about in Ben Head's saloon— crowded on Saturday evenings with visiting farm-hands. Songs were sung and glasses thumped [1] on the bar. At ten o'clock father drove home along a lonely country road, made his horse comfortable for the night and himself went to bed, quite happy in his position in life. He had at that time no notion of trying to rise in the world.

It was in the spring of his thirty-fifth year that father married my mother, then a country school-teacher, and in the following spring I came wriggling[2] and crying into the world. Something happened to the two people. They became ambitious. The American passion for getting up in the world took possession of them.

It may have been that mother was responsible. Being a schoolteacher she had no doubt read books and magazines. She had, I presume, read of how Garfield, Lincoln, and other Americans rose from poverty to fame and greatness [3] and as I lay beside her— in the days of her lying-in— she may have dreamed that I would someday rule men and cities. At any rate she induced father to give up his place as a farm-hand, sell his horse and embark on [4]an independent enterprise of his own. She was a tall silent woman with a long nose and troubled grey eyes. For herself she wanted nothing. For father and myself she was incurably ambitious.

The first venture into which the two people went turned out badly. They rented ten acres of poor stony land on Griggs's Road, eight miles from Bidwell, and launched into chicken raising. I grew into boyhood on the place and got my first impressions of life there. From the beginning they were impressions of disaster and if, in my turn, I am a gloomy man inclined to see the darker side of life, I attribute it to the fact that what should have been for me the happy joyous days of childhood were spent on a chicken farm.

One unversed in such matters can have no notion of the many and tragic things that can happen to a chicken. It is born out of an egg, lives for a few weeks as a tiny fluffy[5] thing such as you will see pictured on Easter[6] cards, then becomes hideously naked, eats quantities of corn and meal bought by the sweat of your father's brow, gets diseases called pip, cholera[7], and other names, stands looking with stupid eyes at the sun, becomes sick and dies. A few hens and now and then a rooster, intended to serve God's mysterious ends, struggle through to maturity. The hens lay eggs out of which come other chickens and the dreadful cycle is thus made complete. It is all unbelievably complex. Most philosophers must have been raised on chicken farms. One hopes for so much from a chicken and is so dreadfully disillusioned. Small chickens, just setting out on the journey of life, look so bright and alert and they are in fact so dreadfully stupid. They are so much like people they mix one up in one's judgments of life. If disease does not kill them they wait until your expectations are thoroughly aroused and then walk under the wheels of a wagon— to go squashed and dead back to their maker[8]. Vermin[9] infest[10] their youth, and fortunes must be spent for curative powders. In later life I have seen how a literature[11] has been built up on the subject of fortunes to be made out of the raising of chickens. It is intended to be read by the gods who have just eaten of the tree of the knowledge of good and evil[12]. It is a hopeful literature and declares that much may be done by simple ambitious people who own a few hens. Do not be led astray by it. It was not written for you. Go hunt for gold on the frozen hills of Alaska, put your faith in the honesty of a politician, believe if you will that the world is daily growing better and that good will triumph over evil, but do not read and believe the literature that is written concerning the hen. It was not written for you.

I, however, digress. My tale does not primarily concern itself with the hen. If correctly told it will center on the egg. For ten years my father and mother struggled to make our chicken farm pay and then they gave up that struggle and began another. They moved into the town of Bidwell, Ohio and embarked in the restaurant business. After ten years of worry with incubators[13] that did not hatch, and with tiny— and in their own way lovely— balls of fluff that passed on into semi-naked pullethood and from that into dead henhood, we threw all aside and packing our belongings on a wagon drove down Griggs's Road toward Bidwell, a tiny caravan of hope looking for a new place from which to start on our upward journey through life.

We must have been a sad looking lot[14], not, I fancy, unlike refugees fleeing from a battlefield. Mother and I walked in the road. The wagon that contained our goods had been borrowed for the day from Mr. Albert Griggs, a neighbor. Out of its sides stuck the legs of cheap chairs and at the back of the pile of beds, tables, and boxes filled with kitchen utensils was a crate of live chickens, and on top of that the baby carriage in which I had been wheeled about in my infancy. Why we stuck to the baby carriage I don't know. It was unlikely other children would be born and the wheels were broken. People who have few possessions cling tightly to those they have. That is one of the facts that make life so discouraging.

Father rode on top of the wagon. He was then a bald-headed man of forty-five, a little fat and from long association with mother and the chickens he had become habitually silent and discouraged. All during our ten years on the chicken farm he had worked as a laborer on neighboring farms and most of the money he had earned had been spent for remedies to cure chicken diseases, on Wilmer's White Wonder Cholera Cure or Professor Bidlow's Egg Producer or some other preparations that mother found advertised in the poultry papers. There were two little patches of hair on father's head just above his ears. I remember that as a child I used to sit looking at him when he had gone to sleep in a chair before the stove on Sunday afternoons in the winter. I had at that time already begun to read books and have notions of my own and the bald path that led over the top of his head was, I fancied, something like a broad road, such a road as Caesar might have made on which to lead his legions out of Rome and into the wonders of an unknown world. The tufts of hair that grew above father's ears were, I thought, like forests. I fell into a half-sleeping, half-waking state and dreamed I was a tiny thing going along the road into a far beautiful place where there were no chicken farms and where life was a happy eggless affair.

One might write a book concerning our flight from the chicken farm into town. Mother and I walked the entire eight miles— she to be sure that nothing fell from the wagon and I to see the wonders of the world. On the seat of the wagon beside father was his greatest treasure. I will tell you of that.

On a chicken farm where hundreds and even thousands of chickens come out of eggs, surprising things sometimes happen. Grotesques[15] are born out of eggs as out of people. The accident does not often occur— perhaps once in a thousand births. A chicken is, you see, born that has four legs, two pairs of wings, two heads or what not. The things do not live. They go quickly back to the hand of their maker that has for a moment trembled. The fact that the poor little things could not live was one of the tragedies of life to father. He had some sort of notion that if he could but bring into henhood or roosterhood a five-legged hen or a two-headed rooster his fortune would be made. He dreamed of taking the wonder about to county fairs and of growing rich by exhibiting it to other farm-hands.

At any rate he saved all the little monstrous things that had been born on our chicken farm. They were preserved in alcohol and put each in its own glass bottle. These he had carefully put into a box and on our journey into town it was carried on the wagon seat beside him. He drove the horses with one hand and with the other clung to the box. When we got to our destination the box was taken down at once and the bottles removed. All during our days as keepers of a restaurant in the town of Bidwell, Ohio, the grotesques in their little glass bottles sat on a shelf back of the counter. Mother sometimes protested but father was a rock on the subject of his treasure. The grotesques were, he declared, valuable. People, he said, liked to look at strange and wonderful things.

Did I say that we embarked in the restaurant business in the town of Bidwell, Ohio? I exaggerated a little. The town itself lay at the foot of a low hill and on the shore of a small river. The railroad did not run through the town and the station was a mile away to the north at a place called Pickleville. There had been a cider mill and pickle factory at the station, but before the time of our coming they had both gone out of business. In the morning and in the evening busses came down to the station along a road called Turner's Pike from the hotel on the main street of Bidwell. Our going to the out of the way place to embark in the restaurant business was mother's idea. She talked of it for a year and then one day went off and rented an empty store building opposite the railroad station. It was her idea that the restaurant would be profitable. Travelling men, she said, would be always waiting around to take trains out of town and town people would come to the station to await incoming trains. They would come to the restaurant to buy pieces of pie and drink coffee. Now that I am older I know that she had another motive in going. She was ambitious for me. She wanted me to rise in the world, to get into a town school and become a man of the towns.

At Pickleville father and mother worked hard as they always had done. At first there was the necessity of putting our place into shape to be a restaurant. That took a month. Father built a shelf on which he put tins of vegetables. He painted a sign on which he put his name in large red letters. Below his name was the sharp command— "EAT HERE"— that was so seldom obeyed. A show case was bought and filled with cigars and tobacco. Mother scrubbed the floor and the walls of the room. I went to school in the town and was glad to be away from the farm and from the presence of the discouraged, sad-looking chickens. Still I was not very joyous. In the evening I walked home from school along Turner's Pike and remembered the children I had seen playing in the town school yard. A troop of little girls had gone hopping about and singing. I tried that. Down along the frozen road I went hopping solemnly on one leg. "Hippity Hop to the Barber Shop," I sang shrilly. Then I stopped and looked doubtfully about. I was afraid of being seen in my gay mood. It must have seemed to me that I was doing a thing that should not be done by one who, like myself, had been raised on a chicken farm where death was a daily visitor.

Mother decided that our restaurant should remain open at night. At ten in the evening a passenger train went north past our door followed by a local freight[16]. The freight crew had switching to do in Pickleville and when the work was done they came to our restaurant for hot coffee and food. Sometimes one of them ordered a fried egg. In the morning at four they returned north-bound and again visited us. A little trade began to grow up. Mother slept at night and during the day tended the restaurant and fed our boarders while father slept. He slept in the same bed mother had occupied during the night and I went off to the town of Bidwell and to school. During the long nights, while mother and I slept, father cooked meats that were to go into sandwiches for the lunch baskets of our boarders. Then an idea in regard to getting up in the world came into his head. The American spirit took hold of him. He also became ambitious.

In the long nights when there was little to do father had time to think. That was his undoing. He decided that he had in the past been an unsuccessful man because he had not been cheerful enough and that in the future he would adopt a cheerful outlook on life. In the early morning he came upstairs and got into bed with mother. She woke and the two talked. From my bed in the corner I listened.

Chapter 4　The Literature of the Realistic Period

  It was father's idea that both he and mother should try to entertain the people who came to eat at our restaurant. I cannot now remember his words, but he gave the impression of one about to become in some obscure way a kind of public entertainer. When people, particularly young people from the town of Bidwell, came into our place, as on very rare occasions they did, bright entertaining conversation was to be made. From father's words I gathered that something of the jolly inn-keeper effect was to be sought. Mother must have been doubtful from the first, but she said nothing discouraging. It was father's notion that a passion for the company of himself and mother would spring up in the breasts of the younger people of the town of Bidwell. In the evening bright happy groups would come singing down Turner's Pike. They would troop shouting with joy and laughter into our place. There would be song and festivity. I do not mean to give the impression that father spoke so elaborately of the matter. He was as I have said an uncommunicative man. "They want some place to go. I tell you they want some place to go, " he said over and over. That was as far as he got. My own imagination has filled in the blanks.

  For two or three weeks this notion of father's invaded our house. We did not talk much, but in our daily lives tried earnestly to make smiles take the place of glum[17] looks. Mother smiled at the boarders and I, catching the infection, smiled at our cat. Father became a little feverish in his anxiety to please. There was no doubt, lurking somewhere in him, a touch of the spirit of the showman. He did not waste much of his ammunition on the railroad men he served at night but seemed to be waiting for a young man or woman from Bidwell to come in to show what he could do. On the counter in the restaurant there was a wire basket kept always filled with eggs, and it must have been before his eyes when the idea of being entertaining was born in his brain. There was something pre-natal[18] about the way eggs kept themselves connected with the development of his idea. At any rate an egg ruined his new impulse in life. Late one night I was awakened by a roar of anger coming from father's throat. Both mother and I sat upright in our beds. With trembling hands she lighted a lamp that stood on a table by her head. Downstairs the front door of our restaurant went shut with a bang and in a few minutes father tramped up the stairs. He held an egg in his hand and his hand trembled as though he were having a chill. There was a half insane light in his eyes. As he stood glaring at us I was sure he intended throwing the egg at either mother or me. Then he laid it gently on the table beside the lamp and dropped on his knees beside mother's bed. He began to cry like a boy and I, carried away by his grief, cried with him. The two of us filled the little upstairs room with our wailing voices. It is ridiculous, but of the picture we made I can remember only the fact that mother's hand continually stroked the bald path that ran across the top of his head. I have forgotten what mother said to him and how she induced him to tell her of what had happened downstairs. His explanation also has gone out of my mind. I remember only my own grief and fright and the shiny path over father's head glowing in the lamp light as he knelt by the bed.

As to what happened downstairs. For some unexplainable reason I know the story as well as though I had been a witness to my father's discomfiture[19]. One in time gets to know many unexplainable things. On that evening young Joe Kane, son of a merchant of Bidwell, came to Pickleville to meet his father, who was expected on the ten o'clock evening train from the South. The train was three hours late and Joe came into our place to loaf about and to wait for its arrival. The local freight train came in and the freight crew were fed. Joe was left alone in the restaurant with father.

From the moment he came into our place the Bidwell young man must have been puzzled by my father's actions. It was his notion that father was angry at him for hanging around. He noticed that the restaurant keeper was apparently disturbed by his presence and he thought of going out. However, it began to rain and he did not fancy the long walk to town and back. He bought a five-cent cigar and ordered a cup of coffee. He had a newspaper in his pocket and took it out and began to read. "I'm waiting for the evening train. It's late, " he said apologetically.

For a long time father, whom Joe Kane had never seen before, remained silently gazing at his visitor. He was no doubt suffering from an attack of stage fright[20]. As so often happens in life he had thought so much and so often of the situation that now confronted him that he was somewhat nervous in its presence.

For one thing, he did not know what to do with his hands. He thrust one of them nervously over the counter and shook hands with Joe Kane. "How-de-do, " he said. Joe Kane put his newspaper down and stared at him. Father's eye lighted on the basket of eggs that sat on the counter and he began to talk. "Well, " he began hesitatingly, "well, you have heard of Christopher Columbus, eh?" He seemed to be angry. "That Christopher Columbus was a cheat, " he declared emphatically. "He talked of making an egg stand on its end. He talked, he did, and then he went and broke the end of the egg. "

My father seemed to his visitor to be beside himself at the duplicity of Christopher Columbus. He muttered[21] and swore. He declared it was wrong to teach children that Christopher Columbus was a great man when, after all, he cheated at the critical moment. He had declared he would make an egg stand on end and then when his bluff had been called he had done a trick. Still grumbling at Columbus, father took an egg from the basket on the counter and began to walk up and down. He rolled the egg between the palms of his hands. He smiled genially. He began to mumble words regarding the effect to be produced on an egg by the electricity that comes out of the human body. He declared that without breaking its shell and by virtue of[22] rolling it back and forth in his hands he could stand the egg on its end. He explained that the warmth of his hands and the gentle rolling movement he gave the egg created a new center of gravity, and Joe Kane was mildly interested. "I have handled thousands of eggs, " father said. "No one knows more about eggs than I do."

He stood the egg on the counter and it fell on its side. He tried the trick again and again, each time rolling the egg between the palms of his hands and saying the words regarding the wonders of electricity and the laws of gravity. When after a half hour's effort he did succeed in making the egg stand for a moment he looked up to find that his visitor was no longer watching. By the time he had succeeded in calling Joe Kane's attention to the success of his effort the egg had again rolled over and lay on its side.

Afire with the showman's passion and at the same time a good deal disconcerted by the failure of his first effort, father now took the bottles containing the poultry monstrosities down from their place on the shelf and began to show them to his visitor. "How would you like to have seven legs and two heads like this fellow?" he asked, exhibiting the most remarkable of his treasures. A cheerful smile played over his face. He reached over the counter and tried to slap Joe Kane on the shoulder as he had seen men do in Ben Head's saloon when he was a young farm-hand and drove to town on Saturday evenings. His visitor was made a little ill by the sight of the body of the terribly deformed bird floating in the alcohol in the bottle and got up to go. Coming from behind the counter father took hold of the young man's arm and led him back to his seat. He grew a little angry and for a moment had to turn his face away and force himself to smile. Then he put the bottles back on the shelf. In an outburst of generosity he fairly compelled Joe Kane to have a fresh cup of coffee and another cigar at his expense. Then he took a pan and filling it with vinegar, taken from a jug that sat beneath the counter, he declared himself about to do a new trick. "I will heat this egg in this pan of vinegar," he said. "Then I will put it through the neck of a bottle without breaking the shell. When the egg is inside the bottle it will resume its normal shape and the shell will become hard again. Then I will give the bottle with the egg in it to you. You can take it about with you wherever you go. People will want to know how you got the egg in the bottle. Don't tell them. Keep them guessing. That is the way to have fun with this trick."

Father grinned and winked at his visitor. Joe Kane decided that the man who confronted him was mildly insane but harmless. He drank the cup of coffee that had been given him and began to read his paper again. When the egg had been heated in vinegar father carried it on a spoon to the counter and going into a back room got an empty bottle. He was angry because his visitor did not watch him as he began to do his trick, but nevertheless went cheerfully to work. For a long time he struggled, trying to get the egg to go through the neck of the bottle. He put the pan of vinegar back on the stove, intending to reheat the egg, then picked it up and burned his fingers. After a second bath in the hot vinegar the shell of the egg had been softened a little but not enough for his purpose. He worked and worked and a spirit of desperate determination took possession of him. When he thought that at last the trick was about to be consummated the delayed train came in at the station and Joe Kane started to go nonchalantly[23] out at the door.

Father made a last desperate effort to conquer the egg and make it do the thing that would establish his reputation as one who knew how to entertain guests who came into his restaurant. He worried the egg. He attempted to be somewhat rough with it. He swore and the sweat stood out on his forehead. The egg broke under his hand. When the contents spurted over his clothes, Joe Kane, who had stopped at the door, turned and laughed.

A roar of anger rose from my father's throat. He danced and shouted a string of inarticulate words. Grabbing another egg from the basket on the counter, he threw it, just missing the head of the young man as he dodged through the door and escaped.

Father came upstairs to mother and me with an egg in his hand. I do not know what he intended to do. I imagine he had some idea of destroying it, of destroying all eggs, and that he intended to let mother and me see him begin. When, however, he got into the presence of mother something happened to him. He laid the egg gently on the table and dropped on his knees by the bed as I have already explained. He later decided to close the restaurant for the night and to come upstairs and get into bed. When he did so he blew out the light and after much muttered conversation both he and mother went to sleep. I suppose I went to sleep also, but my sleep was troubled. I awoke at dawn and for a long time looked at the egg that lay on the table. I wondered why eggs had to be and why from the egg came the hen who again laid the egg. The question got into my blood. It has stayed there, I imagine, because I am the son of my father. At any rate, the problem remains unsolved in my mind. And that, I conclude, is but another evidence of the complete and final triumph of the egg— at least as far as my family is concerned.

Notes

1. **thump**: to hit against something loudly.
2. **wriggle**: (cause something to) make quick, short, twisting and turning movements.
3. **how Garfield, Lincoln... greatness**: James A. Garfield (1831-1881) and Abraham Lincoln were both born in log cabins — Garfield in Ohio, Lincoln in Kentucky — and both rose from their humble origins to American president.
4. **embark on**: to start something, especially something new, difficult, or exciting.
5. **fluffy**: light and full of air.
6. **Easter**: the yearly celebration, usually on the first Sunday following the full moon that occurs on or next after March 21, when the Christians remember the death of Christ and his rising from the grave. According to the custom, hen's eggs, painted in bright colors, are to be eaten on this day.
7. **cholera**: infectious and often fatal disease causing severe diarrhoea and vomiting, common in hot countries.
8. **their maker**: referring to God, who is the maker of everything in the universe.
9. **vermin**: certain wild animals and birds (eg rats, foxes, moles, owls) which are

harmful to crops and farmyard animals and birds.
10. **infest**: (of pests, vermin, insects, etc.) live in (a place) persistently and in large numbers.
11. **literature**: the writings dealing with a particular subject; here it refers to a kind of pamphlet telling people how to make a fortune by raising chickens.
12. **It is intended... of good and evil**: the writing is not for ignorant and simple-minded people.
13. **incubator**: a heated container for keeping eggs warm until they hatch.
14. **lot**: a number of persons collectively.
15. **grotesque**: with fantastic or incongruous clothes, make-up, features, etc.
16. **freight**: a railway train carrying goods only.
17. **glum**: moody and melancholy; dejected.
18. **pre-natal**: of or occurring in the period before (giving) birth.
19. **discomfiture**: frustration or disappointment.
20. **stage fright**: nervousness caused by performing in public.
21. **mutter**: complain or grumble privately or in a way that is not openly expressed.
22. **by virtue of**: by way of.
23. **nonchalantly**: behaving in a calm manner, often in a way which suggests lack of interest or care.

Study Questions
1. Do you find any change in father's outlook and disposition? Give evidence to support your answer.
2. Although little attention is directed to the character of mother, how is she a presence in the story?
3. What is meaningful in the author's final reflection on the egg? In what sense can the egg be said to be "triumph" over the family?

Essay Topics
1. At the end of "The Egg", Anderson's narrator writes, "I wondered why eggs had to be and why from the egg came the hen who again laid the egg." Analyze the multiple symbolism of the egg, what it comes to represent by the end of the story, and how Anderson uses it to unify his narrative.
2. What is the theme of the story?

4.9 Katherine Anne Porter

4.9.1 About the author

Katherine Anne Porter (1890-1980) was born in Indian Creek, Texas to a land-poor family. Her mother died when she was two. Raised primarily by her paternal

grandmother, Porter became strong and self-reliant at an early age. The only stable influence in her childhood was her dominant and puritanical paternal grandmother. After her grandmother died, Porter was sent to convent school in New Orleans. Later she managed to get a year of formal high school education at a private girls' school in San Antonio. At the age of sixteen, in an attempt to escape her family and gain financial security, Porter married John Henry Koontz, a railroad clerk, and converted to Catholicism to pacify his family. Their marriage ended nine years later in 1915 when she decided to become an actress.

Porter's writing career began in 1917, when she became a journalist for the *Fort Worth Critic*. In 1918, she took a job with the *Rocky Mountain News* and moved to Denver, where she nearly died in the great influenza epidemic of that year. Finding success as a journalist, Porter moved to New York in 1919. She traveled between there and Mexico City during the 1920s. In 1930, she published her first collection of short stories, *Flowering Judas and Other Stories*, which drew on her firsthand experiences of the revolution in Mexico. This work established her reputation as a highly original writer and earned her a Guggenheim grant, which allowed her to travel to Europe. After staying some time in Germany, Porter settled in Paris for four years. Her second book was *Pale Horse, Pale Rider* (1939), containing three short novels. In the 1940s, she wrote film scripts and began accepting lecture tours as well as teaching appointments in various universities. *The Leaning Tower and Other Stories* was published in 1944. Her only novel is *Ship of Fools*, which was published in 1962. *The Collected Stories of Katherine Anne Porter* (1965) was awarded the National Book Award and the Pulitzer Prize for fiction in 1966. Her non-fiction, entitled *The Collected Essays and Occasional Writings of Katherine Anne Porter*, was published in 1970. In her life, Porter married four more times but remained childless. Her life progression can easily be divided into her time in Mexico, her return to the United States as a middle-aged woman, and her continued successes well into her seniority.

In writing fiction, Porter often drew on her own life, creating rich blends of reality and imagination. Concerned with themes of justice, betrayal, isolation, guilt, and human nature, she wrote from a particularly feminine perspective. Porter strongly believed that the past affects a person's present situation so she incorporated this theme of a haunting past into many of her short story writings. She valued the strong, dominant, feminine personality and despised the ineffectual, indecisive, and malingering male. In the minds of many of her female protagonists there is the wish for a nurturing love and an equal desire for personal independence and autonomy achieved through their own talents and perceptions. Her stories were full of historical texture and local color, each comprising a different setting. Porter was a master of the short story. Her characters were depicted with clarity and detail and her figurative, symbolic language and long sentences lent the tales a poetic air. Her flawless pen and harsh criticism of her times and society made Porter a major voice in the twentieth-century American literature.

4.9.2 "The Jilting of Granny Weatherall"

She flicked her wrist neatly out of Doctor Harry's pudgy careful fingers and pulled the sheet up to her chin. The brat ought to be in knee breeches. Doctoring around the country with spectacles on his nose! "Get along now. Take your schoolbooks and go. There's nothing wrong with me."

Doctor Harry spread a warm paw like a cushion on her forehead where the forked green vein danced and made her eyelids twitch. "Now, now, be a good girl, and we'll have you up in no time."

"That's no way to speak to a woman nearly eighty years old just because she's down. I'd have you respect your elders, young man."

"Well, Missy, excuse me." Doctor Harry patted her cheek. "But I've got to warn you, haven't I? You're a marvel, but you must be careful or you're going to be good and sorry."

"Don't tell me what I'm going to be. I'm on my feet now, morally speaking. It's Cornelia. I had to go to bed to get rid of her."

Her bones felt loose, and floated around in her skin, and Doctor Harry floated like a balloon around the foot of the bed. He floated and pulled down his waistcoat, and swung his glasses on a cord. "Well, stay where you are, it certainly can't hurt you."

"Get along and doctor your sick," said Granny Weatherall. "Leave a well woman alone. I'll call for you when I want you... Where were you forty years ago when I pulled through milk-leg[1] and double pneumonia? You weren't even born. Don't let Cornelia lead you on," she shouted, because Doctor Harry appeared to float up to the ceiling and out. "I pay my own bills, and I don't throw my money away on nonsense!"

She meant to wave good-by, but it was too much trouble. Her eyes closed of themselves, it was like a dark curtain drawn around the bed. The pillow rose and floated under her, pleasant as a hammock in a light wind. She listened to the leaves rustling outside the window. No, somebody was swishing newspapers: no, Cornelia and Doctor Harry were whispering together. She leaped broad awake, thinking they whispered in her ear.

"She was never like this, *never* like this!" "Well, what can we expect?" "Yes, eighty years old..."

Well, and what if she was? She still had ears. It was like Cornelia to whisper around doors. She always kept things secret in such a public way. She was always being tactful and kind. Cornelia was dutiful; that was the trouble with her. Dutiful and good: "So good and dutiful," said Granny, "that I'd like to spank her." She saw herself spanking Cornelia and making a fine job of it.

"What'd you say, mother?"

Granny felt her face tying up in hard knots.

"Can't a body think, I'd like to know?"

"I thought you might like something."

"I do. I want a lot of things. First off, go away and don't whisper."

She lay and drowsed, hoping in her sleep that the children would keep out and let her rest a minute. It had been a long day. Not that she was tired. It was always pleasant to snatch a minute now and then. There was always so much to be done, let me see: tomorrow.

Tomorrow was far away and there was nothing to trouble about. Things were finished somehow when the time came; thank God there was always a little margin over for peace: then a person could spread out the plan of life and tuck in the edges orderly. It was good to have everything clean and folded away, with the hair brushes and tonic bottles sitting straight on the white, embroidered linen: the day started without fuss and the pantry shelves laid out with rows of jelly glasses and brown jugs and white stone-china jars with blue whirligigs[2] and words painted on them: coffee, tea, sugar, ginger, cinnamon, allspice: and the bronze clock with the lion on top nicely dusted off. The dust that lion could collect in twenty-four hours! The box in the attic with all those letters tied up, well, she'd have to go through that tomorrow. All those letters — George's letters and John's letters and her letters to them both — lying around for the children to find afterwards made her uneasy. Yes, that would be tomorrow's business. No use to let them know how silly she had been once.

While she was rummaging around she found death in her mind and it felt clammy and unfamiliar. She had spent so much time preparing for death there was no need for bringing it up again. Let it take care of itself for now. When she was sixty she had felt very old, finished, and went around making farewell trips to see her children and grandchildren, with a secret in her mind: This was the very last of your mother, children! Then she made her will and came down with a long fever. That was all just a notion like a lot of other things, but it was lucky too, for she had once and for all got over the idea of dying for a long time. Now she couldn't be worried. She hoped she had better sense now. Her father had lived to be one hundred and two years old and had drunk a noggin of strong hot toddy on his last birthday. He told the reporters it was his daily habit, and he owed his long life to that. He had made quite a scandal and was very pleased about it. She believed she'd just plague Cornelia a little.

Chapter 4   The Literature of the Realistic Period

"Cornelia! Cornelia!" No footsteps, but a sudden hand on her cheek. "Bless you, where have you been?"

"Here, Mother."

"Well, Cornelia, I want a noggin of hot toddy."

"Are you cold, darling?"

"I'm chilly, Cornelia. Lying in bed stops the circulation. I must have told you a thousand times."

Well, she could just hear Cornelia telling her husband that Mother was getting a little childish and they'd have to humor her. The thing that most annoyed her was that Cornelia thought she was deaf, dumb, and blind. Little hasty glances and tiny gestures tossed around here and over her head saying, "Don't cross her, let her have her way, she's eighty years old," and she sitting there as if she lived in a thin glass cage. Sometimes granny almost made up her mind to pack up and move back to her own house where nobody could remind her every minute that she was old. Wait, wait, Cornelia, till your own children whisper behind your back!

In her day she had kept a better house and had got more work done. She wasn't too old yet for Lydia to be driving eighty miles for advice when one of the children jumped the track, and Jimmy still dropped in and talked things over: "Now, Mammy, you've a good business head, I want to know what you think of this? ···" Old Cornelia couldn't change the furniture around without asking. Little things, little things! They had been so sweet when they were little. Granny wished the old days were back again with the children young and everything to be done over. It had been a hard pull, but not too much for her. When she thought of all the food she had cooked, and all the clothes she had cut and sewed, and all the gardens she had made — well, the children showed it. There they were, made out of her, and they couldn't get away from that. Sometimes she wanted to see John again and point to them and say, Well, I didn't do so badly, did I? But that would have to wait. That was for tomorrow. She used to think of him as a man, but now all the children were older than their father, and he would be a child beside her if she saw him now. It seemed strange and there was something wrong in the idea. Why, he couldn't possibly recognize her. She had fenced in a hundred acres once, digging the post holes herself and clamping the wires with just a negro boy to help. That changed a woman. John would be looking for a young woman with a peaked Spanish comb in her hair and the painted fan. Digging post holes changed a woman. Riding country roads in the winter when women had their babies was another thing: sitting up nights with sick horses and sick negroes and sick children and hardly ever losing one. John, I hardly ever lost one of them! John would see that in a minute, that would be something he could understand, she wouldn't have to explain anything!

It made her feel like rolling up her sleeves and putting the whole place to rights again. No matter if Cornelia was determined to be everywhere at once, there were a great many things left undone on this place. She would start tomorrow and do them. It was good to be strong enough for everything, even if all you made melted and changed and slipped under your hands, so that by the time you finished you almost forgot what you were working for. What was it I set out to do? She asked herself intently, but she could not remember. A fog rose over the valley, she saw it marching across the creek swallowing the trees and moving up the hill like an army of ghosts. Soon it would be at the near edge of the orchard, and then it was time to go in and light the lamps. Come in, children, don't stay out in the night air.

Lighting the lamps had been beautiful. The children huddled up to her and breathed like little calves waiting at the bars in the twilight. Their eyes followed the match and watched the flame rise and settle in a blue curve, then they moved away from her. The lamp was lit, they didn't have to be scared and hang on to mother any more. Never, never, never more. God, for all my life, I thank Thee. Without Thee, my God, I could never have done it. Hail, Mary, full of grace[3].

I want you to pick all the fruit this year and see nothing is wasted. There's always someone who can use it. Don't let good things rot for want of using. You waste life when you waste good food. Don't let things get lost. It's bitter to lose things. Now, don't let me get to thinking, not when I'm tired and taking a little nap before supper...

The pillow rose about her shoulders and pressed against her heart and the memory was being squeezed out of it: oh, push down the pillow, somebody: it would smother her if she tried to hold it. Such a fresh breeze blowing and such a green day with no threats in it. But he had not come, just the same. What does a woman do when she has put on the white veil and set out the white cake for a man and he doesn't come? She tried to remember. No, I swear he never harmed me but in that. He never harmed me but in that... and what if he did? There was the day, the day, but a whirl of dark smoke rose and covered it, crept up and over into the bright field where everything was planted so carefully in orderly rows. That was hell, she knew hell when she saw it. For sixty years she had prayed against remembering him and against losing her soul in the deep pit of hell, and now the two things were mingled in one and the thought of him was a smoky cloud from hell that moved and crept in her head when she had just got rid of Doctor Harry and was trying to rest a minute. Wounded vanity, Ellen, said a sharp voice in the top of her mind. Don't let your wounded vanity get the upper hand of you. Plenty of girls get jilted. You were jilted, weren't you? Then stand up to it. Her eyelids wavered and let in streamers of blue-gray light like tissue paper over her eyes. She must get up and pull the shades down or she'd never sleep. She was in bed again and the shades were not down. How could that happen? Better turn over, hide from the light, sleeping in the light gave you nightmares. "Mother, how do you feel now?" and a stinging wetness on her forehead. But I don't like having my face washed in cold water!

Hapsy? George? Lydia? Jimmy? No, Cornelia and her features were swollen and full

Chapter 4 The Literature of the Realistic Period

of little puddles. "They're coming, darling, they'll all be here soon." Go wash your face, child, you look funny.

Instead of obeying, Cornelia knelt down and put her head on the pillow. She seemed to be talking but there was no sound. "Well, are you tongue-tied? Whose birthday is it? Are you going to give a party?"

Cornelia's mouth moved urgently in strange shapes. "Don't do that, you bother me, daughter."

"Oh no, Mother. Oh, no..."

Nonsense. It was strange about children. They disputed your every word. "No what, Cornelia?"

"Here's Doctor Harry."

"I won't see that boy again. He left just five minutes ago."

"That was this morning, Mother. It's night now. Here's the nurse."

"This is Doctor Harry, Mrs. Weatherall. I never saw you look so young and happy!"

"Ah, I'll never be young again — but I'd be happy if they'd let me lie in peace and get rested."

She thought she spoke up loudly, but no one answered. A warm weight on her forehead, a warm bracelet on her wrist, and a breeze went on whispering, trying to tell her something. A shuffle of leaves in the everlasting hand of God, He blew on them and they danced and rattled. "Mother, don't mind, we're going to give you a little hypodermic." "Look here, daughter, how do ants get in this bed? I saw sugar ants yesterday." Did you send for Hapsy too?

It was Hapsy she really wanted. She had to go a long way back through a great many rooms to find Hapsy standing with a baby on her arm. She seemed to herself to be Hapsy also, and the baby on Hapsy's arm was Hapsy and himself and herself, all at once, and there was no surprise in the meeting. Then Hapsy melted from within and turned flimsy as gray gauze and the baby was a gauzy shadow, and Hapsy came up close and said,"I thought you'd never come," and looked at her very searchingly and said,"You haven't changed a bit!" They leaned forward to kiss, when Cornelia began whispering from a long way off,"Oh, is there anything you want to tell me? Is there anything I can do for you?"

Yes, she had changed her mind after sixty years and she would like to see George. I want you to find George. Find him and be sure to tell him I forgot him. I want him to know I had my husband just the same and my children and my house like any other woman. A good house too and a good husband that I loved and fine children out of him. Better than I had hoped for even. Tell him I was given back everything he took away and more. Oh, no, oh, God, no, there was something else besides the house and the man and the children. Oh, surely they were not all? What was it? Something not given back... Her breath crowded down under her ribs and grew into a monstrous frightening shape with cutting edges; it bored up into her head, and the agony was unbelievable: Yes, John, get the Doctor now, no more talk, the time has come.

When this one was born it should be the last. The last. It should have been born first, for it was the one she had truly wanted. Everything came in good time. Nothing left out, left over. She was strong, in three days she would be as well as ever. Better. A woman needed milk in her to have her full health.

"Mother, do you hear me?"

"I've been telling you —"

"Mother, Father Connolly's here."

"I went to Holy Communion only last week. Tell him I'm not so sinful as all that."

"Father just wants to speak with you."

He could speak as much as he pleased. It was like him to drop in and inquire about her soul as if it were a teething baby, and then stay on for a cup of tea and a round of cards and gossip. He always had a funny story of some sort, usually about an Irishman who made his little mistakes and confessed them, and the point lay in some absurd thing he would blurt out in the confessional showing his struggles between native piety and original sin. Granny felt easy about her soul. Cornelia, where are your manners? Give Father Connolly a chair. She had her secret comfortable understanding with a few favorite saints who cleared a straight road to God for her. All as surely signed and sealed as the papers for the new forty acres. Forever... heirs and assigns[4] forever. Since the day the wedding cake was not cut, but thrown out and wasted. The whole bottom of the world dropped out, and there she was blind and sweating with nothing under her feet and the walls falling away. His hand had caught her under the breast, she had not fallen, there was the freshly polished floor with the green rug on it, just as before. He had cursed like a sailor's parrot and said, "I'll kill him for you." Don't lay a hand on him, for my sake leave something to God. "Now, Ellen, you must believe what I tell you..."

So there was nothing, nothing to worry about anymore, except sometimes in the night one of the children screamed in a nightmare, and they both hustled out and hunting for the matches and calling, "There, wait a minute, here we are!" John, get the doctor now, Hapsy's time has come. But there was Hapsy standing by the bed in a white cap. "Cornelia, tell Hapsy to take off her cap. I can't see her plain."

Her eyes opened very wide and the room stood out like a picture she had seen somewhere. Dark colors with the shadows rising towards the ceiling in long angles. The tall black dresser gleamed with nothing on it but John's picture, enlarged from a little one, with John's eyes very black when they should have been blue. You never saw him, so how do you know how he looked? But the man insisted the copy was perfect, it was very rich and handsome. For a picture, yes, but it's not my husband. The table by the bed had a linen cover and a candle and a crucifix. The light was blue from Cornelia's silk lampshades. No sort of light at all, just frippery[5]. You had to live forty years with

Chapter 4 The Literature of the Realistic Period

kerosene lamps to appreciate honest electricity. She felt very strong and she saw Doctor Harry with a rosy nimbus[6] around him.

"You look like a saint, Doctor Harry, and I vow that's as near as you'll ever come to it."

"She's saying something."

"I heard you Cornelia. What's all this carrying on?"

"Father Connolly's saying —"

Cornelia's voice staggered and jumped like a cart in a bad road. It rounded corners and turned back again and arrived nowhere. Granny stepped up in the cart very lightly and reached for the reins, but a man sat beside her and she knew him by his hands, driving the cart. She did not look in his face, for she knew without seeing, but looked instead down the road where the trees leaned over and bowed to each other and a thousand birds were singing a Mass. She felt like singing too, but she put her hand in the bosom of her dress and pulled out a rosary, and Father Connolly murmured Latin in a very solemn voice and tickled her feet[7]. My God, will you stop that nonsense? I'm a married woman. What if he did run away and leave me to face the priest by myself? I found another a whole world better. I wouldn't have exchanged my husband for anybody except Saint Michael[8] himself, and you may tell him that for me with a thank you in the bargain.

Light flashed on her closed eyelids, and a deep roaring shook her. Cornelia, is that lightning? I hear thunder. There's going to be a storm. Close all the windows. Call the children in... "Mother, here we are, all of us." "Is that you Hapsy?" "Oh, no, I'm Lydia. We drove as fast as we could." Their faces drifted above her, drifted away. The rosary fell out of her hands and Lydia put it back. Jimmy tried to help, their hands fumbled together, and granny closed two fingers around Jimmy's thumb. Beads wouldn't do, it must be something alive. She was so amazed her thoughts ran round and round. So, my dear Lord, this is my death and I wasn't even thinking about it. My children have come to see me die. But I can't, it's not time. Oh, I always hated surprises. I wanted to give Cornelia the amethyst[9] set — Cornelia, you're to have the amethyst set, but Hapsy's to wear it when she wants, and, Doctor Harry, do shut up. Nobody sent for you. Oh, my dear Lord, do wait a minute. I meant to do something about the Forty Acres, Jimmy doesn't need it and Lydia will later on, with that worthless husband of hers. I meant to finish the alter cloth and send six bottles of wine to Sister Borgia for her dyspepsia[10]. I want to send six bottles of wine to Sister Borgia, Father Connolly, now don't let me forget.

Cornelia's voice made short turns and tilted over and crashed. "Oh, mother, oh, mother, oh, mother..."

"I'm not going, Cornelia. I'm taken by surprise. I can't go."

You'll see Hapsy again. What bothered her? "I thought you'd never come." Granny made a long journey outward, looking for Hapsy. What if I don't find her? What then? Her heart sank down and down, there was no bottom to death, she couldn't come to the end of it. The blue light from Cornelia's lampshade drew into a tiny point in the center of her brain, it flickered and winked like an eye, quietly it fluttered and dwindled. Granny laid curled down within herself, amazed and watchful, staring at the point of light that was herself; her body was now only a deeper mass of shadow in an endless darkness and this darkness would curl around the light and swallow it up. God, give a sign!

For a second time there was no sign. Again no bridegroom and the priest in the house. She could not remember any other sorrow because this grief wiped them all away. Oh, no, there's nothing more cruel than this — I'll never forgive it. She stretched herself with a deep breath and blew out the light.

Notes
1. **milk-leg**: painful swelling of the leg, usually as a result of infection during childbirth.
2. **whirligigs**: circular pattern; swirls.
3. **Hail, Mary, full of grace**: beginning of a Roman Catholic prayer to the Virgin Mary.
4. **assigns**: people to whom property is legally transferred.
5. **frippery**: showy, useless display of elegance.
6. **nimbus**: halo; a cloudy radiance.
7. **murmured ... feet**: administered last rites, including prayers and applying holy oil to the feet.
8. **Saint Michael**: an archangel.
9. **amethyst**: purple or violet quartz, used in jewelry.
10. **dyspepsia**: indigestion.

Study Questions
1. What are the qualities Granny possesses which help her live successfully?
2. Does Granny have any weaknesses? If so, what are they?
3. What are the major causes of Granny's acute pain in her heart?
4. How does Porter's use of stream-of-consciousness and flashbacks reflect the themes of Modernism?

Chapter 5 The Literature of the Modernist Period

5.1 An Introduction

The modern period of American literature covered the years between the beginning of World War Ⅰ (1914) and the end of World War Ⅱ (1945). Many historians have characterized the period as the United States' "coming of age". Compared with the second half of the 19th century, American industrialization and urbanization had become even larger factors in American society as the nation moved further from its agricultural roots into a new existence as a large factory nation. At the beginning of the First World War, the American government adopted a neutral policy, which brought America great economic advantages because it would allow America to trade with all the states involved in war. Although America participated in the war later on, its direct involvement was relatively brief (1917 — 1918) and its casualties many fewer than those of its European allies and foes. Since the wars were not fought on the American soil, by the second decade of the twentieth century, the United States had become the most powerful industrialized nation in the world, outstripping Britain and Germany in terms of industrial production. The institution of "big" science and "rational" ways of thinking about space, time, matter, and the universe also began to take place during this era. What is more, the technological revolution had brought about great changes in the life of the American people. The telephone ceased to be a curiosity but became a commonplace. The radio, along with other agencies of mass communication, began imposing its own imagery on the nation at large. By far the most powerful technological innovation in America between the wars was the automobile, which resulted in a mobility unimaginable to the previous generations. Americans began to enjoy the world's highest national average income in this era.

Despite its economic booming, there was a sense of unease and restlessness in American society. Strikes took place in several big cities because of industrial depression and uneven distribution of wealth; the rate of unemployment went up due to the oversupply of goods; farmers were driven off their land owing to the poor harvest of the crops. Following the crash of the stock market in 1929, a depression set in, causing unrest and economic upheaval on a global scale. Besides, political corruptions, organized crimes, the growth of radical labor force, and the terrorist drive of the Ku Klux Klan made an already disorderly American society even more turbulent.

The changes in the non-material system of belief and behavior had also been great. The First World War became the emblem of all wars in the twentieth century, which means violence, devastation, blood and death, and made a big impact on the life of the American people. After the war, the people became less certain about what might arise in this changing world and more cynical about accepted standards of honesty and morality. They seemed to be obsessed with a feeling of skepticism and disillusionment about religion and other established institutions. It was just this uncertainty, this powerlessness and hopelessness of the individual that became the true style of this time. Neither the church nor the government could give sufficient answers to the horrible questions that had been raised. And Eliot's "spiritual wasteland" might be the best phrase to describe the real situations of the first few decades of the twentieth century.

Radical social changes would tend to give rise to different kinds of philosophical ideas. Between the mid-19th century and the first decade of the 20th century, there had been a big flush of new theories in both social and natural sciences, as well as in the field of art, which played an important role in bringing about modernism and modernistic writings. Apart from Darwinism, which was still a big influence over the writers of this period, the two thinkers whose ideas had the greatest impact on the period were Karl Marx and Sigmund Freud. Marx believed that the root cause of all human behavior was economic, and that the leading feature of the economic life was the division of society into antagonistic classes based on a relation to the means of production. Freud propounded an idea of human beings themselves as grounded in the "unconscious" that controlled a great deal of overt behavior, and claimed that the practice of the psychoanalysis of human behavior was something vitally important. It was also worthwhile to mention William James, an American psychologist famous for his theory of "stream of consciousness," and Carl Jung, a Swiss psychiatrist, noted for his "collective unconscious" and "archetypal symbol" as part of modern mythology. Their theories have infused modern American literature and made it possible for most of the writers in the modern period to probe into the inner world of human reality.

Modernism is the result of the general transformation of society caused by industrialism and technology during the 19th century. It was in the big urban centers of Europe that the industrial innovations, the social tensions and the economic problems of modernity were most intensely manifested. Modernism as a literary movement reached its height in Europe between 1910 and 1930. The general thematic concerns of Modernist literature are the deepest problems of modern life that derived from the claim of the individual to preserve the autonomy and individuality of his existence in the face of overwhelming social forces, of historical heritage, of external culture, and of the technique of life. American modernism, which was inspired by the European avant-garde art, was a trend of thought that affirmed the power of human beings to create, improve, and reshape their environment, with the aid of scientific knowledge, technology and practical experimentation, and was thus in its essence both progressive and optimistic. Modernist literature in America dealt with such topics as racial relationships, gender roles and sexuality, to name just a few. It reached its peak in America from the 1920s up to the 1940s.

Chapter 5 The Literature of the Modernist Period

When the First World War broke out, many young American men volunteered to take part in "the war to end wars" only to find that modern warfare was not as glorious or heroic as they thought to be. Disillusioned and disgusted by the frivolous, greedy, and heedless way of life in America, they began to write from their own experiences in the war. Among these young writers were the most prominent figures in American literature, such as Ezra Pound, Ernest Hemingway, F. Scott Fitzgerald, T. S. Eliot, and Sherwood Anderson. They were basically expatriates who left America and formed a community of writers and artists in Paris. These writers were later named by an American writer, Gertrude Stein, also an expatriate, "The Lost Generation".

Modernist poetry is a mode of writing characterized by two main features: the first is technical innovation through the extensive use of free verse, and the second, a move away from the Romantic idea of an unproblematic poetic "self" directly addressing an equally unproblematic ideal reader or audience. Ezra Pound's role as a leading spokesman of the famous Imagist Movement in the history of American literature can never be ignored and his one-image poem best demonstrates his principles of what a new poetry should be. Pound listed three main principles as guidelines for Imagism, including direct treatment of poetic subjects, elimination of merely ornamental or superfluous words, and rhythmical composition should be done with the phrasing of music, not a metronome. While sharing the same pursuit of imagism, William Carlos Williams rooted his poetic imagination in American native tradition. His poems such as "This Is Just to Say" and "The Red Wheel Barrow," with their simple styles and seemingly absent subject matter, set the stage for a quiet poet's revolt against unquestioning convention, be it literary, social, or logical. Focusing more on stylistic exploration, E. E. Cummings' poems challenged readers by intentionally subverting the very rules of grammar that the English language was built upon, presenting a new style of poetry that dealt less with conscious topics and more with associations and dreamlike images. Wallace Stevens is also remembered for his contributions to the twentieth century American poetry. With more cultivated and refined style, he focused his attention on man and things in his world. The folk-oriented poetry of Sterling Brown and Langston Hughes, for example, written in a rhythm fit to be either sung or told as a story, melancholically describes the joyful attitude of Afro-Americans towards life, in spite of all the hardships they were confronted with.

Prose underwent a similar revitalization, as novelists and short story writers felt the same need to create new modes of communication that had pushed poets to such artistic heights. F. Scott Fitzgerald, Ernest Hemingway, and William Faulkner are considered to be the masters in the field of American fiction, each of them producing some distinguished literary works in their lifetime. The Jazz Age of the 1920s characterized by the frivolity and carelessness is brought vividly to life in *The Great Gatsby* (1925), a brilliantly written, economically structured story about the American dream of the self-made man. The anti-heroic war tales of Ernest Hemingway were both controversial yet wildly acclaimed by the reading public. His novels and short stories often dealt frankly with the gross realities of war, while he subtly manipulated his simple, journalistic prose style to express his own bleak view of the world around him, a world outside of simple cause and effect relationships, lacking both logic and philosophy. William Faulkner creates his own mythical kingdom that mirrors not only the decline of the Southern society but also the spiritual wasteland of the whole American society. His works reflected the Modernist movement, showcasing disjointed images, multiple points of view, complex sentences, and stream-of-consciousness narration as newly accepted literary tools to describe the world. Besides, writers like Sherwood Anderson, Sinclair Lewis, and John Steinbeck contributed a great deal to modern American literature in their different treatments of the subjects that concerned the modern man. Anderson explores the motivations and frustrations of his fictional characters in terms of Freud's theory of psychology, particularly in *Winesburg, Ohio* (1919), in which individuals in the small community are depicted as socially alienated and emotionally suppressed, unable to love or to be loved. In contrast, Lewis is a sociological writer and his *Babbit* (1922) presents a documentary picture of the narrow and limited middle-class mind, especially that of the middle-class businessmen. John Steinbeck is a representative of the 1930s, when "novels of social protest" became dominant on the American literary scene. His *The Grapes of Wrath* (1939) proves to be a symbolic journey of man on the way to finding some truth about life and himself, and a record of the dispossessed and the wretched farmers during the Great Depression as well.

The vigorous upsurge of American native drama is a highly important development of the 20th century American literature. The leading playwright is Eugene O'Neill, who is remembered for his tragic view of life. Most of his plays are about the root, the truth of human desires and human frustrations. Besides, his plays are experimental with regard to dramatic structure and ways of theatrical production available through technology, which remind us of the stylized realism or German Expressionism. His *Long Day's Journey Into Night* (1956) is a powerful, extended autobiography in dramatic form, focusing on his own family and their physical and psychological deterioration, as witnessed in the course of one night. Though the scene of American dramas was not so promising as fiction and poetry, Arthur Miller and Tennessee Williams were yet to acclaim the literary recognition and to hold the central position in American drama until the present times.

5.2 Ezra Pound

5.2.1 About the Author

Ezra Pound (1885-1972) was born in Idaho and raised in a suburb of Philadelphia.

Chapter 5 The Literature of the Modernist Period

At the age of twelve he entered Cheltenham, a military school. Then he studied languages at the University of Pennsylvania, where he became the lifelong friend of William Carlos Williams. In 1908 Pound travelled widely in Europe, working as a journalist. Pound spent much of his time concerned with promoting the careers of many of the great writers of the time and was a key figure in the publication of many influential works, including Hemingway's *In Our Time*, and Eliot's *The Waste Land*. He married Dorothy Shakespeare in 1914 and became London editor of the *Little Review* in 1917.

Pound had been called the "inventor" of Chinese poetry, for he pursued a lifelong study of ancient Chinese texts, and translated among others the writings of Confucius. In about 1909 Pound became the founder and, for a time, the leader of the school of poetry called *Imagism*, a movement in poetry which derived its technique from classical Chinese and Japanese poetry — stressing clarity, precision, and economy of language. Pound's own poetry of this period appeared in such volumes as *Personae* (1910), *Cathay* (1915), and *Lustra* (1916). In 1914 Pound started the Vorticist movement, which he describes as setting "the arts in their rightful place as the acknowledged guide and lamp of civilization". In 1920 Pound moved to Paris, where he was a friend of the writers Gertrude Stein and Ernest Hemingway. From 1924 to 1945, he lived in Italy, working on *The Cantos* and promoting Social Credit. During World War II he made a series of pro-fascistic and anti-Semetic radio broadcasts that led to his eventual arrest for treason following the war. Pound spent 12 years in a hospital for the criminally insane in Washington, D. C. After he was released, he returned to Italy, where he spent his remaining years.

Pound's literary talents are extraordinary. As a poet, he has experimented with various verse forms, from short poems focusing on concrete images to his epic masterpiece, *The Cantos*. Written from 1915 to 1970, featuring unexpected juxtapositions and associations, *The Cantos* have combined reminiscence, meditation, and allusions to many cultures, including Renaissance Italy, dynastic China, and 18th-century America. His other poetic works include twelve volumes of verse which were later collected and published in *Collected Early Poems and Ezra Pound* (1982), and *Personae* (1909), and some longer pieces such as *Hugh Selwyn Mauberley* (1920).

Besides his emphasis on concrete images in poetry writing, the other important aspects of Pound's poetic work include his use of myth and personae. The poet, he argued, cannot relate a delightful psychic experience by speaking out directly in the first person; he must "screen himself" and speak indirectly through an impersonal and objective story, which is usually a myth or a piece of the earlier literature, or a "mask", that is, a persona. In this way, Pound can sustain a dialogue between past and present successfully. As to his language, his lines are usually oblique yet marvelously compressed. His poetry is dense with personal, literary, and historical allusions, but at the expense of syntax and summary statements. In spite of all this, Pound's reputation as a chief architect of English and American literary modernism has never been depreciated.

5.2.2 "In a Station of the Metro[1]"

The apparition[2] of these faces in the crowd;
Petals on a wet, black bough.

Notes

1. This little poem looks to be a modern adoption of the Japanese haiku (俳句). Pound wrote an account of its composition, however, which claims that the poem's form was determined by the experience that inspired it, evolving organically rather than being chosen arbitrarily. Whether it is truth or myth, the piece has become a famous document in the history of Imagism. **Metro**: Paris subway.
2. **apparition**: a visible appearance of something not present, and especially of a dead person.

Study Questions

1. What two images are juxtaposed, or placed next to each other, in the poem?
2. Why does Pound use the word "apparition" instead of "appearance" in this poem?
3. What is Pound trying to say about the people in the station?

5.2.3 "A Pact"

> I make a pact with you, Walt Whitman[1]—
> I have detested[2] you long enough.
> I come to you as a grown child
> Who has had a pig-headed[3] father;
> I am old enough now to make friends.
> It was you that broke the new wood[4],
> Now is a time for carving.
> We have one sap and one root —
> Let there be commerce[5] between us.

Notes

1. **Walt Whitman**: (1819-1892) Great American democratic poet (see previous Chapter 3.8). In the cluster of poems named *Leaves of Grass*, Walt Whitman gave America

its first genuine epic poem. The poetic style devised is now called free verse, that is, poetry without a fixed beat or regular rhyme scheme. He is the first great American poet to use this form of poetry.
2. **detest**: dislike intensely.
3. **pig-headed**: stubborn. Here "a pig-headed father" refers to Walt Whitman.
4. **to break new wood**: to make experiments with the conventions of the traditional poetry.
5. **commerce**: the exchange of views, attitudes, etc.

Study Questions
1. What attitude does the poet hold toward Walt Whitman?
2. What does the poet mean by saying "It was you that broke the new wood"?
3. What are the stylistic features of this poem?

5.3 William Carlos Williams

5.3.1 About the Author

William Carlos Williams (1883-1963) was born in Rutherford, New Jersey. In his teenage years, he ventured to Europe with his mother and brother for two years, studying in both Switzerland and France. Then he attended Horace Mann High School, where he began writing poetry. After having passed a special examination, Williams was admitted in 1902 to the medical school of the University of Pennsylvania, where he met and befriended both Ezra Pound and Hilda Doolittle. These friendships supported his growing passion for poetry. After graduation from the university in 1906, Williams moved to New York City to work as an intern at a French Hospital. He published his first book, *Poems*, in 1909. Then he returned to Rutherford in 1910 and began his medical practice. In 1912 he married Florence Herman, with whom he had two sons. Meanwhile, Williams began publishing in small magazines and embarked on a literary career.

Although Williams maintained his primary occupation as a doctor, he had a full literary career. He wrote at night and spent weekends in New York City with literary friends. His work consists of short stories, poems, plays, novels, critical essays, etc. At the height of his artistry, he composed a personal epic, *Paterson* (1946-1958, published entire 1963), which is an attempt to define the duties of the poet in the context of the American environment. His other poetry collections include *The Collected Early Poems* (1938), *The Collected Later Poems* (1950), and *Pictures from Brueghel and*

Other Poems (1962). His most important prose works are *The Great American Novel* (1923), *In the American Grain* (1925), and *White Mule* (1938). In 1963, *Pictures from Brueghel and Other Poems* earned him the Pulitzer Prize and a gold medal from the American Academy of Arts and Letters.

Williams was considered a groundbreaker. His quest for a truly native form of poetry made him a restless experimenter. He tried to invent an entirely fresh form of poetry whose subject matter was centered on everyday circumstances of life and the lives of common people. In shaping his idea of what this new poetry should be, Williams emphasized four qualities. The first was the use of commonplace subjects and themes. The second was the poet's duty to write about real events or objects in a language that all people could understand. The third was specificity, which meant that his poetry made its point by focusing attention on concrete reality. The fourth was the poet's responsibility to write about his or her locale. *The Red Wheelbarrow* is considered a good example of these principles.

Williams is strongly associated with the American Modernist movement in literature, and sees his poetic project as a distinctly American one. Although his influence as a poet spread slowly during the first half of the 20th century, his work received increasing attention later on as younger poets, including Allen Ginsberg and the Beats, were impressed by the accessibility of his language and his openness as a mentor. Today Williams is regarded as one of the most important and original American poets of the 20th century.

5.3.2 "The Red Wheelbarrow"

so much depends
upon

a red wheel
barrow

glazed with rain
water

beside the white
chickens.

Study Questions

1. What is the tension between concrete images and the imagination?
2. What elements of Imagism does this poem exhibit?
3. What philosophy of life does the poem indicate?

Chapter 5 The Literature of the Modernist Period

Essay Topics

Write about the colors that are mentioned in this poem, and their significance to the poem overall.

5.3.3 "Spring and All"

By the road to the contagious[1] hospital
under the surge of the blue
mottled[2] clouds driven from the
northeast — a cold wind. Beyond, the
waste of broad, muddy fields
brown with dried weeds, standing and fallen

patches of standing water
the scattering of tall trees

All along the road the reddish
purplish, forked, upstanding, twiggy
stuff of bushes and small trees
with dead, brown leaves under them
leafless vines —

Lifeless in appearance, sluggish
dazed spring approaches —

They enter the new world naked,
cold, uncertain of all
save that they enter. All about them
the cold, familiar wind —

Now the grass, tomorrow
the stiff curl of wildcarrot leaf
One by one objects are defined —
It quickens: clarity, outline of leaf

But now the stark dignity of
entrance — Still, the profound change
has come upon them: rooted, they
grip down and begin to awaken.

Notes

1. **contagious**: infectious; a contagious disease is one that can be passed from person to person by touch.
2. **mottled**: conveyed with patterns of light and dark colors of different shapes.

Study Questions

1. What kind of landscape does the poet describe in the first part of the poem?
2. How does the poet's observation move with concrete images?
3. What images indicate that spring emerges gradually?
4. What kind of on-going battles can we see through reading the poem?

5.4 Langston Hughes

5.4.1 About the Author

Langston Hughes (1902-1967) was born in Joplin, Missouri. His father left the family when he was very young. So he was brought up mainly by his mother, his maternal grandmother, and a childless couple named Reed. Hughes first attended public schools in Kansas and Illinois, then transferred to a high school in Cleveland, Ohio. After graduation in 1920, he spent a year in Mexico with his father, who tried to discourage him from writing. Upon his return in 1921, Hughes attended Columbia University. But disgusted with the life there, he left the university after a year. In the following years, Hughes held various odd jobs and made extensive travels over West Africa and Europe.

After his return to the United States, Hughes worked in menial jobs and wrote poems. He published his first collection of poetry, *The Weary Blues*, in 1926. His poetry earned him scholarship to Lincoln University in Pennsylvania, where he received his B. A. degree in 1929. Around this time Hughes became active in the Harlem Renaissance, a flowering of creativity among a group of African-American artists and writers. Hughes created a new form of poetry in which he blended the normal verse of poetry with blues and jazz. His work inspired many African American writers and artists to be more creative and prolific. Hughes was also a politically engaged writer. During the 1930s, he wrote and published radical verse and essays in magazines like *New Masses* and *International Literature*; he traveled to the former Soviet Union to participate in an ultimately aborted film about black workers in the United States; and he spent several months in Spain during its civil war, as a correspondent for the black press and a supporter of the anti-fascist forces. In 1942 he made Harlem his permanent home and worked as a newspaper columnist for some years, creating a universal character, Jesse B. Simple.

Hughes was a prolific writer. He wrote sixteen books of poems, two novels, three collections of short stories, twenty plays, and dozens of other books during his life. His works are mainly about racial conflicts, southern violence, Harlem street life, poverty, prejudice, hunger, and hopelessness. His writing style is simple and colloquial, using natural language that could be easily understood and accessible to ordinary people. His art was firmly rooted in race pride and race feeling even as he cherished his freedom as an artist. He was perhaps the most original of African American poets. His literary works helped shape American literature and politics. Through his poetry, novels, plays, essays, and children's books, he promoted equality, condemned racism and injustice, and celebrated African American culture, humor, and spirituality.

5.4.2 "Dreams"

Hold fast to dreams
For if dreams die
Life is a broken-winged bird
That cannot fly.
Hold fast to dreams
For when dreams go
Life is a barren field
Frozen with snow.

Study Questions

1. What is the message the speaker is trying to convey?
2. What does the speaker care about?
3. What may have inspired the poet to write this poem?

5.4.3 "Cross[1]"

My old man's a white old man
And my old mother's black.
If ever I cursed my white old man
I take my curses back.
If ever I cursed my black old mother
And wished she were in hell,
I'm sorry for that evil wish
And now I wish her well
My old man died in a fine big house.
My ma died in a shack.
I wonder where I'm gonna[2] to die,
Being neither white nor black?

Notes

1. **Cross**: cross-bred; person of mixed blood. The word also has rich implied meaning, such as anger, burden, crucifix, crossroad, etc.
2. **gonna**: (American slang) going to.

Study Questions

1. With what tone does the poet discuss this poem?
2. Why did the speaker curse his parents? Why is he repentant now?
3. What is the theme of the poem?

5.5 E. E. Cummings

5.5.1 About the Author

E. E. Cummings (1894-1962) was born in Cambridge, Massachusetts and grew up in a happy and intellectually stimulating household. As a child, his artistic and literary interests were encouraged by his parents, and he determined early that he wanted to become a poet. After graduating from Cambridge Latin School, Cummings entered Harvard, where he became fascinated by avant-garde art. He began to experiment with free verse and to develop as a self-taught cubist painter. He received his Bachelor of Arts degree in 1915 and master's degree in 1916 from Harvard.

During the last years of World War I, Cummings worked as an ambulance driver in France. Because of his outspoken antiwar attitude, he was detained by French authorities on the suspicion of being a spy. He was imprisoned for four months. This incident exemplifies Cummings's disdain for bureaucracy and authority and strengthened his passion for individual freedom, a concern that would help mold his writing, both thematically and stylistically, throughout his career. After the war Cummings moved to New York, entering his cubist paintings in yearly exhibitions and attaining celebrity for the unusual poems he published in the *Dial* and other avant-garde magazines in the 1920s. Cummings published his first book of poems, *Tulips & Chimneys* in 1923, which included lush lyrics from his Harvard years. His other collections of poetry include *Is* 5 (1926), *W* (*ViVa*; 1931), *No Thanks* (1935) and *Ninety-Five Poems* (1958). Cummings reached the height of his popularity during the 1940s and 1950s, receiving the Shelley Memorial Award for poetry (1944) and the Bollinger Prize for Poetry (1958).

Cummings is a combination of an unabashed Romantic in his view of life and an avant-garde modernist seeking to explore unusual means of expression. He values whatever is instinctively human and promoted feeling and imagination. In his work, he has experimented radically with form, punctuation, spelling and syntax, abandoning traditional techniques and structures to create a new, highly idiosyncratic means of poetic expression. His poems are full of wit and ingenuity, of vigorous satire, and of beauty and delicacy. Because he is a painter as well as a poet, he has developed a unique form of literary cubism: he breaks up his material on the page to present it in a new, visually directed way. Thus, Cummings is regarded as one of the most important figures in that remarkable generation of American writers, who carried out a revolution in literary expression in the 20th century.

5.5.2 "Your Little Voice"

your little voice
   Over the wires came leaping
and i felt suddenly
dizzy
   With the jostling[1] and shouting of merry flowers
wee[2] skipping high-heeled flames
courtesied before my eyes
   or twinkling over to my side
Looked up
with impertinently exquisite faces
floating hands were laid upon me
I was whirled and tossed into delicious dancing
up
Up
with the pale important
   stars and the Humorous
      moon
dear girl
How i was crazy how I cried when i heard
   over time
and tide and death
leaping
Sweetly
   your voice

Notes

1. **jostle**: push roughly against (sb), usu. in the crowd.
2. **wee**: little.

Study Questions

1. Identify at least three images that the speaker associates with his dizziness.
2. What ordinary experience of modern life does the poem make extraordinary?
3. How does the speaker feel about the "dear girl"?

5.6 Ernest Hemingway

5.6.1 About the Author

Ernest Hemingway (1899-1961) was born into a middle class family in Oak Park, Illinois. He grew up under the influence of his father who encouraged him to develop outdoor interests such as swimming, fishing and hunting. He attended the local public schools and published his earliest stories and poems in his school newspaper. After graduation in 1917, Hemingway started his career as a reporter for the *Kansas City Star*, covering city crime and writing feature stories. The position helped him develop a journalistic style, which would later become one of the most identifiable characteristics of his fiction. In 1918, he volunteered for war duty and served as an ambulance driver on the Italian front where he suffered a severe leg wound.

After the war, Hemingway went to Paris as a foreign reporter, employed by *The Toronto Star*. In Paris, the center of European modernist movement, he met many significant literary figures, including Gertrude Stein, Ezra Pound, F. Scott Fitzgerald, D. H. Lawrence and T. S. Eliot. And Hemingway became a member of the group of expatriate Americans. In the following years, he entered the booming stage of literary creation. After his first two works, *Three Stories and Ten Poems* (1923) and *In Our Time* (1924), his major novel, *The Sun Also Rises*, came out in 1926, which established his reputation as a literary figure. And 1929 witnessed his second novel, *A Farewell to Arms*, the study of an American ambulance officer's disillusionment in the war. Hemingway used his own experiences as a reporter during the civil war in Spain as the background for his most ambitious novel, *For Whom the Bell Tolls* (1940). In 1952 Hemingway published *The Old Man and the Sea*, a powerful, short, heroic novel about an aged Cuban fisherman, for which he won the 1952 Pulitzer Prize for Fiction. Two years later, Hemingway was awarded the Nobel Prize for Literature.

Hemingway's life was filled with writing and adventure. He was passionately involved with bullfighting in Spain, big game hunting in Africa and deep sea fishing in the Gulf Stream near Cuba. He started drinking quite early and could tolerate large amounts of alcohol, which gradually destroyed his health. In 1960, his health problems, compounded by his three failed marriages and periods of creative stagnation, resulted in a mental breakdown. In the following year on July 2, Hemingway committed suicide in Ketchum, Idaho.

Hemingway's thought and art are shaped by the major influences of Mark Twain, the War and The Bible. By rendering a realistic portrayal of the inter-war period with its disillusionment and disintegration of old values, Hemingway has presented the predicament of the modern man. His protagonists are alienated individuals, fighting a losing battle against the odds of life. However, they exemplify certain principles of honor, courage and endurance in a life of tension and pain. Violence, struggle, suffering and hardships do not make them in any way pessimistic. Men can be physically destroyed but never defeated spiritually. Hemingway's style is characterized by crispness, clearness, and terseness. Short and solid sentences, delightful dialogues, and a painstaking hunt for an apt word or phrase to express the exact truth, are the distinguishing features of his style. Hemingway himself once said, "The dignity of movement of an iceberg is due to only one-eighth of it being above water."

5.6.2 "Indian Camp"

At the lake shore there was another rowboat drawn up[1]. The two Indians stood waiting.

Nick and his father got in the stern[2] of the boat and the Indians shoved it off and one of them got in to row. Uncle George sat in the stern of the camp rowboat. The young Indian shoved the camp boat off and got in to row Uncle George.

The two boats started off in the dark. Nick heard the oarlocks of the other boat quite a way ahead of them in the mist. The Indians rowed with quick choppy strokes[3]. Nick lay back with his father's arm around him. It was cold on the water. The Indian who was rowing them was working very hard, but the other boat moved further ahead in the mist all the time.

"Where are we going, Dad?" Nick asked.

"Over to the Indian camp. There is an Indian lady very sick."

"Oh," said Nick.

Across the bay they found the other boat beached. Uncle George was smoking a cigar in the dark. The young Indian pulled the boat way up on the beach. Uncle George gave both the Indians cigars.

They walked up from the beach through a meadow that was soaking wet[4] with dew, following the young Indian who carried a lantern. Then they went into the woods and followed a trail that led to the logging road that ran back into the hills. It was much lighter on the logging road as the timber was cut away on both sides. The young Indian stopped and blew out his lantern and they all walked on along the road.

They came around a bend[5] and a dog came out barking. Ahead were the lights of the shanties[6] where the Indian bark-peelers[7] lived. More dogs rushed out at them. The two Indians sent them back to the shanties. In the shanty nearest the road there was a light in the window. An old woman stood in the doorway holding a lamp.

Inside on a wooden bunk[8] lay a young Indian woman. She had been trying to have her baby for two days. All the old women in the camp had been helping her. The men had moved off up the road to sit in the dark and smoke out of range of the noise she made[9]. She screamed just as Nick and the two Indians followed his father and Uncle George into the shanty. She lay in the lower bunk, very big under a quilt. Her head was turned to one side. In the upper bunk was her husband. He had cut his foot very badly with an ax three days before. He was smoking a pipe. The room smelled very bad.

Nick's father ordered some water to be put on the stove, and while it was heating he spoke to Nick.

"This lady is going to have a baby, Nick," he said.

"I know," said Nick.

"You don't know," said his father. "Listen to me. What she is going through is called being in labor. The baby wants to be born and she wants it to be born. All her muscles are trying to get the baby born. That is what is happening when she screams."

"I see," Nick said.

Just then the woman cried out.

"Oh, Daddy, can't you give her something to make her stop screaming?" asked Nick.

"No. I haven't any anaesthetic[10]," his father said. "But her screams are not important. I don't hear them because they are not important."

The husband in the upper bunk rolled over against the wall.

The woman in the kitchen motioned to the doctor that the water was hot. Nick's father went into the kitchen and poured about half of the water out of the big kettle into a basin. Into the water left in the kettle he put several things he unwrapped from a handkerchief.

"Those must boil," he said, and began to scrub his hands in the basin of hot water with a cake of soap he had brought from the camp. Nick watched his father's hands scrubbing each other with the soap. While his father washed his hands very carefully and thoroughly, he talked.

"You see, Nick, babies are supposed to be born head first but sometimes they're not. When they're not they make a lot of trouble for everybody. Maybe I'll have to operate on this lady. We'll know in a little while."

When he was satisfied with his hands he went in and went to work.

"Pull back that quilt, will you, George?" he said. "I'd rather not touch it."

Later when he started to operate Uncle George and three Indian men held the woman still. She bit Uncle George on the arm and Uncle George said, "Damn squaw[11] bitch!" and the young Indian who had rowed Uncle George over laughed at him. Nick held the basin for his father. It all took a long time.

His father picked the baby up and slapped it to make it breathe and handed it to the old woman.

"See, it's a boy, Nick," he said. "How do you like being an internee[12]?"

Nick said," All right. " He was looking away so as not to see what his father was doing.

"There. That gets it ," said his father and put something into the basin.

Nick didn't look at it.

"Now," his father said, "there's some stitches to put in. You can watch this or not, Nick , just as you like. I'm going to sew up the incision[13] I made. "

Nick did not watch. His curiosity had been gone for a long time.

His father finished and stood up. Uncle George and the three Indian men stood up. Nick put the basin out in the kitchen.

Uncle George looked at his arm. The young Indian smiled reminiscently.

"I'll put some peroxide[14] on that ,George," the doctor said.

He bent over the Indian woman. She was quiet now and her eyes were closed. She looked very pale. She did not know what had become of the baby or anything.

"I'll be back in the morning. " the doctor said , standing up. "The nurse should be here from St. Ignace by noon and she'll bring everything we need. "

He was feeling exalted and talkative as football players are in the dressing room after a game.

"That's one for the medical journal, George," he said. "Doing a Caesarian with a jack-knife[15] and sewing it up with nine-foot, tapered gut leaders[16]. "

Uncle George was standing against the wall, looking at his arm.

"Oh, you're a great man, all right," he said.

"Ought to have a look at the proud father. They're usually the worst sufferers in these little affairs," the doctor said. "I must say he took it all pretty quietly. "

He pulled back the blanket from the Indian's head. His hand came away wet. He mounted on the edge of the lower bunk with the lamp in one hand and looked in. The Indian lay with his face toward the wall. His throat had been cut from ear to ear. The blood had flowed down into a pool where his body sagged the bunk[17]. His head rested on his left arm. The open razor lay, edge up, in the blankets.

"Take Nick out of the shanty, George," the doctor said.

There was no need of that. Nick, standing in the door of the kitchen, had a good view of the upper bunk when his father, the lamp in one hand, tipped the Indian's head back.

It was just beginning to be daylight when they walked along the logging road back toward the lake.

"I'm terribly sorry I brought you along, Nickie," said his father, all his post-operative exhilaration gone. " It was an awful mess to put you through. "[18]

"Do ladies always have such a hard time having babies?" Nick asked.

"No, that was very, very exceptional."

"Why did he kill himself, Daddy?"

"I don't know, Nick. He couldn't stand things, I guess."

"Do many men kill themselves, Daddy?"

"Not very many, Nick."

"Do many women?"

"Hardly ever."

"Don't they ever?"

"Oh, yes. They do sometimes."

"Daddy?"

"Yes."

"Where did Uncle George go?"

"He'll turn up all right."[19]

"Is dying hard, Daddy?"

"No, I think it's pretty easy, Nick. It all depends."

They were seated in the boat, Nick in the stern, his father rowing. The sun was coming up over the hills. A bass[20] jumped, making a circle in the water. Nick trailed his hand in the water. It felt warm in the sharp chill of the morning.

In the early morning on the lake sitting in the stern of the boat with his father rowing, he felt quite sure that he would never die.

Notes

1. **drawn up**: led to a stop.
2. **stern**: The rear part of a ship or boat.
3. **The Indians rowed with quick choppy strokes**: The Indians rowed hard and quickly, cutting the water into pieces with the oar.
4. **soaking wet**: very wet.
5. **bend**: curve or turn.
6. **shanties**: rough huts or cabins.
7. **bark-peelers**: those people who take the skin on boughs and trunks off a tree.
8. **bunk**: bed fixed to a wall.
9. **The men had moved... the noise she made**: The men had moved away from the camp to sit along the road in darkness and smoke without hearing the scream she made.
10. **anaesthetic**: substance that stops one feeling pain.
11. **squaw**: American Indian woman.
12. **internee**: An advanced student or a recent graduate undergoing supervised practical training.
13. **incision**: A cut into a body tissue or organ, especially one made during surgery.

14. **peroxide**: A compound, such as sodium peroxide, Na_2O_2, that contains a peroxyl group and yields hydrogen peroxide when treated with an acid.
15. **jack-knife**: large pocket-knife with a folding blade.
16. **tapered gut leaders**: made the contents of leading articles.
17. **where his body sagged the bunk**: where the bunk sank down under the weight of his body.
18. **It was an awful mess to put you through**: It was terrible for you to experience it.
19. **He'll turn up all right**: He will get better.
20. **bass**: kind of fish.

Study Questions
1. Why did nick's father apologize to him after the husband was found dead?
2. Why did the husband kill himself?
3. What does the last sentence mean?

Essay topics
1. What is the effect of the young husband's death on Nick Adams?
2. What did Nick learn from his witnessing both birth and death over one night?

5.7 F. Scott Fitzgerald

5.7.1 About the Author

F. Scott Fitzgerald (1896-1940) was born in St. Paul, Minnesota of mixed Southern and Irish descent. He attended private schools for his early educations. And in 1913, he entered Princeton University. Although he was socially and literally successful in Princeton, Fitzgerald was poor in academic records. He left Princeton in 1917 and took up a commission in the US Army. While stationed in Montgomery, Alabama, he met and soon fell in love with the eighteen-year-old Zelda Sayre, the daughter of a judge. During this time, he was also working on his first novel,

This Side of Paradise, which was published in 1920. Capturing a mood of spiritual desolation in the aftermath of World War I and a growing, devil-may-care pursuit of pleasure among the American upper classes, *This Side of Paradise* earned both money and fame for Fitzgerald to convince Zelda to marry him. After marriage, the young couple moved to New York City, where they indulged themselves in heavy drinking and parting. They were the darling couple, the daring ones, the rule breakers, leading the lifestyle of characters chronicled in his novels. Fitzgerald therefore gained a reputation as the symbol of the Jazz Age.

To support his expensive life style with Zelda, Fitzgerald contributed commercial stories to various magazines to earn money. After the birth of their daughter in 1921, the Fitzgeralds spent much time in Paris, becoming part of a celebrated circle of American expatriates. His second novel, *The Beautiful and Damned* (1922), increased his popularity. Cynical yet poignant, *The Great Gatsby* (1925) was a devastating portrait of the so-called American Dream, which measured success and love in terms of money. As the giddiness of the Roaring Twenties dissolved into the bleakness of the Great Depression, Zelda suffered a nervous breakdown and Fitzgerald battled alcoholism, which hampered his writing. However, he wrote one more important novel, *Tender is the Night* (1934), in which he traces the decline of a young American psychiatrist whose marriage to a beautiful and wealthy patient drains his personal energies and corrodes his professional career. The 1930s brought relentless decline for Fitzgerald with a series of misfortunes: his reputation declined, his wealth fell, his health failed, and what's more, Zelda had suffered from some serious mental breakdowns which confined her in a sanitarium for the rest of her life. In 1937 Fitzgerald moved to Los Angeles, California, where he worked as a scriptwriter. He died of a heart attack at the age of 44, leaving his last novel *The Last Tycoon* unfinished.

Fitzgerald's writing explores the poignant dilemma of the young man who is neither poor nor rich but falls in love with a golden girl, wealthy, beautiful, and often cruel. He is best known for his novels *The Great Gatsby* (1925) and *Tender Is the Night* (1934), both of which depict disillusion with the American dream of self-betterment, wealth, and success through hard work and perseverance. Apart from his novels, his short stories are also valuable for their insight into his characteristic, thematic concerns. Fitzgerald is regarded as a profound and sensitive artist, as well as the unmatched voice of the Jazz Age. His style, closely related to his themes, is explicit and chilly. His accurate dialogues, his careful observation of mannerism, styles, models and attitudes provide the reader with a vivid sense of reality. The accurate details, the completely original diction and metaphors, the bold impressionistic and colorful quality have all proved his expert artistry.

5.7.2 An Excerpt from Chapter 3 of *The Great Gatsby*

There was music from my neighbor's house through the summer nights. In his blue gardens men and girls came and went like moths among the whisperings and the champagne and the stars. At high tide in the afternoon I watched his guests diving from the tower of his raft, or taking the sun on the hot sand of his beach while his two motor-boats slit the waters of the Sound[1], drawing aquaplanes over cataracts of foam. On week-ends his Rolls-Royce[2] became an omnibus, bearing parties to and from the city between nine in the morning and long past midnight, while his station wagon scampered like a brisk yellow bug to meet all trains. And on Mondays eight servants, including an extra gardener, toiled all day with mops and scrubbing-brushes and hammers and garden-shears, repairing the ravages of the night before.

Every Friday five crates of oranges and lemons arrived from a fruiterer in New York — every Monday these same oranges and lemons left his back door in a pyramid of pulpless halves. There was a machine in the kitchen which could extract the juice of two hundred oranges in half an hour if a little button was pressed two hundred times by a butler's thumb.

At least once a fortnight a corps of caterers came down with several hundred feet of canvas and enough colored lights to make a Christmas tree of Gatsby's enormous garden. On buffet tables, garnished with glistening hors-d' oeuvre[3], spiced baked hams crowded against salads of harlequin designs and pastry pigs and turkeys bewitched to a dark gold. In the main hall a bar with a real brass rail was set up, and stocked with gins and liquors and with cordials so long forgotten that most of his female guests were too young to know one from another.

By seven o'clock the orchestra has arrived, no thin five-piece affair[4], but a whole pitful of[5] oboes and trombones and saxophones and viols and cornets and piccolos, and low and high drums. The last swimmers have come in from the beach now and are dressing up-stairs; the cars from New York are parked five deep in the drive, and already the halls and salons and verandas are gaudy with primary colors, and hair shorn in strange new ways, and shawls beyond the dreams of Castile[6]. The bar is in full swing, and floating rounds of cocktails permeate the garden outside, until the air is alive with chatter and laughter, and casual innuendo[7] and introductions forgotten on the spot, and enthusiastic meetings between women who never knew each other's names.

The lights grow brighter as the earth lurches away from the sun, and now the orchestra is playing yellow cocktail music, and the opera of voices pitches a key higher. Laughter is easier minute by minute, spilled with prodigality, tipped out at a cheerful word. The groups change more swiftly, swell with new arrivals, dissolve and form in the same breath; already there are wanderers, confident girls who weave here and there among the stouter and more stable, become for a sharp, joyous moment the centre of a group, and then, excited with triumph, glide on through the sea-change of faces and voices and color under the constantly changing light.

Suddenly one of the gypsies, in trembling opal, seizes a cocktail out of the air, dumps it down for courage and, moving her hands like Frisco[8], dances out alone on the canvas platform. A momentary hush; the orchestra leader varies his rhythm obligingly for her, and there is a burst of chatter as the erroneous news goes around that she is Gilda Gray's understudy from the FOLLIES[9]. The party has begun.

I believe that on the first night I went to Gatsby's house I was one of the few guests who had actually been invited. People were not invited — they went there. They got into automobiles which bore them out to Long Island, and somehow they ended up at Gatsby's door. Once there they were introduced by somebody who knew Gatsby, and after that they conducted themselves according to the rules of behavior associated with amusement parks. Sometimes they came and went without having met Gatsby at all, came for the party with a simplicity of heart that was its own ticket of admission.

I had been actually invited. A chauffeur in a uniform of robin's-egg blue[10] crossed my lawn early that Saturday morning with a surprisingly formal note from his employer: the honor would be entirely Gatsby's, it said, if I would attend his "little party" that night. He had seen me several times, and had intended to call on me long before, but a peculiar combination of circumstances had prevented it — signed Jay Gatsby, in a majestic hand.

Dressed up in white flannels I went over to his lawn a little after seven, and wandered around rather ill at ease among swirls and eddies of people I didn't know — though here and there was a face I had noticed on the commuting train. I was immediately struck by the number of young Englishmen dotted about; all well dressed, all looking a little hungry, and all talking in low, earnest voices to solid and prosperous Americans. I was sure that they were selling something: bonds or insurance or automobiles. They were at least agonizingly aware of the easy money in the vicinity and convinced that it was theirs for a few words in the right key[11].

As soon as I arrived I made an attempt to find my host, but the two or three people of whom I asked his whereabouts stared at me in such an amazed way, and denied so vehemently any knowledge of his movements, that I slunk off in the direction of the cocktail table — the only place in the garden where a single man could linger without looking purposeless and alone.

I was on my way to get roaring drunk from sheer embarrassment when Jordan Baker came out of the house and stood at the head of the marble steps, leaning a little backward and looking with contemptuous interest down into the garden.

Welcome or not, I found it necessary to attach myself to some one before I should begin to address cordial remarks to the passers-by.

"Hello!" I roared, advancing toward her. My voice seemed unnaturally loud across the garden.

"I thought you might be here," she responded absently as I came up. "I remembered you lived next door to —" She held my hand impersonally, as a promise that she'd take care of me in a minute, and gave ear to two girls in twin yellow dresses, who stopped at the foot of the steps.

"Hello!" they cried together. "Sorry you didn't win."

That was for the golf tournament. She had lost in the finals the week before.

"You don't know who we are," said one of the girls in yellow, "but we met you

Chapter 5　The Literature of the Modernist Period

here about a month ago."

"You've dyed your hair since then," remarked Jordan, and I started, but the girls had moved casually on and her remark was addressed to the premature moon, produced like the supper, no doubt, out of a caterer's basket. With Jordan's slender golden arm resting in mine, we descended the steps and sauntered about the garden. A tray of cocktails floated at us through the twilight, and we sat down at a table with the two girls in yellow and three men, each one introduced to us as Mr. Mumble.

"Do you come to these parties often?" inquired Jordan of the girl beside her.

"The last one was the one I met you at," answered the girl, in an alert confident voice. She turned to her companion: "Wasn't it for you, Lucille?"

It was for Lucille, too.

"I like to come," Lucille said. "I never care what I do, so I always have a good time. When I was here last I tore my gown on a chair, and he asked me my name and address — inside of a week I got a package from Croirier's with a new evening gown in it."

"Did you keep it?" asked Jordan.

"Sure I did. I was going to wear it to-night, but it was too big in the bust and had to be altered. It was gas blue with lavender beads. Two hundred and sixty-five dollars."

"There's something funny about a fellow that'll do a thing like that," said the other girl eagerly. "He doesn't want any trouble with *anybody*."

"Who doesn't?" I inquired.

"Gatsby. Somebody told me — "

The two girls and Jordan leaned together confidentially.

"Somebody told me they thought he killed a man once."

A thrill passed over all of us. The three Mr. Mumbles bent forward and listened eagerly.

"I don't think it's so much *that*, " argued Lucille sceptically; "it's more that he was a German spy during the war."

One of the men nodded in confirmation.

"I heard that from a man who knew all about him, grew up with him in Germany," he assured us positively.

"Oh, no," said the first girl, "it couldn't be that, because he was in the American army during the war." As our credulity switched back to her she leaned forward with enthusiasm. "You look at him sometimes when he thinks nobody's looking at him. I'll bet he killed a man."

She narrowed her eyes and shivered. Lucille shivered. We all turned and looked around for Gatsby. It was testimony to the romantic speculation he inspired that there were whispers about him from those who found little that it was necessary to whisper about in this world.

The first supper — there would be another one after midnight — was now being served, and Jordan invited me to join her own party, who were spread around a table on the other side of the garden. There were three married couples and Jordan's escort, a persistent undergraduate given to violent innuendo, and obviously under the impression that sooner or later Jordan was going to yield him up her person[12] to a greater or lesser degree. Instead of rambling, this party had preserved a dignified homogeneity, and assumed to itself the function of representing the staid nobility of the country-side — East Egg condescending to West Egg[13], and carefully on guard against its spectroscopic gayety.

"Let's get out," whispered Jordan, after a somehow wasteful and inappropriate half-hour. "This is much too polite for me."

We got up, and she explained that we were going to find the host: I had never met him, she said, and it was making me uneasy. The undergraduate nodded in a cynical, melancholy way.

The bar, where we glanced first, was crowded, but Gatsby was not there. She couldn't find him from the top of the steps, and he wasn't on the veranda. On a chance we tried an important-looking door, and walked into a high Gothic[14] library, panelled with carved English oak, and probably transported complete from some ruin overseas.

A stout, middle-aged man, with enormous owl-eyed spectacles, was sitting somewhat drunk on the edge of a great table, staring with unsteady concentration at the shelves of books. As we entered he wheeled excitedly around and examined Jordan from head to foot.

"What do you think?" he demanded impetuously.

"About what?" He waved his hand toward the book-shelves.

"About that. As a matter of fact you needn't bother to ascertain. I ascertained. They're real."

"The books?"

He nodded.

"Absolutely real — have pages and everything. I thought they'd be a nice durable cardboard. Matter of fact, they're absolutely real. Pages and — Here! Lemme show you."

Taking our scepticism for granted, he rushed to the bookcases and returned with Volume One of the "Stoddard Lectures[15]."

"See!" he cried triumphantly. "It's a bona-fide[16] piece of printed matter. It fooled me. This fella's[17] a regular Belasco[18]. It's a triumph. What thoroughness! What realism! Knew when to stop, too — didn't cut the pages. But what do you want? What do you expect?"

He snatched the book from me and replaced it hastily on its shelf, muttering that if one brick was removed the whole library was liable to collapse.

Chapter 5　The Literature of the Modernist Period

"Who brought you?" he demanded. "Or did you just come? I was brought. Most people were brought."

Jordan looked at him alertly, cheerfully, without answering.

"I was brought by a woman named Roosevelt," he continued. "Mrs. Claud Roosevelt. Do you know her? I met her somewhere last night. I've been drunk for about a week now, and I thought it might sober me up to sit in a library."

"Has it?"

"A little bit, I think. I can't tell yet. I've only been here an hour. Did I tell you about the books? They're real. They're — "

"You told us." We shook hands with him gravely and went back outdoors.

There was dancing now on the canvas in the garden; old men pushing young girls backward in eternal graceless circles, superior couples holding each other tortuously, fashionably, and keeping in the corners — and a great number of single girls dancing individualistically or relieving the orchestra for a moment of the burden of the banjo or the traps. By midnight the hilarity had increased. A celebrated tenor had sung in Italian, and a notorious contralto[19] had sung in jazz, and between the numbers people were doing "stunts" all over the garden, while happy, vacuous bursts of laughter rose toward the summer sky. A pair of stage twins, who turned out to be the girls in yellow, did a baby act in costume, and champagne was served in glasses bigger than finger-bowls. The moon had risen higher, and floating in the Sound was a triangle of silver scales, trembling a little to the stiff, tinny drip of the banjoes on the lawn.

I was still with Jordan Baker. We were sitting at a table with a man of about my age and a rowdy little girl, who gave way upon the slightest provocation to uncontrollable laughter. I was enjoying myself now. I had taken two finger-bowls of champagne, and the scene had changed before my eyes into something significant, elemental, and profound.

At a lull in the entertainment the man looked at me and smiled.

"Your face is familiar," he said, politely. "Weren't you in the Third Division during the war?"

"Why, yes. I was in the Ninth Machine-gun Battalion."

"I was in the Seventh Infantry until June nineteen-eighteen. I knew I'd seen you somewhere before."

We talked for a moment about some wet, gray little villages in France. Evidently he lived in this vicinity, for he told me that he had just bought a hydroplane, and was going to try it out in the morning.

"Want to go with me, old sport?[20] Just near the shore along the Sound."

"What time?"

"Any time that suits you best."

It was on the tip of my tongue to ask his name when Jordan looked around and smiled.

"Having a gay time now?" she inquired.

"Much better." I turned again to my new acquaintance. "This is an unusual party for me. I haven't even seen the host. I live over there — " I waved my hand at the invisible hedge in the distance, "and this man Gatsby sent over his chauffeur with an invitation." For a moment he looked at me as if he failed to understand.

"I'm Gatsby," he said suddenly.

"What!" I exclaimed. "Oh, I beg your pardon."

"I thought you knew, old sport. I'm afraid I'm not a very good host."

He smiled understandingly — much more than understandingly. It was one of those rare smiles with a quality of eternal reassurance in it that you may come across four or five times in life. It faced — or seemed to face — the whole external world for an instant, and then concentrated on you with an irresistible prejudice in your favor. It understood you just so far as you wanted to be understood, believed in you as you would like to believe in yourself, and assured you that it had precisely the impression of you that, at your best, you hoped to convey. Precisely at that point it vanished — and I was looking at an elegant young rough-neck, a year or two over thirty, whose elaborate formality of speech just missed being absurd. Some time before he introduced himself I'd got a strong impression that he was picking his words with care.

Almost at the moment when Mr. Gatsby identified himself, a butler hurried toward him with the information that Chicago was calling him on the wire. He excused himself with a small bow that included each of us in turn.

"If you want anything just ask for it, old sport," he urged me. "Excuse me. I will rejoin you later."

When he was gone I turned immediately to Jordan — constrained to assure her of my surprise. I had expected that Mr. Gatsby would be a florid and corpulent person in his middle years.

"Who is he?" I demanded.

"Do you know?"

"He's just a man named Gatsby."

"Where is he from, I mean? And what does he do?"

"Now *you're* started on the subject," she answered with a wan smile. "Well, he told me once he was an Oxford man." A dim background started to take shape behind him, but at her next remark it faded away.

"However, I don't believe it."

"Why not?" "I don't know," she insisted, "I just don't think he went there."

Something in her tone reminded me of the other girl's "I think he killed a man," and had the effect of stimulating my curiosity. I would have accepted without question the information that Gatsby sprang from the swamps of Louisiana or from the lower East Side of New York[21]. That was comprehensible. But young men didn't — at least in my provincial inexperience I believed they didn't — drift coolly out of nowhere and buy a palace on Long Island Sound.

"Anyhow, he gives large parties," said Jordan, changing the subject with an urbane distaste for the concrete. "And I like large parties. They're so intimate. At small parties there isn't any privacy."

There was the boom of a bass drum, and the voice of the orchestra leader rang out suddenly above the echolalia[22] of the garden.

"Ladies and gentlemen," he cried. "At the request of Mr. Gatsby we are going to play for you Mr. Vladimir Tostoff's latest work, which attracted so much attention at Carnegie Hall[23] last May. If you read the papers, you know there was a big sensation." He smiled with jovial condescension, and added: "Some sensation!" Whereupon everybody laughed.

"The piece is known," he concluded lustily, "as Vladimir Tostoff's *Jazz History of the World*."

The nature of Mr. Tostoff's composition eluded me, because just as it began my eyes fell on Gatsby, standing alone on the marble steps and looking from one group to another with approving eyes. His tanned skin was drawn attractively tight on his face and his short hair looked as though it were trimmed every day. I could see nothing sinister about him. I wondered if the fact that he was not drinking helped to set him off from his guests, for it seemed to me that he grew more correct as the fraternal hilarity increased. When the *Jazz History of the World* was over, girls were putting their heads on men's shoulders in a puppyish, convivial way[24], girls were swooning backward playfully into men's arms, even into groups, knowing that some one would arrest their falls — but no one swooned backward on Gatsby, and no French bob[25] touched Gatsby's shoulder, and no singing quartets were formed with Gatsby's head for one link.

"I beg your pardon."

Gatsby's butler was suddenly standing beside us.

"Miss Baker?" he inquired. "I beg your pardon, but Mr. Gatsby would like to speak to you alone."

"With me?" she exclaimed in surprise.

"Yes, madame."

She got up slowly, raising her eyebrows at me in astonishment, and followed the butler toward the house. I noticed that she wore her evening-dress, all her dresses, like sports clothes — there was a jauntiness about her movements as if she had first learned to walk upon golf courses on clean, crisp mornings.

I was alone and it was almost two. For some time confused and intriguing sounds had issued from a long, many-windowed room which overhung the terrace. Eluding Jordan's undergraduate, who was now engaged in an obstetrical conversation with two chorus girls, and who implored me to join him, I went inside.

The large room was full of people. One of the girls in yellow was playing the piano, and beside her stood a tall, red-haired young lady from a famous chorus, engaged in song. She had drunk a quantity of champagne, and during the course of her song she had decided, ineptly, that everything was very, very sad — she was not only singing, she was weeping too. Whenever there was a pause in the song she filled it with gasping, broken sobs, and then took up the lyric again in a quavering soprano[26]. The tears coursed down her cheeks — not freely, however, for when they came into contact with her heavily beaded eyelashes they assumed an inky color, and pursued the rest of their way in slow black rivulets. A humorous suggestion was made that she sing the notes on her face[27], whereupon she threw up her hands, sank into a chair, and went off into a deep vinous sleep.

"She had a fight with a man who says he's her husband," explained a girl at my elbow.

I looked around. Most of the remaining women were now having fights with men said to be their husbands. Even Jordan's party, the quartet from East Egg, were rent asunder by dissension. One of the men was talking with curious intensity to a young actress, and his wife, after attempting to laugh at the situation in a dignified and indifferent way, broke down entirely and resorted to flank attacks — at intervals she appeared suddenly at his side like an angry diamond, and hissed: "You promised!" into his ear.

The reluctance to go home was not confined to wayward men. The hall was at present occupied by two deplorably sober men and their highly indignant wives. The wives were sympathizing with each other in slightly raised voices.

"Whenever he sees I'm having a good time he wants to go home."

"Never heard anything so selfish in my life."

"We're always the first ones to leave."

"So are we."

"Well, we're almost the last to-night," said one of the men sheepishly. "The orchestra left half an hour ago."

In spite of the wives' agreement that such malevolence was beyond credibility, the dispute ended in a short struggle, and both wives were lifted, kicking, into the night.

As I waited for my hat in the hall the door of the library opened and Jordan Baker and Gatsby came out together. He was saying some last word to her, but the eagerness in his manner tightened abruptly into formality as several people approached him to say good-bye.

Jordan's party were calling impatiently to her from the porch, but she lingered for a moment to shake hands.

"I've just heard the most amazing thing," she whispered. "How long were we in there?"

"Why, about an hour." "It was — simply amazing," she repeated abstractedly. "But I swore I wouldn't tell it and here I am tantalizing you[28]." She yawned gracefully in my face: "Please come and see me... Phone book... Under the name of Mrs. Sigourney Howard... My aunt..." She was hurrying off as she talked — her brown hand waved a jaunty salute as she melted into her party at the door.

Rather ashamed that on my first appearance I had stayed so late, I joined the last of Gatsby's guests, who were clustered around him. I wanted to explain that I'd hunted for him early in the evening and to apologize for not having known him in the garden.

"Don't mention it," he enjoined me eagerly. "Don't give it another thought, old sport." The familiar expression held no more familiarity than the hand which reassuringly brushed my shoulder. "And don't forget we're going up in the hydroplane to-morrow morning, at nine o'clock."

Then the butler, behind his shoulder: "Philadelphia wants you on the 'phone, sir."

"All right, in a minute. Tell them I'll be right there... good night."

"Good night."

"Good night." He smiled — and suddenly there seemed to be a pleasant significance in having been among the last to go, as if he had desired it all the time. "Good night, old sport... good night."

...

Notes

1. **the Sound**: Long Island Sound, a narrow finger of the Atlantic Ocean between Long Island and the state of Connecticut on the mainland, just east of New York City.
2. **Rolls-Royce**: a very expensive and luxurious British automobile.
3. **hors-d'oeuvre**: (French) small dishes served with cocktails or before a meal.
4. **no thin five-piece affair**: not a small band composed of only five musical instruments.
5. **a whole pitful of**: full of; the pit is the place where the musicians sit, usually in front of the stage.
6. **Castile**: a region of Spain, once an independent kingdom, renowned for its lace and embroidered shawls.
7. **innuendo**: allusive remark.
8. **like Frisco**: (slang) rapidly and vigorously; Frisco is short for San Francisco.
9. **the FOLLIES**: the Ziegfeld Follies, a satirical musical produced by Florence Ziegfeld, very popular in the 1920s. Gilda Gray was one of its famous stars.
10. **robin's-egg blue**: greenish blue.
11. **in the right key**: spoken in a right proper manner.
12. **to yield him up her person**: to yield up to him physically and mentally.
13. **East Egg, West Egg**: West Egg is where middle-class families live and the place Gatsby is living in; East Egg is where the eminent wealthy families live.

14. **Gothic**: a style of architecture which originated in France in the 12th century characterized by great height in the buildings, pointed arches, rib vaulting and large window space.
15. "**Stoddard Lecture**": a collection of lectures in ten volumes by John Lawson Stoddard (1850—1931), a famous American public lecturer and writer.
16. **bona-fide**: (Latin) genuine.
17. **This fella's**: This fellow is.
18. **Belasco**: David Belasco (1853—1931) American theatrical producer, manager and writer, known for his minutely detailed and spectacular stage settings.
19. **contralto**: woman singer with a lowest voice.
20. **old sport**: (slang) a friendly casual address to a person of any age.
21. **the lower East Side of New York**: a slum area of the City in the 1920s.
22. **echoladia**: the often pathological repetition of what is said by others as if echoing them.
23. **Carnegie Hall**: a famous concert-hall of the New York City named after its founder, Andrew Carnegie (1835—1919), American industrialist and patron of many cultural institutions.
24. **in a puppyish, convivial way**: in a playful and merry-making way.
25. **French bob**: hair that is cut short, a female hair style of the period in vogue, referring to a fashionable woman.
26. **in a quavering soprano**: in the highest, shaking singing voice.
27. **she sing the notes on her face**: her eye make-up mixed with tears leaves stains on her face, like musical notes.
28. **tantalizing you**: making you feel hopeful and excited, and then not allowing you to have what you want.

Study Questions
1. What kind of parties does Gatsby give on Saturdays according to the narrator?
2. What kind of people would attend the parties according to the narrator?
3. Why did Gatsby call the narrator "old sport"?
4. What is your impression on Gatsby after reading the text?

Essay Topics
1. Is Nick a reliable narrator? How does his point of view color the reality of the novel?
2. How does Gatsby represent the American dream? What does the novel have to say about the condition of the American dream in the 1920s?

5.8　William Faulkner

5.8.1　About the Author

William Faulkner (1897-1962) was born in New Albany, Mississippi. While he was still a child, the family moved to Oxford, Mississippi. Faulkner's education was irregular after the fifth grade. Although he attended high school for a period and later took courses at the University of Mississippi, he never earned a degree. In 1918 he was refused admission into the armed forces because of his size. Determined to fight in World War I, he enlisted in the Royal Canadian Air Force and had basic training in Toronto. But the war was over before he could make his first solo flight.

After the war he studied literature at the University of Mississippi for a short time. He published his first collection of poems entitled *The Marble Faun* in 1924. Despite his desire to be a poet, he had come to realize that his talent was for prose. In 1926 he published his first novel, *Soldier's Pay*. Then he traveled to Europe, where he learned the experimental writing of James Joyce and the psychoanalysis of Sigmund Freud, thus widening his vision further. In 1929 Faulkner published his most ambitious work, *The Sound and the Fury*, in which he portrayed the decline of an aristocratic family, by the technique of allowing the main characters to tell the story in internal monologues. His other four novels, *As I Lay Dying* (1930), *Light in August* (1932), *Absalom, Absalom*! (1936), and *Go Down, Moses* (1942), are all considered masterpieces of modernist fiction.

In 1929, Faulkner married Estelle Oldham, his childhood sweetheart, who had recently divorced her husband. Next year he purchased the traditional Southern pillared house in Oxford, which he named Rowan Oak. To earn money to support his wife and children, Faulkner worked over the next 20 years in Hollywood on several screenplays. Faulkner received the 1949 Nobel Prize for Literature and the 1954 Pulitzer Prize for his novel *The Fable*. During the last years of his life, besides his problems with alcohol, his wife's drug addiction and declining health shadowed his life.

As a writer, Faulkner depicts people facing the problems of living in modern society. He believed that human beings possess the ability to overcome overwhelming challenges by drawing on qualities that are distinctly human, including virtue, love, loyalty, and humor. His genius lies in the artistic union of the universal and the particular: the treatment of cosmic themes through vivid, sympathetic portraits of believable characters. Many of his novels are set in Yoknapatawpha county, an imaginary area in Mississippi with a colorful history and a richly varied population. Using the decay and corruption of the South after the American Civil War as a background, Faulkner portrayed the tragedy that occurred when the traditional values of a society disintegrated.

Faulkner was particularly noted for the eloquent richness of his prose style and for the unique blend of tragedy and humor in his works. He was also a brilliant literary technician, making frequent use of convoluted time sequences and of the stream-of-consciousness technique. He borrowed cinematic devices, experimented with multiple narrators, and interrupted simple stories with rambling interior monologues. The language of his characters is based on popular Southern speech, and can be foul, funny, brilliantly metaphorical, savage, and exciting. Thus, Faulkner has been considered America's greatest novelist in the modern period. The best of his fictions rank among the most enduring of world literature. In writing about his land and about man in the ageless, eternal struggles, Faulkner speaks for both his people and humanity.

5.8.2 *A Rose for Emily*

I

When Miss Emily Grierson died, our whole town went to her funeral: the men through a sort of respectful affection for a fallen monument[1], the women mostly out of curiosity to see the inside of her house, which no one save an old man-servant — a combined gardener and cook — had seen in at least ten years.

It was a big, squarish frame house that had once been white, decorated with cupolas and spires and scrolled balconies in the heavily lightsome style of the seventies[2], set on what had once been our most select street. But garages and cotton gins had encroached and obliterated even the august names of that neighborhood; only Miss Emily's house was left, lifting its stubborn and coquettish decay above the cotton wagons and the gasoline pumps — an eyesore among eyesores[3]. And now Miss Emily had gone to join the representatives of those august names where they lay in the cedar — bemused cemetery among the ranked and anonymous graves of Union and Confederate soldiers who fell at the battle of Jefferson.

Alive, Miss Emily had been a tradition, a duty, and a care; a sort of hereditary obligation upon the town, dating from that day in 1894 when Colonel Sartoris, the mayor — he who fathered the edict that no Negro woman should appear on the streets without an apron — remitted her taxes, the dispensation dating from the death of her father on into perpetuity. Not that Miss Emily would have accepted charity. Colonel Sartoris invented an involved tale to the effect that Miss Emily's father had loaned money to the

Chapter 5 The Literature of the Modernist Period

town, which the town, as a matter of business, preferred this way of repaying. Only a man of Colonel Sartoris generation and thought could have invented it, and only a woman could have believed it.

When the next generation, with its more modern ideas, became mayors and aldermen[4], this arrangement created some little dissatisfaction. On the first of the year they mailed her a tax notice. February came, and there was no reply. They wrote her a formal letter, asking her to call at the sheriff's office at her convenience. A week later the mayor wrote her himself, offering to call or to send his car for her, and received in reply a note on paper of an archaic shape, in a thin, flowing calligraphy in faded ink, to the effect that she no longer went out at all. The tax notice was also enclosed, without comment.

They called a special meeting of the Board of Aldermen. A deputation waited upon her, knocked at the door though which no visitor had passed since she ceased giving china-painting lessons eight or ten years earlier. They were admitted by the old Negro into a dim hall from which a stairway mounted into sill more shadow. It smelled of dust and disuse — a close, dank smell. The Negro led them into the parlor. It was furnished in heavy, leather-covered furniture. When the Negro opened the blinds of one window, they could see that the leather was cracked; and when they sat down, a faint dust rose sluggishly about their thighs, spinning with slow motes in the single sun-ray. On a tarnished gilt easel before the fireplace stood a crayon portrait of Miss Emily's father.

They rose when she entered — a small, fat woman in black, with a thin gold chain descending to her waist and vanishing into her belt, leaning on an ebony cane with a tarnished gold head. Her skeleton was small and spare; perhaps that was why what would have been merely plumpness in another was obesity in her[5]. She looked bloated, like a body long submerged in motionless water, and of that pallid hue. Her eyes, lost in the fatty ridges of her face, looked like two small pieces of coal pressed into a lump of dough as they moved from one face to another while the visitors stated their errand.

She did not ask them to sit. She just stood in the door and listened quietly until the spokesman came to a stumbling halt[6]. Then they could hear the invisible watch ticking at the end of the gold chain.

Her voice was dry and cold. "I have no taxes in Jefferson. Colonel Sartoris explained it to me. Perhaps one of you can gain access to the city records and satisfy yourselves."

"But we have. We are the city authorities, Miss Emily. Didn't you get a notice from the sheriff, signed by him?"

"I received a paper, yes," Miss Emily said. "Perhaps he considers himself the sheriff... I have no taxes in Jefferson."

"But there is nothing on the books to show that, you see. We must go by the —"

"See Colonel Sartoris. I have no taxes in Jefferson."

"But, Miss Emily —"

"See Colonel Sartoris." (Colonel Sartoris had been dead almost ten years.) "I have no taxes in Jefferson. Tobe!" The Negro appeared. "Show these gentlemen out."

II

So she vanquished them, horse and foot[7], just as she had vanquished their fathers thirty years before about the smell. That was two years after her father's death and a short time after her sweetheart — the one we believed would marry her — had deserted her. After her father's death she went out very little; after her sweetheart went away, people hardly saw her at all. A few of the ladies had the temerity to call, but were not received, and the only sign of life about the place was the Negro man — a young man then — going in and out with a market basket.

"Just as if a man — any man — could keep a kitchen properly," the ladies said; so they were not surprised when the smell developed. It was another link between the gross, teeming world and the high and mighty Griersons.

A neighbor, a woman, complained to the mayor, Judge Stevens, eighty years old.

"But what will you have me do about it, madam?" he said.

"Why, send her word to stop it," the woman said. "Isn't there a law?"

"I am sure that won't be necessary," Judge Stevens said. "It's probably just a snake or a rat that nigger of hers killed in the yard. I'll speak to him about it."

The next day he received two more complaints, one from a man who came in diffident deprecation. "We really must do something about it, Judge. I'd be the last one in the world to bother Miss Emily, but we've got to do something." That night the Board of Aldermen met — three graybeards and one younger man, a member of the rising generation.

"It's simple enough," he said. "Send her word to have her place cleaned up. Give her a certain time to do it in, and if she don't...."

"Dammit, sir," Judge Stevens said, "will you accuse a lady to her face of smelling bad?"

So the next night, after midnight, four men crossed Miss Emily's lawn and slunk about the house like burglars, sniffing along the base of the brickwork and at the cellar openings while one of them performed a regular sowing motion with his hand out of a sack slung from his shoulder. They broke open the cellar door and sprinkled lime there, and in all the outbuildings[8]. As they recrossed the lawn, a window that had been dark was lighted and Miss Emily sat in it, the light behind her, and her upright torso[9] motionless as that of an idol. They crept quietly across the lawn and into the shadow of the locusts that lined the street. After a week or two the smell went away.

That was when people had begun to feel really sorry for her. People in our town, remembering how old lady Wyatt, her great-aunt, had gone completely crazy at last, believed that the Griersons held themselves a little too high for what they really were. None of the young men were quite good enough for Miss Emily and such. We had long thought of them as a tableau. Miss Emily a slender figure in white in the background, her father a spraddled silhouette[10] in the foreground, his back to her and clutching a horsewhip, the two of them framed by the back-flung front door[11]. So when she got to be thirty and was still single, we were not pleased exactly, but vindicated; even with insanity in the family she wouldn't have turned down all of her chances if they had really materialized.

When her father died, it got about that the house was all that was left to her; and in a way, people were glad. At last they could pity Miss Emily. Being left alone, and a pauper, she had become humanized. Now she too would know the old thrill and the old despair of a penny more or less[12].

The day after his death all the ladies prepared to call at the house and offer condolence and aid, as is our custom. Miss Emily met them at the door, dressed as usual and with no trace of grief on her face. She told them that her father was not dead. She did that for three days, with the ministers calling on her, and the doctors, trying to persuade her to let them dispose of the body. Just as they were about to resort to law and force[13], she broke down, and they buried her father quickly.

We did not say she was crazy then. We believed she had to do that. We remembered all the young men her father had driven away, and we knew that with nothing left, she would have to cling to that which had robbed her, as people will.

III

She was sick for a long time. When we saw her again, her hair was cut short, making her look like a girl, with a vague resemblance to those angels in colored church windows — sort of tragic and serene.

The town had just let the contracts for paving the sidewalks, and in the summer after her father's death they began the work. The construction company came with niggers and mules and machinery, and a foreman named Homer Barron, a Yankee — a big, dark, ready man, with a big voice and eyes lighter than his face. The little boys would follow in groups to hear him cuss the niggers, and the niggers singing in time to the rise and fall of picks. Pretty soon he knew everybody in town. Whenever you heard a lot of laughing anywhere about the square, Homer Barron would be in the center of the group. Presently we began to see him and Miss Emily on Sunday afternoons driving in the yellow-wheeled buggy and the matched team of bays[14] from the livery stable.

At first we were glad that Miss Emily would have an interest, because the ladies all said, "Of course a Grierson would not think seriously of a Northerner, a day laborer."

But there were still others, older people, who said that even grief could not cause a real lady to forget *noblesse oblige*[15]— without calling it *noblesse oblige*. They just said, "Poor Emily. Her kinsfolk should come to her." She had some kin in Alabama; but years ago her father had fallen out with[16] them over the estate of old lady Wyatt, the crazy woman, and there was no communication between the two families. They had not even been represented at the funeral.

And as soon as the old people said, "Poor Emily," the whispering began. "Do you suppose it's really so?" they said to one another. "Of course it is. What else could..." This behind their hands[17]; rustling of craned silk and satin behind jalousies[18] closed upon the sun of Sunday afternoon as the thin, swift clop-clop-clop of the matched team passed: "Poor Emily."

She carried her head high enough — even when we believed that she was fallen[19]. It was as if she demanded more than ever the recognition of her dignity as the last Grierson; as if it had wanted that touch of earthiness to reaffirm her imperviousness[20]. Like when she bought the rat poison, the arsenic. That was over a year after they had begun to say "Poor Emily," and while the two female cousins were visiting her.

"I want some poison," she said to the druggist. She was over thirty then, still a slight woman, though thinner than usual, with cold, haughty black eyes in a face the flesh of which was strained across the temples and about the eye sockets as you imagine a lighthouse-keeper's face[21] ought to look. "I want some poison," she said.

"Yes, Miss Emily. What kind? For rats and such? I'd recom — "

"I want the best you have. I don't care what kind."

The druggist named several. "They'll kill anything up to an elephant. But what you want is — "

"Arsenic," Miss Emily said. "Is that a good one?"

"Is... arsenic? Yes, ma'am. But what you want — "

"I want arsenic."

The druggist looked down at her. She looked back at him, erect, her face like a strained flag. "Why, of course," the druggist said. "If that's what you want. But the law requires you to tell what you are going to use it for."

Miss Emily just stared at him, her head tilted back in order to look him eye for eye, until he looked away and went and got the arsenic and wrapped it up. The Negro delivery boy brought her the package; the druggist didn't come back. When she opened the package at home there was written on the box, under the skull and bones: "For rats."

IV

So the next day we all said, "She will kill herself"; and we said it would be the best thing. When she had first begun to be seen with Homer Barron, we had said, "She will marry him." Then we said, "She will persuade him yet," because Homer himself had remarked — he liked men, and it was known that he drank with the younger men in the Elks' Club — that he was not a marrying man. Later we said, "Poor Emily" behind the jalousies as they passed on Sunday afternoon in the glittering buggy, Miss Emily with her head high and Homer Barron with his hat cocked and a cigar in his teeth, reins and whip in a yellow glove.

Then some of the ladies began to say that it was a disgrace to the town and a bad example to the young people. The men did not want to interfere, but at last the ladies forced the Baptist minister — Miss Emily's people were Episcopal — to call upon her. He would never divulge what happened during that interview, but he refused to go back again. The next Sunday they again drove about the streets, and the following day the minister's wife wrote to Miss Emily's relations in Alabama.

So she had blood-kin under her roof again and we sat back to watch developments. At first nothing happened. Then we were sure that they were to be married. We learned that Miss Emily had been to the jeweler's and ordered a man's toilet set in silver, with the letters H. B. on each piece. Two days later we learned that she had bought a complete outfit of men's clothing, including a nightshirt, and we said, "They are married." We were really glad. We were glad because the two female cousins were even more Grierson than Miss Emily had ever been.

So we were not surprised when Homer Barron — the streets had been finished some time since — was gone. We were a little disappointed that there was not a public blowing-off[22], but we believed that he had gone on to prepare for Miss Emily's coming, or to give her a chance to get rid of the cousins. (By that time it was a cabal[23], and we were all Miss Emily's allies to help circumvent the cousins.) Sure enough, after another week they departed. And, as we had expected all along, within three days Homer Barron was back in town. A neighbor saw the Negro man admit him at the kitchen door at dusk one evening.

And that was the last we saw of Homer Barron. And of Miss Emily for some time. The Negro man went in and out with the market basket, but the front door remained closed. Now and then we would see her at the window for a moment, as the men did that night when they sprinkled the lime, but for almost six months she did not appear on the streets. Then we knew that this was to be expected too; as if that quality of her father which had thwarted her woman's life so many times had been too virulent and too furious to die.

When we next saw Miss Emily, she had grown fat and her hair was turning gray. During the next few years it grew grayer and grayer until it attained an even pepper-and-salt iron-gray, when it ceased turning. Up to the day of her death at seventy-four it was still that vigorous iron-gray, like the hair of an active man.

From that time on her front door remained closed, save for a period of six or seven years, when she was about forty, during which she gave lessons in china-painting. She fitted up a studio in one of the downstairs rooms, where the daughters and granddaughters of Colonel Sartoris' contemporaries were sent to her with the same regularity and in the same spirit that they were sent to church on Sundays with a twenty-five-cent piece for the collection plate[24]. Meanwhile her taxes had been remitted.

Then the newer generation became the backbone and the spirit of the town, and the painting pupils grew up and fell away and did not send their children to her with boxes of color and tedious brushes and pictures cut from the ladies' magazines. The front door closed upon the last one and remained closed for good. When the town got free postal delivery, Miss Emily alone refused to let them fasten the metal numbers above her door and attach a mailbox to it. She would not listen to them.

Daily, monthly, yearly we watched the Negro grow grayer and more stooped, going in and out with the market basket. Each December we sent her a tax notice, which would be returned by the post office a week later, unclaimed. Now and then we would see her in one of the downstairs windows — she had evidently shut up the top floor of the house — like the carven torso of an idol in a niche, looking or not looking at us, we could never tell which. Thus she passed from generation to generation — dear, inescapable, impervious, tranquil, and perverse.

And so she died. Fell ill in the house filled with dust and shadows, with only a doddering Negro man to wait on her. We did not even know she was sick; we had long since given up trying to get any information from the Negro. He talked to no one, probably not even to her, for his voice had grown harsh and rusty, as if from disuse.

She died in one of the downstairs rooms, in a heavy walnut bed with a curtain, her gray head propped on a pillow yellow and moldy with age and lack of sunlight.

V

The Negro met the first of the ladies at the front door and let them in, with their hushed, sibilant voices and their quick, curious glances, and then he disappeared. He walked right through the house and out the back and was not seen again.

The two female cousins came at once. They held the funeral on the second day, with the town coming to look at Miss Emily beneath a mass of bought flowers, with the crayon face of her father musing profoundly above the bier and the ladies sibilant and macabre[25]; and the very old men — some in their brushed Confederate uniforms — on the porch and the lawn, talking of Miss Emily as if she had been a contemporary of theirs, believing that they had danced with her and courted her perhaps, confusing time with its mathematical progression, as the old do, to whom all the past is not a diminishing road but, instead, a huge meadow which no winter ever quite touches, divided from them now by the narrow bottle-neck[26] of the most recent decade of years.

Already we knew that there was one room in that region above stairs which no one had seen in forty years, and which would have to be forced. They waited until Miss Emily was decently in the ground before they opened it.

The violence of breaking down the door seemed to fill this room with pervading dust. A thin, acrid pall as of the tomb seemed to lie everywhere upon this room decked and furnished as for a bridal: upon the valance curtains[27] of faded rose color, upon the rose-shaded lights, upon the dressing table, upon the delicate array of crystal and the man's toilet things backed with tarnished silver, silver so tarnished that the monogram[28] was obscured. Among them lay a collar and tie, as if they had just been removed, which, lifted, left upon the surface a pale crescent in the dust. Upon a chair hung the suit, carefully folded; beneath it the two mute shoes and the discarded socks.

The man himself lay in the bed.

For a long while we just stood there, looking down at the profound and fleshless grin. The body had apparently once lain in the attitude of an embrace, but now the long sleep that outlasts love, that conquers even the grimace of love, had cuckolded him[29]. What was left of him, rotted beneath what was left of the nightshirt, had become inextricable from the bed in which he lay; and upon him and upon the pillow beside him lay that even coating of the patient and biding dust.

Then we noticed that in the second pillow was the indentation of a head. One of us lifted something from it, and leaning forward, that faint and invisible dust dry and acrid in the nostrils, we saw a long strand of iron-gray hair.

Notes

1. **a fallen monument**: Emily is regarded as the symbol of tradition and the old way of life. Thus her death is like the falling of a monument.
2. **seventies**: Here it refers to the 1870's.
3. **an eyesore among eyesores**: the most unpleasant thing to look at.
4. **aldermen**: members of the city council.
5. **what would have been merely plumpness in another was obesity in her**: Because of her small frame, a little extra weight, which made women of larger frame look fat, made her look excessively fat.
6. **a stumbling halt**: a pause caused by hesitation in the speaking.
7. **horse and foot**: (idiom) completely.
8. **outbuildings**: buildings, e. g. a shed of stable, separate from the main building.
9. **her upright torso**: the trunk of her body in erect posture.
10. **a spraddled silhouette**: a dark image, whose legs are wide apart.
11. **framed by the back-flung front door**: The front door flung back and served as a frame for a picture.
12. **the old thrill and the old despair of a penny more or less**: the great excitement and

despair caused by the gain or loss of a small amount of money.
13. **resort to law and force**: make use of law and force for help.
14. **the matched team of bays**: a pair of reddish-brown horses.
15. **noblesse oblige**: (Fr.) noble obligation expected of people of high social position.
16. **fallen out with**: quarreled with and afterwards on bad terms with.
17. **This behind their hands**: They whispered gossips with their hands' covering the mouths.
18. **rustling of craned silk and satin**: the rustling sound of their silk and satin dresses caused by the movements.
19. **fallen**: morally degraded.
20. **that touch of earthiness to reaffirm her imperviousness**: the dignity to show that she was unaffected by the outside world.
21. **a lighthouse-keeper's face**: a face with the same strained and intense expression as a lighthouse-keeper's.
22. **a public blowing-off**: a big sensation.
23. **cabal**: a group of people who carry on secret intrigue.
24. **collection plate**: the plate used to collect money during a church service.
25. **the ladies sibilant and macabre**: the ladies whispering about the death.
26. **bottle-neck**: a short, narrow passage; here it refers to something that connects the past and the future.
27. **valance curtains**: short curtains around the frame of a bed.
28. **monogram**: a person's initials combined in one design.
29. **cuckolded him**: made him the man whose wife has committed adultery.

Study Questions
1. Under what kind of historical background does this story take place?
2. What are the major themes of this story?
3. What is the symbolical meaning of the "rose"?
4. Why is Miss Emily called "the fallen monument"?
5. What is the relationship between the past and the present reflected in this story?

5.9 Eugene O'Neill

5.9.1 About the Author

Eugene O'Neill (1888-1953) was born into a theatrical family in New York. At the age of seven he was sent to a Catholic boarding school. The strict rules and lack of emotional warmth at the school profoundly affected his future life. At the age of fourteen, O'Neill attended Betts Academy in Stamford, Connecticut. In 1906 he entered Princeton University, where he stayed only one year. Thereafter he drifted, doing all kinds of odd jobs in a variety of places. He also traveled widely, acquiring experiences that familiarized him with the life of sailors, stevedores, and the outcasts who populate many of his plays.

In 1912, ill with tuberculosis and haunted by his "rebellious dissipations," he reached a personal low point and even attempted suicide. Then he was sent to a sanatorium, where he had what he called his "rebirth." While spending five months there, he studied the master dramatists of the world and set out to become a playwright. After leaving the sanitarium, O'Neill studied the techniques of playwriting at Harvard University for one year under the famous theater scholar George Pierce Baker. He then moved to Greenwich Village, New York, where he became involved with an avant-garde group of artists and radicals. O'Neill's first full-length play to be produced was *Beyond the Horizon* (1920), a grim domestic drama set in New England. The play won the first Pulitzer Prize for O'Neill. Following the success of *Beyond the Horizon*, O'Neill went into an incredibly productive period, writing many of his greatest plays. A four-time Pulitzer Prize winner, O'Neill is the only American dramatist to date to win the Nobel Prize for literature (1936).

O'Neill, who drank heavily at times, battled ill health and depression throughout his adult life. During the last ten years of his life, he suffered from an undiagnosed neurological disorder that made writing difficult. However, his failing health did not prevent him from writing two of the greatest works the American stage has ever seen. *The Iceman Cometh* (1946) is a complex, ironic, deeply moving exploration of human existence, written out of a profound insight into human nature and constructed with tremendous skill and logic. *Long Day's Journey Into Night* (1956) is equally impressive. The play can be read autobiographically, since some parts of the story are closely based on O'Neill's own family. However, like most great works of literature, the play reaches beyond its immediate subject. As a product of hard-won art, *Long Day's Journey Into Night* has gained its status as a world classic and simultaneously marks the climax of O'Neill's literary career and the coming of age of American drama.

During all his career as a dramatist, O'Neill wrote and published about forty-nine plays altogether of various lengths. Most of them are tragedies, dealing with the basic issues of human existence and predicament: life and death, illusion and disillusion, alienation and communication, dream and reality, self and society, and desire and frustration. As a playwright, O'Neill was a technical innovator. He was constantly experimenting with new styles and forms for his plays, especially during the twenties when Expressionism was in full swing. Many of his plays are marked by new theatrical techniques and symbolic devices that express religious and philosophical ideas and give his characters psychological depth. Through his efforts, the American theatre grew up during the 1920s, developing into a cultural medium that could take its place with the best in American fiction, painting, and music. We can safely say that it is O'Neill who set the pace for the blossoming of the Broadway theatre.

5.9.2 An Excerpt from ACT 2, SCENE II of *Long Day's Journey into Night*

SCENE: The same, about a half hour later.[1] *The tray with the bottle of whiskey has been removed from the table. The family are returning from lunch as the curtain rises. Mary*[2] *is the first to enter from the back parlor. Her husband*[3] *follows. He is not with her as he was in the similar entrance after breakfast at the opening of Act One. He avoids touching her or looking at her. There is condemnation in his face, mingled now with the beginning of an old weary, helpless resignation.*[4] *Jamie*[5] *and Edmund*[6] *follow their father. Jamie's face is hard with defensive cynicism. Edmund tries to copy this defense but without success. He plainly shows he is heart-sick as well as physically ill.*

Mary is terribly nervous again, as if the strain of sitting through lunch with them had been too much for her. Yet at the same time, in contrast to this, her expression shows more of that strange aloofness which seems to stand apart from her nerves and the anxieties which harry them.

She is talking as she enters — a stream of words that issues casually, in a routine of family conversation, from her mouth. She appears indifferent to the fact that their thoughts are not on what she is saying any more than her own are. As she talks, she comes to the left of the table and stands, facing front, one hand fumbling with the bosom of her dress, the other playing over the table top. Tyrone lights a cigar and goes to the screen door, staring out. Jamie fills a pipe from a jar on top of the bookcase at rear. He lights it as he goes to look out the window at right. Edmund sits in a chair by the table, turned half away from his mother so he does not have to watch her.

MARY: It's no use finding fault with Bridget[7]. She doesn't listen. I can't threaten her, or she'd threaten she'd leave. And she does do her best at times. It's too bad they seem to be just the times you're sure to be late, James. Well, there's this consolation: It's difficult to tell from her cooking whether she's doing her best or her worst.

She gives a little laugh of detached amusement — indifferently.

Never mind. The summer will soon be over, thank goodness. Your season will open again and we can go back to second-rate hotels and trains. I hate them, too, but at least I don't expect them to be like a home, and there's no housekeeping to worry about. It's unreasonable to expect Bridger or Cathleen[8] to act as if this was a home. They know it isn't as well as we know it. It never has been and it never will be.

TYRONE: (*Bitterly without turning around.*) No, it never can be now. But it was once, before you —[9]

MARY: (*Her face instantly set in blank denial.*) Before I what?

There is a dead silence. She goes on with a return of her detached air.

No, no. Whatever you mean, it isn't true, dear. It was never a home. You've always preferred the Club or a barroom. And for me it's always been as lonely as a dirty room in a one-night stand hotel. In a real home one is never lonely. You forget I know from experience what a home is like. I gave up one to marry you — my father's home.

At once, through an association of ideas she turns to Edmund. Her manner becomes tenderly solicitous, but there is the strange quality of detachment in it.

I'm worried about you, Edmund. You hardly touched a thing at lunch. That's no way to take care of yourself. It's all right for me not to have an appetite. I've been growing too fat. But you must eat.

(*Coaxingly maternal.*) Promise me you will, dear, for my sake.

EDMUND: (*Dully.*) Yes, Mama.

MARY: (*Pats his cheek as he tries not to shrink away.*) That's a good boy.

There is another pause of dead silence. Then the telephone in the front hall rings and all of them stiffen startledly.

TYRONE: (*Hastily.*) I'll answer. McGuire[10] said he'd call me.

He goes out through the front parlor.

MARY: (*Indifferently.*) McGuire. He must have another piece of property on his list that no one would think of buying except your father. It doesn't matter any more, but it's always seemed to me your father could afford to keep on buying property but never to give me a home.

She stops to listen as TYRONE's voice is heard from the hall.

TYRONE: Hello. (*With forced heartiness.*) Oh, how are you, Doctor?

Jamie turns from the window. Mary's fingers play more rapidly on the table top. Tyrone's voice, trying to conceal, reveals that he is hearing bad news.

I see. (*Hurriedly.*) Well, you'll explain all about it when you see him this afternoon. Yes, he'll be in without fail. Four o'clock. I'll drop in myself and have a talk with you before that. I have to go uptown on business, anyway. Goodbye, Doctor.

EDMUND: (*Dully.*) That didn't sound like glad tiding.

Jamie gives him a pitying glance — then looks out the window again. Mary's face is terrified and her hands flutter distractedly. Tyrone comes in. The strain is obvious in his casualness as he addresses Edmund.

TYRONE: It was Doctor Hardy[11]. He wants you to be sure and see him at four.

EDMUND: (*Dully.*) What did he say? Not that I give a damn now.

MARY: (*Bursts out excitedly.*) I wouldn't believe him if he swore on a stack of Bibles. You mustn't pay attention to a word he says, EDMUND.

TYRONE: (*Sharply.*) Mary!

MARY: (*More excitedly.*) Oh, we all realized why you like him, James! Because he's cheap! But please don't try to tell me! I know all about Doctor Hardy. Heaven knows I ought to after all these years. He's an ignorant fool! There should be a law to keep men like him from practicing. He hasn't the slightest idea — When you're in agony and half insane, he sits and holds your hand and delivers sermons on will power!

Her face is drawn in an expression of intense suffering by the memory. For the moment, she loses all caution. With bitter hatred.

He deliberately humiliates you! He makes you beg and plead! He treats you like a criminal! He understands nothing! And yet it was exactly the same type of cheap quack who first gave you the medicine — and you never knew what it was until too late![12]

(*Passionately.*) I hate doctors! They'll do anything — anything to keep you coming to them. They'll sell their souls! What's worse, they'll sell yours, and you never know it till one day you find yourself in hell!

EDMUND: Mama! For God's sake, stop talking.

TYRONE: (*Shakenly.*) Yes, Mary, it's no time —

MARY: (*Suddenly is overcome by guilty confusion — stammers.*) I— Forgive me, dear. You're right. It's useless to be angry now.

There is again a pause of dead silence. When she speaks again, her face has cleared and is calm, and the quality of uncanny detachment is in her voice and manner.

I'm going upstairs for a moment, if you'll excuse me. I have to fix my hair.

(*She adds smilingly.*) That is if I can find my glasses. I'll be right down.

TYRONE: (*As she starts through the doorway — pleading and rebuking.*) Mary!

MARY: (*Turns to stare at him calmly.*) Yes, dear? What is it?

TYRONE: (*Helplessly.*) Nothing.

MARY: (*With a strange derisive smile.*) You're welcome to come up and watch me if you're so suspicious.

TYRONE: As if that could do any good! You'd only postpone it. And I'm not your jailor. This isn't prison.

MARY: No. I know you can't help thinking it's a home.

(*She adds quickly with a detached contrition.*) I'm sorry, dear. I don't mean to be bitter. It's not your fault.

She turns and disappears through the back parlor. The three in the room remain silent. It is as if they were waiting until she got upstairs before speaking.

JAMIE: (*Cynically brutal.*) Another shot in the arm!

EDMUND: (*Angrily.*) Cut out that kind of talk!

TYRONE: Yes! Hold your foul tongue and your rotten Broadway loafer's lingo[13]! Have you no pity or decency?

(*Losing his temper.*) You ought to be kicked out in the gutter! But if I did it, you know damned well who'd weep and plead for you, and excuse you and complain till I let you come back.

JAMIE: (*A spasm of pain crosses his face.*) Christ, don't I know that? No pity? I have all the pity in the world for her. I understand what a hard game to beat she's up against — which is more than you ever have! My lingo didn't mean I had no feeling. I was merely putting bluntly what we all know, and have to live with now, again.

(*Bitterly.*) The cures are no damned good except for a while. The truth is there is no cure and we've been saps to hope — (*Cynically.*) They[14] never come back!

EDMUND: (*Scornfully parodying his brother's cynicism.*) They never come back! Everything is in the bag! It's all a frame-up! We're all fall guys and suckers and we can't beat the game!

(*Disdainfully.*) Christ, if I felt the way you do — !

JAMIE: (*Stung for a moment — then shrugging his shoulders, dryly.*) I thought you did. Your poetry isn't very cheery. Nor the stuff you read and claim you admire.

(*He indicates the small bookcase at rear.*) Your pet with the unpronounceable name, for example.

EDMUND: Nietzsche[15]. You don't know what you're talking about. You haven't read him.

JAMIE: Enough to know it's a lot of bunk!

TYRONE: Shut up, both of you! There's little choice between the philosophy you learned from Broadway loafers, and the one Edmund got from his books. They're both rotten to the core. You've both flouted the faith you were born and brought up in — the one true faith of the Catholic Church — and your denial has brought nothing but self-destruction!

His two sons stare at him contemptuously. They forget their quarrel and are as one against him on this issue.

EDMUND: That's the bunk[16], Papa!

JAMIE: We don't pretend, at any rate.

(*Caustically.*) I don't notice you've worn any holes in the knees of your pants going to Mass.

TYRONE: It's true I'm a bad Catholic in the observance, God forgive me. But I believe!

(*Angrily.*) And you're a liar! I may not go to church but every night and morning of my life I get on my knees and pray!

EDMUND: (*Bitingly.*) Did you pray for Mama?

TYRONE: I did. I've prayed to God these many years for her.

EDMUND: Then Nietzsche must be right.

(*He quotes from Thus Spake Zarathustra*[17].) "God is dead: of His pity for man hath God died."

TYRONE: (*Ignores this.*) If your mother had prayed, too — She hasn't denied her faith, but she's forgotten it, until now there's no strength of the spirit left in her to fight against her curse.

(*Then dully resigned.*) But what's the good of talk? We've lived with this before and now we must again. There's no help for it.

(*Bitterly.*) Only I wish she hadn't led me to hope this time. By God, I never will again!

EDMUND: That's a rotten thing to say, Papa!

(*Defiantly.*) Well, I'll hope! She's just started. It can't have got a hold on her yet. She can still stop. I'm going to talk to her.

JAMIE: (*Shrugs his shoulders.*) You can't talk to her now. She'll listen but she won't listen. She'll be here but she won't be here, you know the way she gets.

TYRONE: Yes, that's the way the poison acts on her always. Every day from now on, there'll be the same drifting away from us until by the end of each night —

EDMUND: (*Miserably.*) Cut it out, Papa!

(*He jumps up from his chair.*) I'm going to get dressed.

(*Bitterly, as he goes.*) I'll make so much noise she can't suspect I've come to spy on her.

He disappears through the front parlor and can be heard stamping noisily upstairs.

JAMIE: (*After a pause.*) What did Doc Hardy say about the Kid?

TYRONE: (*Dully.*) It's what you thought. He's got consumption[18].

JAMIE: God damn it!

TYRONE: There is no possible doubt, he said.

JAMIE: He'll have to go to a sanatorium.

TYRONE: Yes, and the sooner the better, Hardy said, for him and everyone around him. He claims that in six months to a year Edmund will be cured, if he obeys orders.

(*He sighs — gloomily and resentfully.*)

I never thought a child of mine — It doesn't come from my side of the family. There wasn't one of us that didn't have lungs as strong as an ox.

JAMIE: Who gives a damn about that part of it! Where does Hardy want to send him?

TYRONE: That's what I'm to see him about.

JAMIE: Well, for God's sake, pick out a good place and not some cheap dump[19]!

TYRONE: (*Stung.*) I'll send him wherever Hardy thinks best!

JAMIE: Well, don't give Hardy your old over-the-hills-to-the-poorhouse song about taxes and mortgages.

TYRONE: I'm no millionaire who can throw money away! Why shouldn't I tell Hardy the truth?

JAMIE: Because he'll think you want him to pick a cheap dump, and because he'll know it isn't the truth — especially if he hears afterwards you've seen McGuire and let that flannel-mouth, gold-brick merchant ting you with another piece of bum[20] property!

TYRONE: (*Furiously.*) Keep your nose out of my business!

JAMIE: This is Edmund's business. What I'm afraid of is, with your Irish bogtrotter idea that consumption is fatal, you'll figure it would be a waste of money to spend any more than you can help.

TYRONE: You liar!

JAMIE: All right. Prove I'm a liar. That's what I want. That's why I brought it up.

TYRONE: (*His rage still smouldering.*) I have every hope Edmund will be cured. And keep your dirty tongue off Ireland! You're a fine one to sneer, with the map of it on your face[21]!

JAMIE: Not after I wash my face.

Then before his father can react to this insult to the old Sod, he adds dryly, shrugging his shoulders.

Well, I've said all I have to say. It's up to you.

(*Abruptly.*) What do you want me to do this afternoon, now you're going uptown? I've done all I can do on the hedge until you cut more of it. You don't want me to go ahead with your clipping, I know that.

TYRONE: No. You'd get it crooked, as you get everything else.

JAMIE: Then I'd better go uptown with Edmund. The bad news coming on top of what's happened to Mama may hit him hard.

TYRONE: (*Forgetting his quarrel.*) Yes, go with him, Jamie. Keep up his spirits, if you can.

(*He adds caustically.*) If you can without making it an excuse to get drunk!

JAMIE: What would I use for money? The last I heard they were still selling booze, not giving it away.

(*He starts for the front-parlor doorway.*) I'll get dressed.

He stops in the doorway as he sees his mother approaching from the hall, and moves aside to let her come in. Her eyes look brighter, and her manner is more detached. This change becomes more marked as the scene goes on.

MARY: (*Vaguely.*) You haven't seen my glasses anywhere, have you, Jamie?

She doesn't look at him. He glances away, ignoring her question but she doesn't seem to expect an answer, she comes forward, addressing her husband without looking at him.

You haven't seen them, have you, James?

Behind her Jamie disappears through the front parlor.

TYRONE: (*Turns to look out the screen door.*) No, Mary.

MARY: What's the matter with Jamie? Have you been nagging at him again? You shouldn't treat him with such contempt all the time. He's not to blame. If he'd been brought up in a real home, I'm sure he would have been different.

...

Notes

1. **The same, about a half hour later:** The sitting room of the summer home of the Tyrone family, about 1:30 p.m., one day in August 1912.
2. **Mary:** Mary Tyrone, a handsome, nervous woman.
3. **Her husband:** James Tyrone, an aging former matinee idol, regarded as a miser.
4. This sentence shows that James has found by now that Mary, recently released from an institution as cured of her drug addiction, is in fact not cured.
5. **Jamie:** the eldest son of Mary and James at 33, a hard-drinking, cynical Broadway hanger-on.
6. **Edmund:** the youngest son of Mary and James, a sickly, morbid intellectual.
7. **Bridget:** the cook of the Tyrone family.
8. **Cathleen:** the housemaid.
9. **before you:** before you went on drugs.
10. **McGuire:** a real estate businessman.
11. **Doctor Hardy:** a quack doctor chosen by James to treat Mary.
12. Mary recalls how Hardy, a cheap quack, treated her with morphine after her sickness in giving birth to Edmund and made her go on drugs.
13. **Broadway loafer's lingo:** Broadway loafer's jargon that we are not familiar with.
14. **they:** the healthy and happy days.
15. **Nietzsche:** Friedrich Wilhelm Nietzsche (1844-1900), German philosopher and poet.
16. **bunk:** (slang) buncombe.
17. ***Thus Spake Zarathustra:*** (Also *sprach Zarathustra*, published between 1883 and 1885), one of the important books written by Nietzsche, a rhapsodical series of sermons of an imaginary prophet, written in a poetic prose modeled on that of the Bible.
18. **consumption:** tuberculosis of the lungs, a wasting disease.
19. **dump:** (slang) an ugly, run-down place.
20. **bum:** (colloq.) a loafer; vagrant.
21. **with the map of it on your face:** your face presents the striking features of an Irishman.

Chapter 5 The Literature of the Modernist Period

Study Questions

1. How do drugs and alcohol function within the play?
2. Which member of the family has gone wrong?
3. What problems in a family are presented in this play?

Essay Topics

1. What are the major conflicts in the play? How, if at all, are they resolved?
2. Discuss O'Neill's use of broken dreams in the play. What do they mean to the characters, and what do they symbolize?

Chapter 6 The Literature since World War II

6.1 An Introduction

The United States emerged from World War II in excellent economic shape. In sharp contrast to the economic devastation and loss of human life of its allies like Great Britain and the former Soviet Union, American territory had not been damaged from the ravages of war. In the postwar years, America experienced fast economic growth and enjoyed a long period of prosperity. It can be safely said that the postwar period is characterized as an era during which the United States attained unprecedented levels of political, economic, and military power on a global scale. Americans increasingly dedicated to a materialistic standard of living in the second half of the twentieth century. Suburbs and corporations grew, families became more mobile in search of better-paying jobs, and the center of the population moved westward along newly constructed highways. The change that most transformed American society, however, was the rise of the mass media and mass culture. First radio, then movies, and now an all-powerful television presence changed greatly the way of American life at its roots, giving rise to mass consumerism in an urban society.

However, there were crises of course — for example, the anti-Communist McCarthy hearings and the Cold War with the former Soviet Union, which gave rise to a mutual fear and hostility. Besides, the Korean War in the early 1950s and the Vietnam War in the 1960s broadened the gap between the government and the people. The assassination of John F. Kennedy and of Martin Luther King, and Nixon's Water-Gate scandal intensified the terror and tossed the whole nation again into grief and despair. The Civil Rights movement in the 1950s and 1960s and the feminist movement of the 1960s and 1970s left extensive and enduring effects on the people, inspiring American ethnic minorities to fight for their own rights. The American young people were not satisfied with traditional values and rebelled in various ways. One typical example is the Hippies. They rebelled against traditional values, rejected what they viewed as Western materialism, and practiced a kind of nonviolent anarchy. They grew long hair and beards, wore strange clothes, smoked marijuana and advocated free sex. Another anti-cultural group of the 1960s was the Yippies who opposed capitalism, demanded an end to racism and the Vietnam War, and advocated "sex and drugs and rock 'n' roll".

Literature in the postwar United States was likewise dazzlingly diverse, exciting, and evolving. New voices arose from many quarters, challenging old ideas and adapting literary traditions to suit changing conditions of the national life. American fiction from 1945 onwards was a bigger story than poetry and drama. First of all, a group of new writers who survived the war wrote about their traumatic experience within the military machine. Norman Mailer and Herman Wouk might be examples of this group. Robert Penn Warren and Flannery O'Conner were representatives of the talented southern writers, who followed Faulkner's footsteps in portraying the decadence and evil in the Southern society. By the 1950s a significant group of Jewish-American writers had appeared and one of them was Saul Bellow. Their work, drawing on the Jewish experience and tradition, examined subtly the dismantling of the self by an intolerable modern history. Black fiction began to attract critical attention during this period too. The two major figures were Richard Wright and Ralph Ellison, both of whom captured the wide attention of the white readers by truthfully, openly, and shockingly describing the life of black people as they knew it from their own experience. For the first time in the history of American writings, African-Americans started to question their identity as a group and as an individual. Other important writers who were writing at the time include J. D. Salinger and John Updike. Salinger is considered to be a spokesman for the alienated youth in the post-war era and his *The Catcher in the Rye* (1951) is regarded as a students' classic. Updike's Rabbit novels examine the middle-class values and portray the troubled relationships in people's private life and their internal decay under the stress of the modern times.

American Fiction in the 1960s and 1970s proves to be different from its predecessors in that the writers started to depart from the conventions of the novel writing and experimented with some new forms. Hence, it is always referred to as "new fiction", with Kurt Vonnegut, Joseph Heller, John Bath, and Thomas Pynchon at its forefront. Roughly speaking, these writers shared almost the same belief that human beings are trapped in a meaningless world and that neither God nor man can make sense of the human condition. What's more, this absurdist vision is integrated with an absurd form, which is characterized by comic exaggerations, ironic uses of parodies, multiple realities, often two-dimensional characters, and a combination of fantastic events with realistic presentations.

Like fiction, poetry also flourished in various forms in the postwar period. Lots of poets actively took part in all kinds of political or literary movements with their pens, to express their views, to utter their uneasiness about the uses of social power and industrial power, in poems. "The Beats" of the 1950s took Ginsburg's *Howl* as their manifesto and deliberately punned downtrodden elements in society, including radicalism and homosexuality. Poets in the 1960s identified with political causes such as the black power movement, women's liberation, the antiwar movement, and gay rights. They also adopted new forms in their poetry writing, emphasizing the importance of exposing rather than composing the self. Postmodern poetry, as it emerged, was skeptical of single versions of reality; instead, it became increasingly pluralistic. During this period, poets drew inspiration from minority, as well as international cultural forms, in creating new poetic styles as well as new poetic content. In addition, they borrowed techniques from film and video technology such as jump cuts, shifting angles, split screens, and open-endedness to create new poetic styles that questioned the very categories of knowledge production. They also became more visible in American public life, offering public readings, workshops, and conferences. The most extraordinary poets of this period are Theodore Roethke, Robert Lowell, Richard Wilbur, Richard Eberhart, Allen Ginsberg, Gary Snyder, Sylvia Plath, and Delmore Schwarts.

During the postwar period, American drama had a hard life under the squeeze of movies and television. However, new and young playwrights waded on with unremitting efforts. They were struggling to broaden the ways and forms of theatrical language in the narrowing art space. Two playwrights emerged who would dominate dramatic activity for the next 15 years or so: Arthur Miller and Tennessee Williams. Miller combined realistic characters and a social agenda while writing modern tragedy, most notably in *Death of a Salesman* (1949), a tale of the life and death of the ordinary working man Willy Loman. Williams contributed many plays about social misfits and outsiders. His play, *A Streetcar Named Desire* (1947), is concerned about a neurotic, impoverished Southern woman who fights to maintain her illusions of gentility when forced to confront the truth about her life by her sister's working-class husband. In the late 1950s African American playwriting received a tremendous boost with the highly acclaimed *Raisin in the Sun* (1959), which, written by Lorraine Hansberry, was the story of a black family and how they handle a financial windfall. Edward Albee introduced the tradition of the Theater of the Absurd in *The Zoo Story* (1958), catching the American imagination with their psychological danger and intelligent dialogue. *The Serpent* (1968) by Jean-Claude Van Itallie recreated Biblical stories through the depiction of modern events such as the assassination of John F. Kennedy. Megan Terry's play, *Calm Down Mother* (1965), experimented with traditional dramatic structure through actor transformations. Sam Shepard and David Mamet loomed large in American drama of the 1970s and 1980s with *Buried Child* (1978) and *Glengarry Glen Ross* (1983) as their represented works.

More recently American literature is alive with a diversity of interests. Writers from different ethnic and multicultural backgrounds, including women writers, African-Americans, Asian-Americans, and Latino-Americans, are beginning to make their voices heard and they are writing about American experience and consciousness from quite a fresh outlook, hence bringing vitality to the American literary creation.

6.2 Saul Bellow

6.2.1 About the Author

Saul Bellow (1915-2005) was born in a working-class suburb of Montreal, Canada. His parents were Jewish immigrants from Russia. The family moved to Chicago, USA in 1924. Bellow attended Lafayette School, Columbus Elementary School, and Sabin Junior

High. In 1933 Bellow entered the University of Chicago, but transferred to Northwestern University, where he studied anthropology and sociology and graduated in 1937. Then he taught at Pestalozzi-Froebel Teachers' College, Chicago, from 1938 to 1942. During World War II, Bellow joined in the Merchant Marine of the United States. While in the service, he wrote his first novel *The Dangling Man* (1944), which deals with the anxiety and discomfort of a young man waiting to be drafted in wartime. At the beginning of his career, Bellow was influenced by Trotskyism and the Partisan Review group of intellectuals. He became engaged with a wide range of cultural fields and tradition — Nietzsche, Oedipal conflicts, popular culture, and Russian-Jewish heritage.

After the war, Bellow returned to teaching, holding various posts at the Universities of Minnesota, New York, Princeton and Puerto Rico. From 1948 to 1950, he wrote and worked in Paris, traveled in Europe, and began work on *The Adventures of Augie March*, which gave a vivid, often humorous picture of Jewish life in Chicago and of a young man's search for identity. The novel appeared in 1956 and won him the first National Book Award. His next major work, *Seize the Day* (1956) is a novella concerning the theme of modern humanity, threatened with loss of identity but not destroyed in spirit. *Henderson the Rain King* (1959) told the story of a millionaire who travels to Africa, searching in vain for a meaning in his life. *Herzog* (1964), which was inspired by Bellow's failed marriage, centers on a middle-aged Jewish intellectual, Moses E. Herzog, who has experienced a spiritual and emotional paralysis, triggered by the breakup of his marriage and his contemplation of the wasteland of modern life. Bellow's subsequent works include *To Jerusalem and Back* (1976), *The Dean's December* (1982), *More Die of Heartbreak* (1987), and *Ravelstein* (2000). He published also short stories and plays. In 1976 Bellow won the Nobel Prize for Literature. He also received the Pulitzer Prize (1976), and three National Book Awards.

Bellow is one of the greatest American novelists of the second half of the 20th century. No other post-WW II American writer has analyzed so completely and so humanely the effects of American cultural anxiety with the age of technology and rationalism, existentialism, and the legacy of high modernism. Bellow's protagonist is invariably an Everyman whose primary function is to embody the progress of a state of mind. To bring his characters alive, Bellow has developed a style of dialogue that actually reflects the rhythms and sounds of living conversation. The short, terse, explosive speech patterns, which are sprinkled with colloquialisms, ring true to his character and the occasion. Distance and point of view are employed in Bellow's narrative, mostly first-person, to create a dual vision for the sake of his thematic concern. Besides, the narrative, usually in the confessional mode of autobiography, journal, memoir, or letter, gives the reader an insight into the deeper layers of the protagonist's consciousness in the midst of flux.

6.2.2　An Excerpt from *Seize the Day*

Ass! Idiot! Wild boar! Dumb mule! Slave! Lousy, wallowing hippopotamus! Wilhelm called himself as his bending legs carried him from the dining room. His pride! His inflamed feelings! His begging and feebleness! And trading insults with his old father — and spreading confusion over everything. Oh, how poor, contemptible, and ridiculous he was! When he remembered how he had said, with great reproof, "You ought to know your own son," — Why, how corny[1] and abominable it was.

He could not get out of the sharply brilliant dining room fast enough. He was horribly worked up[2]; his neck and shoulders, his entire chest ached as though they had been tightly tied with ropes. He smelled the salt odor of tears in his nose.

But at the same time, since there were depths in Wilhelm not unsuspected by himself, he received a suggestion from some remote element in his thoughts that the business of life, the real business — to carry his peculiar burden, to feel shame and importance, to taste these quelled tears — the only important business, the highest business was being done. Maybe the making of mistakes expressed the very purpose of his life and the essence of his being here. Maybe he was supposed to make them and suffer from them on this earth. And though he had raised himself above Mr. Perls and his father because they adored money, still they were called to act energetically and this was better than to yell and cry, pray and beg, poke and blunder and go by fits and starts[3] and fall upon the thorns[4] of life, and finally sink beneath that watery floor — would that be tough luck, or would it be good riddance[5]?

But he raged once more against his father. Other people with money, while they're still alive, want to see it do some good. Granted, he shouldn't support me. But have I ever asked him to do that? Have I ever asked for dough at all, either for Margaret or for the kids or for myself? It isn't the money, but only the assistance; not even assistance, but just the feeling. But he may be trying to teach me that a grown man should be cured of such feeling. Feeling got me in dutch[6] at Rojax. I had the feeling that I belonged to the firm, and my feelings were hurt when they put Gerber in over me. Dad thinks I'm too simple. But I'm not so simple as he thinks. What about his feelings? He doesn't forget death for one single second, and that's what makes him like this. And not only is death on his mind but through money he forces me to think about it, too. It gives him power over me. He forces me that way, he himself, and then he's sore. If he was poor, I could care for him and show it. The way I could care, too, if I only had a chance. He'd see

Chapter 6 The Literature since World War II

how much love and respect I had in me. It would make him a different man, too. He'd put his hands on me and give me his blessing.

Someone in a gray straw hat with a wide cocoa-colored band spoke to Wilhelm in the lobby. The light was dusky, splotched with red underfoot; green, the leather furniture; yellow, the indirect lighting.

"Hey, Tommy. Say, there."

"Excuse me," said Wilhelm, trying to reach a house phone. But this was Dr. Tamkin, whom he was just about to call.

"You have a very obsessional look on your face," said Dr. Tamkin.

Wilhelm thought. Here he is, here he is. If I could only figure this guy out.

"Oh," he said to Tamkin. "Have I got such a look? Well, whatever it is, you name it and I'm sure to have it."

The sight of Dr. Tamkin brought his quarrel with his father to a close. He found himself flowing into another channel.

"What are we doing?" he said. "What's going to happen to lard today?"

"Don't worry yourself about that. All we have to do is hold on to it and it's sure to go up. But what's made you so hot under the collar[7], Wilhelm?"

"Oh, one of those family situations." This was the moment to take a new look at Tamkin, and he viewed him closely but gained nothing by the new effort. It was conceivable that Tamkin was everything that he claimed to be, and all the gossip false. But was he a scientific man, or not? If he was not, this might be a cause for the district attorney's office to investigate. Was he a liar? That was a delicate question. Even a liar might be trustworthy in some ways. Could he trust Tamkin — could he? He feverishly, fruitlessly sought an answer.

But the time for his question was past, and he had to trust him now. After a long struggle to come to a decision, he had given him the money. Practical judgment was in abeyance[8]. He had worn himself out, and the decision was no decision. How had this happened? But how had his Hollywood career begun? It was not because of Maurice Venice, who turned out to be a pimp[9]. It was because Wilhelm himself was ripe for the mistake. His marriage, too, had been like that. Through such decisions somehow his life had taken from. And so, from the moment when he tasted the peculiar flavor of fatality in Dr. Tamkin, he could no longer keep back the money.

Five days ago Tamkin had said, "Meet me tomorrow, and we'll go to the market." Wilhelm, therefore, had had to go. At eleven o'clock they had walked to the brokerage office. On the way, Tamkin broke the news to Wilhelm that though this was an equal partnership he couldn't put up his half of the money just yet; it was tied up for a week or so in one of his patents. Today he would be two hundred dollars short; next week, he'd make it up. But neither of them needed an income from the market, of course. This was only a sporting[10] proposition anyhow, Tamkin said. Wilhelm had to answer, "Of

219

course." It was too late to withdraw. What else could he do? Then came the formal part of the transaction, and it was frightening. The very shade of green of Tamkin's check looked wrong; it was a false, disheartening color. His handwriting was peculiar, even monstrous; the e's were like i's, the t's and i's the same, and the h's like wasps' bellies. He wrote like a fourth-grader. Scientists, however, dealt mostly in symbols; they printed. This was Wilhelm's explanation.

Dr. Tamkin had given him his check for three hundred dollars. Whilhelm, in a blinded and convulsed aberration, pressed and pressed to try to kill[11] the trembling of his hand as he wrote out his check for a thousand. He set his lips tight, crouched with his huge back over the table, and wrote with crumbling, terrified fingers, knowing that if Tamkin's check bounced[12] his own would not be honored either. His sole cleverness was to set the date ahead by one day to give the green check time to clear.

Next he had signed a power of attorney[13], allowing Tamkin to speculate with his money, and this was an even more frightening document. Tamkin had never said a word about it, but here they were and it had to be done.

After delivering his signatures, the only precaution Wilhelm took was to come back to the manager of the brokerage office and ask him privately, "Uh, about Doctor Tamkin. We were in here a few minutes ago, remember?"

That day had been a weeping, smoky one and Wilhelm had gotten away from Tamkin on the pretext of having to run to the post office. Tamkin had gone to lunch alone, and here was Wilhelm, back again, breathless, his hat dripping, needlessly asking the manager if he remembered.

"Yes, sir, I know", the manager had said. He was a cold, mild, lean German who dressed correctly and around his neck wore a pair of opera glasses with which he read the board. He was an extremely correct person except that he never shaved in the morning, not caring, probably, how he looked to the fumblers and the old people and the operators and the gamblers and the idlers of Broadway uptown. The market closed at three. Maybe, Wilhelm guessed, he had a thick beard and took a lady out to dinner later and wanted to look fresh-shaven.

"Just a question," said Wilhelm. "A few minutes ago I signed a power of attorney so Doctor Tamkin could invest for me. You gave me the blanks."

"Yes, sir, I remember."

"Now this is what I want to know," Wilhelm had said. "I'm no lawyer and I only gave the paper a glance. Does this give Doctor Tamkin power of attorney over any other assets of mine — money, or property?"

The rain had dribbled from Wilhelm's deformed, transparent raincoat; the buttons of his shirt, which always seemed tiny, were partly broken, in pearly quarters of the moon, and some of the dark, thick golden hairs that grew on his belly stood out. It was the manager's business to conceal his opinion of him; he was shrewd, gray, correct (although unshaven) and had little to say except on matters that came to his desk. He must have recognized in Wilhelm a man who reflected long and then made the decision he had rejected twenty separate times. Silvery, cook, level, long-profiled, experienced, indifferent, observant, with unshaven refinement, he scarcely looked at Wilhelm, who trembled with fearful awkwardness. The manager's face, low-colored, long-nostriled, acted as a unit of perception; his eyes merely did their reduced share. Here was a man, like Rubin, who knew and knew and knew. He, a foreigner, knew; Wilhelm, in the city of his birth, was ignorant.

The manager had said, "No, sir, it does not give him."

"Only over the funds I deposited with you?"

"Yes, that is right, sir."

"Thank you, that's what I wanted to find out," Wilhelm had said, grateful.

The answer comforted him. However, the question had no value. None at all. For Wilhelm had no other assets. He had given Tamkin his last money. There wasn't enough of it to cover his obligations anyway, and Wilhelm had reckoned that he might as well go bankrupt now as next month. "Either broke or rich," was how he had figured, and that formula had encouraged him to make the gamble. Well, not rich; he did not expect that, but perhaps Tamkin might really show him how to earn what he needed in the market. By now, however, he had forgotten his own reckoning and was aware only that he stood to lose his seven hundred dollars to the last cent.

Dr. Tamkin took the attitude that they were a pair of gentlemen experimenting with lard and grain futures[14]. The money, a few hundred dollars, meant nothing much to either of them. He said to Wilhelm, "Watch. You'll get a big kick out of this[15] and wonder why more people don't go into it. You think the Wall Street guys are so smart — geniuses? That's because most of us are psychologically afraid to think about the details. Tell me this. When you're on the road, and you don't understand what goes on under the hood of your car, you'll worry what'll happen if something goes wrong with the engine. Am I wrong?" No, he was right, "Well," said Dr. Tamkin with an expression of quiet triumph about his mouth, almost the suggestion of a jeer. "It's the same psychological principle, Wilhelm. They are rich because you don't understand what goes on. But it's no mystery, and by putting in a little money and applying certain principles of observation, you begin to grasp it. It can't be studied in the abstract. You have to take a specimen risk[16] so that you feel the process, the money-flow, the whole complex. To know how it feels to be a seaweed you have to get in the water. In a very short time we'll take out a hundred-percent profit." Thus Wilhelm had had to pretend at the outset that his interest in the market was theoretical.

"Well," said Tamkin when he met him now in the lobby, "what's the problem, what is this family situation? Tell me." He put himself forward as the keen mental scientist. Whenever this happened Wilhelm didn't know what to reply. No matter what he said or did it seemed that Dr. Tamkin saw through him.

"I had some words with my dad."

Dr. Tamkin found nothing extraordinary in this. "it's the eternal same story," he said. "The elemental conflict of parent and child. It won't end, ever. Even with a fine old gentleman like your dad."

"I don't suppose it will. I've never been able to get anywhere with him[17]. He objects to my feelings. He thinks they're sordid. I upset him and he gets mad at me. But maybe all old men are alike."

"Sons, too, take it from one of them," said Dr. Tamkin. "All the same, you should be proud of such a fine old patriarch of a father. It should give you hope. The longer he lives, the longer your life-expectancy becomes."

Wilhelm answered, brooding, "I guess so. But I think I inherit more from my mother's side, and she died in her fifties."

"A problem arose between a young fellow I'm treating and his dad — I just had a consultation," said Dr. Tamkin as he removed his dark gray hat.

"So early in the morning?" said Wilhelm with suspicion.

"Over the telephone, of course."

What a creature Tamkin was when he took off his hat! The indirect light showed the many complexities of his bald skull, his gull's nose, his rather handsome eyebrows, his vain mustache, his deceiver's brown eyes. His figure was stocky, rigid, short in the neck, so that the large ball of the occiput touched his collar. His bones were peculiarly formed, as though twisted twice where the ordinary human bone was turned only once, and his shoulders rose in two pagoda-like points. At midbody he was thick. He stood pigeon-toed[18], a sign perhaps that he was devious or had much to hide. The skin of his hands was aging, and his nails were moonless, concave, clawlike, and they appeared loose. His eyes were as brown as beaver fur and full of strange lines. The two large brown naked balls looked thoughtful — but were they? And honest — but was Dr. Tamkin honest? There was a hypnotic power in his eyes, but this was not always of the same strength, nor was Wilhelm convinced that it was completely natural. He felt that Tamkin tried to make his eyes deliberately conspicuous, with studied[19] art, and that he brought forth his hypnotic effect by an exertion[20]. Occasionally it failed or drooped, and when this happened, the sense of his face passed downward to his heavy (possibly foolish?) red underlip.

Wilhelm wanted to talk about the lard holdings, but Dr. Tamkin said, "This father-and-son case of mine would be instructive to you. It's a different psychological type completely than your dad. This man's father thinks that he isn't his son."

"Why not?"

"Because he has found out something about the mother carrying on with a friend of the family for twenty-five years."

"Well, what do you know!" said Wilhelm. His silent thought was pure bull. Nothing but bull!

"You must note how interesting the woman is, too. She had two husbands. Whose are the kids? The fellow detected her and she gave a signed confession that two of the four children were not the father's."

"It's amazing," said Wilhelm, but he said it in a rather distant way. He was always hearing such stories from Dr. Tamkin. If you were to believe Tamkin, most of the world was like this. Everybody in the hotel had a mental disorder, a secret history, a concealed disease. The wife of Rubin at the newsstand was supposed to be kept by Carl, the yelling, loud-mouthed gin-rummy player. The wife of Frank in the barbershop had disappeared with a GL[21] while he was waiting for her to disembark at the French Lines pier. Everyone was like the faces on a laying card, upside down either way. Every public figure had a character-neurosis. Maddest of all were the businessmen, the heartless, flaunting, boisterous business class who ruled this country with their hard manners and their bold lies and their absurd words that nobody could believe. They were crazier than anyone. They spread the plague. Wilhelm, thinking of the Rojax Corporation, was inclined to agree that many businessmen were insane. And he supposed that Tamkin, for all his peculiarities, spoke a kind of truth and did some people a sort of good. It confirmed Wilhelm's suspicions to hear that there was a plague, and he said, "I couldn't agree with you more. They trade on anything, they steal everything, they're cynical right to the bones."

"You have to realize," said Tamkin, speaking of his patient, or his client, "that the mother's confession isn't good. It's a confession of duress. I try to tell the young fellow he shouldn't worry about a phony[22] confession. But what does it help him if I am rational with him?"

"No?" said Wilhelm, intensely nervous. "I think we ought to go over to the market. It'll be opening pretty soon."

"Oh, come on," said Tamkin. "It isn't even nine o'clock, and there isn't much trading the first hour anyway. Things don't get hot in Chicago until half-past ten, and they're an hour behind us, don't forget. Anyway, I say lard will go up, and it will. Take my word. I've made a study of the guilt-aggression cycle which is behind it. I ought to know something about that. Straighten your collar."

"But meantime," said Wilhelm, "we have taken a licking this week. Are you sure your insight is at its best? Maybe when it isn't, we should lay off and wait."

"Don't you realize," Dr. Tamkin told him, "you can't march in a straight line to the victory? You fluctuate toward it. From Euclid to Newton there were straight lines. The modern age analyzes the wavers. On my own accounts, I took a licking in hides and coffee. But I have confidence. I'm sure I'll outguess them." He gave Wilhelm a narrow smile, friendly, calming, shrewd, and wizard-like, patronizing, secret, potent. He saw his fears and smiled at them. "It's something," he remarked, "to see how the competition-factor will manifest itself in different individuals."

"So? Let's go over."

"But I haven't had my breakfast yet."

"I've had mine."

"Come, have a cup of coffee."

"I wouldn't want to meet my dad." Looking through the glass doors, Wilhelm saw that his father had left by the other exit. Wilhelm thought. He didn't want to run into me, either. He said to Dr. Tamkin, "Okay, I'll sit with you, but let's hurry it up because I'd like to get to the market while there's still a place to sit. Everybody and his uncle get in ahead of you."

"I want to tell you about this boy and his dad. It's highly absorbing. The father was a nudist. Everybody went naked in the house. Maybe the women found men with clothes attractive. Her husband didn't believe in cutting his hair, either. He practiced dentistry. In his office he wore riding pants and a pair of boots, and he wore a green eyeshade."

"Oh, come off it,"[23] said Wilhelm.

"This is a true case history."

Without warning, Wilhelm began to laugh. He himself had had no premonition of his change of humor. His face became warm and pleasant, and he forgot his father, his anxieties; he panted earlike, happily, through his teeth. "This sounds like a horse-dentist. He wouldn't have to put on pants to treat a horse. Now what else are you going to tell me? Did the wife play the mandolin? Does the boy join the cavalry? Oh Tamkin, you really are a killer-diller."[24]

"Oh, you think I'm trying to amuse you," said Tamkin. "That's because you aren't familiar with my outlook. I deal in fact. Facts always are sensational. I'll say that a second time. Facts always are sensational."

Wilhelm was reluctant to part with his good mood. The doctor had little sense of humor. He was looking at him earnestly.

"I'd bet you any amount of money," said Tamkin, "that the facts about you are sensational."

"Oh — ha, ha! You want them? You can sell them to a true confession magazine."

"People forget how sensational the things are that they do. They don't see it on themselves. It blends into the background of their daily life."

Wilhelm smiled. "Are you sure this boy tells you the truth?"

"Yes, because I've known the whole family for years."

"And you do psychological work with your own friends? I didn't know that was allowed."

"Well, I'm a radical in the profession. I have to do good wherever I can."

Wilhelm's face became ponderous again and pale. His whitened gold hair lay heavy

Chapter 6　The Literature since World War Ⅱ

on his head, and he clasped uneasy fingers on the table. Sensational, but oddly enough, dull, too. Now how do you figure that out? It blends with the background. Funny but unfunny. True but false. Casual but laborious, Tamkin was. Wilhelm was most suspicious of him when he took his driest tone.

"With me," said Dr. Tamkin,"I am at my most efficient when I don't need the fee, when I only love without a financial reward. I remove myself from the social influence, especially money. The spiritual compensation is what I look for. Bringing people into the here-and-now, the real universe. That's the present moment. The past is no good to us. The future is full of anxiety. Only the present is real — the here-and-now. Seize the day."

"Well," said Wilhelm, his earnestness returning. "I know you are a very unusual man. I like what you say about here-and-now. Are all the people who come to see your personal friends and patients too? Like that tall handsome girl, the one who always wears those beautiful broomstick skirts and belts?"

"She was an epileptic, and a most bad and serious pathology, too. I'm curing her successfully. She hasn't had a seizure in six months, and she used to have one every week."

"And that young cameraman, the one who showed us those movies from the jungles of Brazil, isn't he related to her?"

"Her brother. He's under my care, too. He has some terrible tendencies, which are to be expected when you have an epileptic sibling. I came into their lives when they needed help desperately, and took hold of them. A certain man forty years older than she had her in his control and used to give her fits by suggestion whenever she tried to leave him. If you only knew one percent of what goes on in the city of New York! You see, I understand what it is when the lonely person begins to feel like an animal. When the night comes, he feels like howling from his window like a wolf. I'm taking complete care of that young fellow and his sister. I have to steady him down or he'll go from Brazil to Australia the next day. The way I keep him in the here-and-now is by teaching him Greek."

This was a complete surprise! "What, do you know Greek?"

"A friend of mine taught me when I was in Cairo. I studied Aristotle with him to keep from being idle."

Wilhelm tried to take in these new claims and examine them. Howling from the window like a wolf when night comes sounded genuine to him. That was something really to think about. But the Greek! He realized that Tamkin was watching to see how he took it. More elements were continually being added. A few days ago Tamkin had hinted that he had once been in the underworld, one of the Detroit Purple Gang. He was once head of a mental clinic in Toledo. He had worked with a Polish inventor on an unsinkable ship. He was a technical consultant in the field of television. In the life of a

225

man of genius, all of these things might happen. But had they happened to Tamkin? Was he a genius? He often said that he had attended some of the Egyptian royal family as a psychiatrist. "But everybody is alike, common or aristocrat," he told Wilhelm. "The aristocrat knows less about life."

An Egyptian princess, whom he had treated in California, for horrible disorders he had described to Wilhelm, retained him to come back to the old country with her, and there he had had many of her friends and relatives under his care. They turned over a villa on the Nile to him. "For ethical reasons, I can't tell you many of the details about them," he said — but Wilhelm had already heard all these details, and strange and shocking they were, if true. If true — he could not be free from doubt. For instance, the general who had to wear ladies' silk stockings and stand otherwise naked before the mirror — and all the rest. Listening to the doctor when he was so strangely factual, Wilhelm had to translate his words into his own language, and he could not translate fast enough or find terms to fit what he heard.

"Those Egyptian big shots invested in the market, too, for the heck of it[25]. What did they need extra money for? By association. I almost became a millionaire myself, and if I had played it smart there's no telling what might have happened. I could have been the ambassador." The American? The Egyptian ambassador? "A friend of mine tipped me off on the cotton[26]. I made a heavy purchase of it. I didn't have that kind of money, but everybody there knew me. It never entered their minds that a person of their social circle didn't have dough[27]. The sale was made on the phone. Then, while the cotton shipment was at sea, the price tripled. When the stuff suddenly became so valuable all hell broke loose on the world cotton market[28], they looked to see who was the owner of this big shipment. Me! They canceled. This was illegal. I sued them. But as I didn't have the money to fight them I sold the suit to a Wall Street lawyer for twenty thousand dollars. He fought it and was winning. They settled with him out of court for more than a million. But on the way back from Cairo, flying, there was a crash. All on board died. I have this guilt on my conscience, of being the murderer of that lawyer although he was a crook."

Wilhelm thought, I must be a real jerk to sit and listen to such impossible stories. I guess I am a sucker for people who talk about the deeper things of life, even the way he does.

"We scientific men speak of irrational guilt, Wilhelm," said Dr. Tamkin, as if Wilhelm were a pupil in his class. "But in such a situation, because of the money, I wished him harm. I realize it. This isn't the time to describe all the details, but the money made me guilty. Money and Murder both begin with M. Machinery, Mischief."

Wilhelm, his mind thinking for him at random, said, "What about Mercy? Milk-of-human-kindness[29]?"

"One fact should be clear to you by now. Money-making is aggression. That's the whole thing. The functionalistic explanation is the only one. People come to the market

Chapter 6　The Literature since World War Ⅱ

to kill. They say, 'I'm going to make a killing. ' It's not accidental. Only they haven't got the genuine courage to kill, and they erect a symbol of it. The money. They make a killing by a fantasy. Now, counting and number is always a sadistic activity. Like hitting. In the Bible, the Jews wouldn't allow you to count them. They knew it was sadistic. "

"I don't understand what you mean," said Wilhelm. A strange uneasiness tore at him. The day was growing too warm and his head felt dim. "What makes them want to kill?"

"By and by, you'll get the drift," Dr. Tamkin assured him. His amazing eyes had some of the rich dryness of a brown fur. Innumerable crystalline hairs of spicules of light glittered in their bold surfaces. "You can't understand without first spending years on the study of the ultimates of human and animal behavior, the deep chemical, organismic, and spiritual secrets of life. I am a psychological poet. "

"If you're this kind of poet," said Wilhelm, whose fingers in his pocket were feeling in the little envelopes for the Phenaphen capsules, "what are you doing on the market?"

"That's a good question. Maybe I am better at speculation because I don't care. Basically, I don't wish hard enough for money, and therefore I come with a cool head to it. "

Wilhelm thought, Oh, sure! That's an answer, is it? I bet that if I took a strong attitude he'd back down on everything. He'd grovel in front of me. The way he looks at me on the sly[30], to see if I'm being taken in! He swallowed his Phenaphen pill with a long gulp of water. The rims of his eyes grew red as it went down. And then he felt calmer.

"Let me see if I can give you an answer that will satisfy you," said Dr. Tamkin. His flapjacks were set before him. He spread the butter on them, poured on brown maple syrup, quartered them, and began to eat with hard, active, muscular jaws which sometimes gave a creak at the hinges. He pressed the handle of his knife against his chest and said, "In here, the human bosom — mine, yours, everybody's — there isn't just one soul. There's a lot of souls. But there are two main ones, the real soul and a pretender soul. Now! Every man realizes that he has to love something or somebody. He feels that he must go outward. 'If thou canst not love, what art thou?' Are you with me?"

"Yes, Doc, I think so," said Wilhelm listening — a little skeptically but nonetheless hard.

"'What art thou?' Nothing. That's the answer. Nothing. In the heart of hearts — Nothing! So of course you can't stand that and want to be Something, and you try. But instead of being this Something, the man puts it over on everybody instead. You can't be that strict to yourself. You love a little. Like you have a dog" (Scissors!) "or give

227

some money to a charity drive. Now that isn't love, is it? What is it? Egotism, pure and simple. It's a way to love the pretender soul. Vanity. Only vanity, is what it is. And social control. The interest of the pretender soul is the same as the interest of the social life, the society mechanism. This is the main tragedy of human life. Oh, it is terrible! Terrible! You are not free. Your own betrayer is inside of you and sells you out. You have to obey him like a slave. He makes you work like a horse. And for what? For who?"

"Yes, for what?" The doctor's words caught Wilhelm's heart. "I couldn't agree more," he said, "When do we get free?"

"The purpose is to keep the whole thing going. The true soul is the one that pays the price. It suffers and gets sick, and it realizes that the pretender can't be loved. Because the pretender is a lie. The true soul loves the truth. And when the true soul feels like this, it wants to kill the pretender. The love has turned into hate. Then you become dangerous. A killer. You have to kill the deceiver."

"Does this happen to everybody?"

The doctor answered simply, "Yes, to everybody. Of course, for simplification purposes, I have spoken of the soul; it isn't a scientific term but it helps you to understand it. Whenever the slayer slays, he wants to slay the soul in him which has gypped and deceived him. Who is his enemy? Him. And his lover? Also. Therefore, all suicide is murder, and all murder is suicide. It's the one and identical phenomenon. Biologically, the pretender soul takes away the energy of the true soul and makes it feeble, like a parasite. It happens unconsciously, unawarely, in the depths of the organism. Ever take up parasitology?"

"No, it's my dad who's the doctor."

"You should read a book about it."

Wilhelm said, "But this means that the world is full of murderers. So it's not the world. It's a kind of hell."

"Sure," the doctor said. "At least a kind of purgatory. You walk on the bodies. They are all around. I can hear them cry de profundis[31] and wring their hands. I hear them, poor human beasts. I can't help hearing. And my eyes are open to it. I have to cry, too. This is the human tragedy-comedy."

...

Notes

1. **corny**: derived from corn-fed; dull, simple.
2. **worked up**: very excited.
3. **by fits and starts**: continually starting and stopping.
4. **the thorns**: annoyance.
5. **good riddance**: a rude way of saying you are glad someone has left.
6. **in dutch**: in trouble.

Chapter 6 The Literature since World War II

7. **what's made you so hot under the collar**: what's made you so angry or worried.
8. **in abeyance**: something such as a custom, rule, or system that is in abeyance is not being used at the present time.
9. **pimp**: a man who makes money by controlling prostitutes.
10. **sporting**: fair.
11. **kill**: stop, put an end to.
12. **bounced**: returned by the bank as worthless.
13. **power of attorney**: power to act for another. Here it means Wilhelm signed on an official paper, committing his money to Tamkin to invest in shares.
14. **lard and grain future**: referring to lard and grain business they invested.
15. **get a big kick out of this**: enjoy it very much, e.g. make a big money.
16. **take a specimen risk**: take an experimental risk.
17. **I've never been able to get anywhere with him**: we never agree on anything; we can never reach any agreement.
18. **pigeon-toed**: with his toes pointing inward.
19. **studied**: carefully considered.
20. **exertion**: effort.
21. **GL**: (abbreviation) girls love.
22. **phony**: pretended; false.
23. **come off it**: don't be silly; don't try to deceive me.
24. **killer-diller**: a man good at amusing or making jokes.
25. **for the heck of it**: heck = hell; for fun.
26. **tip me off on the cotton**: give me secret information about the cotton market.
27. **dough**: American money.
28. **all hell broke loose on the world cotton market**: everything in the cotton market become completely confused.
29. **Milk-of-human-kindness**: compassion, sympathy.
30. **on the sly**: secretly.
31. **de profundis**: (Latin) from the bottom of heart; "Out of the Depth" first words of Psalm 130.

Study Questions

1. What business did Wilhelm trust Dr. Tamkin to do?
2. What has Tommy Wilhelm finally realized?
3. What does Dr. Tamkin mean by saying "Only the present is real — the here-and-now. Seize the day"?

Essay Topics

1. What kind of hero is Wilhelm? Is he an anti-hero?

2. What is the role of psychology in the novel?

6.3 Arthur Miller

6.3.1 About the Author

Arthur Miller (1915-2005) was born into a Jewish-American family in New York City. His father lost his business in the 1929 Depression and the family was forced to move to a smaller home in Brooklyn. Miller spent his boyhood playing football and reading adventure stories. After finishing his high school studies in 1932, young Miller worked in an automobile parts warehouse to earn money for college. In 1934, he entered the University of Michigan, where he won awards for playwriting. After graduation in 1938 with a degree in English, Miller returned to New York and began a series of jobs involving playwriting. During World War II, Miller tried to enlist, but a school football injury kept him out of the armed forces. Then in 1940 he married Mary Slattery, his college sweetheart, with whom he had two children.

In 1947 Miller wrote his first successful play, *All My Sons*, which established him as a significant American playwright. But it was *Death of a Salesman* in 1949 that brought him international fame and secured his position as one of American foremost playwrights. In the play, Miller tells a tale of the life and death of the ordinary working man Willy Loman, by mixing the tradition of social realism with a more expressionistic structure. As Willy Loman becomes more and more absorbed by scenes from his past, the action progressively takes place in his mind. And through Willy Loman, Miller examines the myth of the American Dream and the shallow promise of happiness through material wealth. Miller wrote *The Crucible* (1953), by taking witch-hunting as an analogy for the contemporary situation. The play became an enduring metaphor not only for McCarthyism, but also for any system of domestic repression. Miller's *A View From the Bridge* (1955), a play of obsession and betrayal, ultimately took its place as a popular classic of the international stage. In 1955, Miller divorced his first wife, and in the following year he married Marilyn Monroe, the famous Hollywood actress. But the two divorced in 1961, the year of Monroe's death. In 1962, Miller married his third wife, professional photographer Inge Morath.

Not content to rest on the great achievements of his past, Miller continued to experiment with forms of drama, creating a variety of plays throughout the 1970s and 1980s. In his life, Miller had received two Pulitzer Prizes, the Prince of Asturias Literary Prize (2002), the Tony Award (1938), the Gold Medal of Arts and Literature (1959), and the Anglo American Theater Award (1966).

Miller writes movingly about a variety of important issues, including personal responsibility, self-delusion, family and marital conflicts, city corruption and political persecution. By creating plays that show the human will as inexhaustible and irrepressible, Miller expresses a vision of humanity that shows that transcendence is coexistent with consciousness. His characters have the ability to face and accept what is real and thereby to discover the truth about their lives and identities. Miller believes that as long as we continue to wrestle with our givens, resist the forces of chaos, and struggle to impose order on the natural world and our mental landscape, we will have an opportunity for a meaningful life. As a symbol of artistic and moral integrity, Miller's bravery and his willingness to fight for what he believes in his chosen art form has made him a great American playwright whose name will live on in world letters.

6.3.2 An Excerpt from Act II of *The Death of a Salesman*

...

BIFF: No, you're going to hear the truth — what you are and what I am!
LINDA: Stop it!
WILLY: Spite![1]
HAPPY: (*Coming down toward Biff*) You cut it now!
BIFF: (*to Happy*) The man don't know who we are! The man is gonna know! (*To Willy*) We never told the truth for ten minutes in this house!
HAPPY: We always told the truth!
BIFF: (*Turning on him*) You big blow,[2] are you the assistant buyer? You're one of the two assistants to the assistant, aren't you?
HAPPY: Well, I'm practically —
BIFF: You're practically full of it! We all are! And I'm through with it. (*To Willy*) Now hear this, Willy, this is me.
WILLY: I know you!
BIFF: You know why I had no address for three months? I stole a suit in Kansas City and I was in jail. (*To Linda, who is sobbing*) Stop crying. I'm through with it.
Linda turns away from them, her hands covering her face.
WILLY: I suppose that's my fault!
BIFF: I stole myself out of every good job since high school!
WILLY: And whose fault is that?
BIFF: And I never got anywhere because you blew me so full of hot air I could never stand taking orders from anybody! That's whose fault is!
WILLY: I hear that!
LINDA: Don't, Biff!
BIFF: It's goddam time you heard that! I had to be boss big shot in two weeks, and I'm

through with it!

WILLY: Then hang yourself! For spite, hang yourself!

BIFF: NO! Nobody's hanging himself, Willy! I ran down eleven flights with a pen in my hand today. And suddenly I stopped, you hear me? And in the middle of that office building, do you hear this? I stopped in the middle of that building and I saw — the sky. I saw the things that I love in this world. The work and the food and time to sit and smoke. And I looked at the pen and said to myself, what the hell am I grabbing this for? Why am I trying to become what I don't want to be? What am I doing in an office, making a contemptuous, begging fool of myself, when all I want is out there, waiting for me the minute I say I know who I am! Why can't I say that, Willy?

He tries to make Willy face him, but Willy pulls away and moves to the left.

WILLY: (*With hatred, threateningly*) The door of your life is wide open!

BIFF: Pop! I'm a dime a dozen,³ and so are you!

WILLY: (*Turning on him now in an uncontrolled outburst*) I am not a dime a dozen! I am Willy Loman, and you are Biff Loman!

Biff starts for Willy, but is blocked by Happy. In his fury, Biff seems on the verge of attacking his father.

BIFF: I am not a leader of men, Willy, and neither are you. You were never anything but a hard-working drummer who landed in the ash can like all the rest of them! I'm one dollar an hour, Willy! I tried seven states and couldn't raise it. A buck an hour! Do you gather my meaning? I'm not bringing home any prizes any more, and you're going to stop waiting for me to bring them home!

WILLY: (*Directly to Biff*) You vengeful, spite mut!⁴

Biff breaks from Happy. Willy, in fright, starts up the stairs. Biff grabs him.

BIFF: (*At the peak of his fury*) Pop, I'm nothing! I'm nothing, Pop. Can't you understand that? There's no spite in it any more. I'm just what I am, that's all.

Biff's fury has spent itself, and he breaks down, sobbing, holding on to Willy, who dumbly fumbles for Biff's face.

WILLY: (*Astonished*) What're you doing? What're you doing? (*To Linda*) Why is he crying?

BIFF: (*Crying, broken*) Will you let me go, for Christ's sake? Will you take that phony dream and burn it before something happens?

(*Struggling to contain himself, he pulls away and moves to the stairs.*) I'll go in the morning. Put him — put him to bed.

Exhausted, Biff moves up the stairs to his room.

WILLY: (*After a long pause, astonished, elevated*) Isn't that — isn't that remarkable? Biff — he likes me!

LINDA: He loves you, Willy!

HAPPY: (*Deeply moved*) Always did, Pop.

WILLY: Oh, Biff! (*Staring wildly*) He cried! Cried to me. (*He is choking with his love, and now cries out his promise.*) That boy — that boy is going to be magnificent!
Ben appears in the light just outside the kitchen. [5]
BEN: Yes, outstanding, with twenty thousand behind him.
LINDA: (*Sensing the racing of his mind, fearfully, carefully*) Now come to bed, Willy. It's all settled now. [6]
WILLY: (*Finding it difficult not to rush out of the house*) Yes, we'll sleep. Come on. Go to sleep, Hap.
BEN: And it does take a great kind of a man to crack the jungle. [7]
　In accents of dread, Ben's idyllic music starts up.
HAPPY: (*His arm around Linda*) I'm getting married, Pop, don't forget it. I'm changing everything. I'm gonna run that department before the year is up. You'll see, Mom. (*He kisses her.*)
BEN: The jungle is dark but full of diamonds, Willy.
　Willy turns, moves, listening to Ben.
LINDA: Be good. You're both good boys, just act that way, that's all.
HAPPY: 'Night, Pop. (*He goes upstairs.*)
LINDA: (*To Willy*) Come dear.
BEN: (*With greater force*) One must go in to fetch a diamond out.
WILLY: (*To Linda, as he moves slowly along the edge of the kitchen, toward the door*) I just want to get settled down, Linda. Let me sit alone for a little.
LINDA: (*Almost uttering her fear*) I want you upstairs.
WILLY: (*Taking her in his arms*) In a few minutes, Linda. I couldn't sleep right now. Go on, you look awful tired. (*He kissed her.*)
BEN: Not like an appointment at all. A diamond is rough and hard to the touch.
WILLY: Go on now. I'll be right up.
LINDA: I think this is the only way, Willy.
WILLY: Sure, it's the best thing.
BEN: Best thing!
WILLY: The only way. Everything is gonna be — go on, kid, get to bed. You look so tired.
LINDA: Come right up.
WILLY: Two minutes.
　Linda goes into the living-room, then reappears in her bedroom. Willy moves just outside the kitchen door.
WILLY: Loves me. (*Wonderingly*) Always loved me. Isn't that a remarkable thing? Ben, he'll worship me for it!
BEN: (*With promise*) It's dark there, but full of diamonds.
WILLY: Can you imagine that magnificence with twenty thousand dollars in his pocket?

LINDA: (*Calling from her room*) Willy! Come up!

WILLY: (*Calling into the kitchen*) Yes! Yes. Coming! It's very smart, you realize that, don't you, sweetheart? Even Ben sees it. I gotta go, baby. 'By! By!

(*Going over to Ben, almost dancing*) Imagine? When the mail comes he'll be ahead of Bernard again!

BEN: A perfect proposition all round.

WILLY: Did you see how he cried to me? Oh, if I could kiss him, Ben!

BEN: Time, William, time!

WILLY: Oh, Ben, I always knew one way or another we were gonna make it, Biff and I!

BEN: (*Looking at his watch*) The boat. We'll be late. (*He moves slowly off into the darkness.*)

WILLY: (*Elegiacally, turning to the house*) Now when you kick off, boy, I want a seventy-yard boot, and get right down the field under the ball, and when you hit, hit low and hit hard, because it's important, boy. (*He swings around and faces the audience.*) There's all kinds of important people in the stands, and the first thing you know... (*Suddenly realizing he is alone*) Ben! Ben, where do I...? (*He makes a sudden movement of search.*) Ben, how do I...?

LINDA: (*Calling*) Willy, you coming up?

WILLY: (*Uttering a gasp of fear, whirling about as if to quiet her*) Sh! (*He turns around as if to find his way; sounds, faces, voices, seem to be swarming in upon him and he flicks at them, crying.*) Sh! Sh! (*Suddenly music, faint and high, stops him. It rises in intensity, almost to an unbearable scream. He goes up and down on his toes, and rushes off around the house.*) Shhh!

LINDA: Willy!

There is no answer. Linda waits. Biff gets up off his bed. He is still in his clothes. Happy sits up. Biff stands listening.

LINDA: (*With real fear*) Willy, answer me! Willy!

There is the sound of a car starting and moving away at full speed.

LINDA: No!

BIFF: (*Rushing down the stairs*) Pop!

As the car speeds off, the music crashes down in the frenzy of sound, which becomes the soft pulsation of a single cello string. Biff slowly returns to his bedroom. He and Happy gravely don their jackets. Linda slowly walks out of her room. The music has developed into a dead march. The leaves of day are appearing over everything. Charley and Bernard somberly dressed, appear and knock on the kitchen door. Biff and Happy slowly descend the stairs to the kitchen as Charley and Bernard enter. All stop a moment when Linda, in clothes of mourning, bearing a little bunch of roses, comes through the draped doorway into the kitchen. She goes to Charley and takes his arm. Now all move toward the audience, through the wall-line of the kitchen. At the limit of the apron, Linda lays down the flowers, kneels, and sits back on her heels. All stare down at the grave.

Notes

1. **spite**: a mean or evil feeling toward another, characterized by the inclination to hurt, humiliate, annoy, frustrate, and so on.
2. **blow**: (Informal) to brag; boast.
3. **dime a dozen**: an expression used to imply that something is available in large quantities. The fact that the item is not rare suggests that it is not of great value.
4. **mutt**: a mixed-breed dog; an insult if applied to a human being.
5. ***Ben appears in the light just outside the kitchen***: This is only a vision, in which Ben is not a remembered figure, but a personification of Willy's own feelings, speaking for Willy's subconscious mind.
6. **It's all settled now**: The words have different meanings to the two of them. For Linda it means Biff will leave and Willy won't fight anymore; for Willy it means Biff loves him and the only thing he has left to give him is the $20 000 insurance money after his death.
7. **the jungle**: The jungle, or woods, represents the chaotic yet rewarding nature of life. In many ways, the jungle also represents the twentieth century free market economy. Ben tells Willy, "the jungle is dark but full of diamonds." So like Ben, Willy hopes to strike it rich in the business world of New England.

Study Questions

1. What is the cause of the conflict between Willy Loman and his son Biff?
2. What is a hallucination? What causes them?
3. What forces entrap Willy and drive him to self-destruction?

Essay Topics

Write a character analysis of Willy, discussing his strengths and weaknesses.

6.4 J. D. Salinger

6.4.1 About the Author

J. D. Salinger (1919-) was born in Manhattan, New York, to a Jewish father and an Irish Catholic mother. As a child, he attended various private schools but was expelled for not making an effort to do the work. However, he managed to get graduated from Valley Forge Military Academy in 1936. Then he started his freshman year at New York University in 1937, but dropped out the next spring to work on a cruise ship. He

 spent the late 1930s studying in Europe and turned to writing while taking an evening short story course at Columbia University in 1939. He started publishing short stories in the 1940s in magazines including the *Saturday Evening Post*, *Colliers*, and especially the *New Yorker*. Salinger entered military service in 1942 and served until the end of World War II, participating in the Normandy campaign and the liberation of France.

After returning to the States, Salinger's career as a writer of serious fiction took off. His story, "Slight Rebellion off Madison," appeared in the *New Yorker* in 1946. In 1951, he published his best known novel, *The Catcher in the Rye*. The novel tells the tale of Holden Caulfield, a troubled adolescent who leaves his fancy prep school for an urban walkabout. The sales of the book grew rapidly as teenagers began reading the novel not only to satisfy class requirements, but also as a source of answers, guidance, and inspiration in their own lives. Favoring the short-story form, however, Salinger also wrote numerous "coming of age" stories about the eccentric and melancholic Glass family. In 1953 he published a collection of seven short stories entitled *Nine Stories*.

Salinger was first married to a European girl but soon after World War II ended he divorced her. His second marriage was to a Dartmouth College student named Claire Douglas in 1955. With her, Salinger had two children. Claire developed a gradual hate for Salinger, and later divorced him. His current wife is Colleen, a nurse who is very active in their community. Always a private man, Salinger becomes increasingly reclusive in his later part of life. He refuses requests for interviews and has not published since 1965, though he reportedly continues to write at his remote home in Cornish, New Hampshire.

Best known for his novel *The Catcher in the Rye*, Salinger is recognized as one of the most popular and influential authors of American fiction to emerge after World War II. In his long and short fictions, he shows his major concerns with children's growing-up problems, which are presented in the confrontation of the protagonist's innocence with the knowledge of the evils of the world. His characters, children or adolescents, feel suffocated by a world which denies innocence. In order to survive they withdraw into mysticism, to find a tranquilizing spiritual world undisturbed by human vices where innocence is incorruptible. However, human beings have to learn the evil, the corruption of the world before they grow up. Hence there is a gradual movement of the enlightened hero from innocence to knowledge, from rejection to reconciliation, and from the disgust with the world to a desire for human compassion, sympathy and love.

Salinger's artistry in fiction writing is outstanding. His works are humorous and ironic. He writes in vivid, colloquial English, using a lot of slang and ungrammatical or short sentences. Actually Salinger's style has a lot to do with his religious vision, which is related to primitive Christianity and Zen Buddhism. His vision entails a reverence for language, a delight in everyday speech, a customary use of simple words and images to convey complex themes, thus revealing the very depths of human lives.

6.4.2 An Excerpt from Chapter 21 of *The Catcher in the Rye*

The best break I had in years, when I got home the regular night elevator boy, Pete, wasn't on the car. Some new guy I'd never seen was on the car, so I figured that if I didn't bump smack into my parents and all I'd be able to say hello to old Phoebe and then beat it and nobody'd even know I'd been around.

It was really a terrific break. What made it even better, the new elevator boy was sort of on the stupid side. I told him, in this very casual voice, to take me up to the Dicksteins'. The Dicksteins were these people that had the other apartment on our floor. I'd already taken off my hunting hat, so as not to look suspicious or anything. I went in the elevator like I was in a terrific hurry.

He had the elevator doors all shut and all, and was all set to take me up, and then he turned around and said, "They ain't in. They're at a party on the fourteenth floor."

"That's all right," I said. "I'm supposed to wait for them. I'm their nephew."

He gave me this sort of stupid, suspicious look.

"You better wait in the lobby, fella," he said.

"I'd like to — I really would," I said. "But I have a bad leg. I have to hold it in a certain position. I think I'd better sit down in the chair outside their door."

He didn't know what the hell I was talking about, so all he said was "Oh" and took me up. Not bad, boy. It's funny. All you have to do is say something nobody understands and they'll do practically anything you want them to.

I got off at our floor — limping like a bastard — and started walking over toward the Dicksteins' side. Then, when I heard the elevator doors shut, I turned around and went over to our side. I was doing all right. I didn't even feel drunk anymore.

Then I took out my door key and opened our door, quiet as hell. Then, very, very carefully and all, I went inside and closed the door. I really should've been a crook.

It was dark as hell in the foyer[1], naturally, and naturally I couldn't turn on any lights. I had to be careful not to bump into anything and make a racket. I certainly knew I was home, though. Our foyer has a funny smell that doesn't smell like anyplace else. I don't know what the hell it is. It isn't cauliflower and it isn't perfume — I don't know what the hell it is — but you always know you're home. I started to take off my coat and hang it up in the foyer closet, but that closet's full of hangers that rattle like madmen when you open the door, so I left it on. Then I started walking very, very slowly back toward old Phoebe's room. I knew the maid wouldn't hear me because she had only one eardrum. She had this brother that stuck a straw down her ear when she was a kid, she once told me. She was pretty deaf and all.

But my parents, especially my mother, she has ears like a goddam bloodhound. So I took it very, very easy when I went past their door. I even held my breath, for God's sake. You can hit my father over the head with a chair and he won't wake up, but my mother, all you have to do to my mother is cough somewhere in Siberia and she'll hear you. She's nervous as hell. Half the time she's up all night smoking cigarettes.

Finally, after about an hour, I got to old Phoebe's room. She wasn't there, though. I forgot about that. I forgot she always sleeps in D. B.'s room when he's away in Hollywood or some place. She likes it because it's the biggest room in the house. Also because it has this big old madman desk in it that D. B. bought off some lady alcoholic in Philadelphia, and this big, gigantic bed that's about ten miles wide and ten miles long. I don't know where he bought that bed. Anyway, old Phoebe likes to sleep in D. B.'s room when he's away, and he lets her. You ought to see her doing her homework or something at that crazy desk. It's almost as big as the bed. You can hardly see her when she's doing her homework. That's the kind of stuff she likes, though. She doesn't like her own room because it's too little, she says. She says she likes to spread out. That kills me. What's old Phoebe got to spread out? Nothing.

Anyway, I went into D. B.'s room quiet as hell, and turned on the lamp on the desk. Old Phoebe didn't even wake up. When the light was on and all, I sort of looked at her for a while. She was laying there asleep, with her face sort of on the side of the pillow. She had her mouth way open. It's funny. You take adults, they look lousy when they're asleep and they have their mouths way open, but kids don't. Kids look all right. They can even have spit all over the pillow and they still look all right.

I went around the room, very quiet and all, looking at stuff for a while. I felt swell[2], for a change. I didn't even feel like I was getting pneumonia or anything any more. I just felt good, for a change. Old Phoebe's clothes were on this chair right next to the bed. She's very neat, for a child. I mean she doesn't just throw her stuff around, like some kids. She's no slob. She had the jacket to this tan suit my mother bought her in Canada hung up on the back of the chair. Then her blouse and stuff were on the seat. Her shoes and socks were on the floor, right underneath the chair, right next to each other. I never saw the shoes before. They were new. They were these dark brown loafers, sort of like this pair I have, and they went swell with that suit my mother bought her in Canada. My mother dresses her nice. She really does. My mother has terrific taste in some things. She's no good at buying ice skates or anything like that, but clothes, she's perfect. I mean Phoebe always has some dress on that can kill you. You take most little kids, even if their parents are wealthy and all, they usually have some terrible dress on. I wish you could see old Phoebe in that suit my mother bought her in Canada. I'm not kidding.

Chapter 6 The Literature since World War Ⅱ

I sat down on old D. B.'s desk and looked at the stuff on it. It was mostly Phoebe's stuff, from school and all. Mostly books. The one on top was called Arithmetic Is Fun! I sort of opened the first page and took a look at it. This is what old Phoebe had on it:

PHOEBE WEATHERFIELD CAULFIELD 4B-1

That killed me. Her middle name is Josephine, for God's sake, not Weatherfield. She doesn't like it, though. Every time I see her she's got a new middle name for herself.

The book underneath the arithmetic was a geography, and the book under the geography was a speller.

She's very good in spelling. She's very good in all her subjects, but she's best in spelling. Then, under the speller, there were a bunch of notebooks. She has about five thousand notebooks. You never saw a kid with so many notebooks. I opened the one on top and looked at the first page. It had on it:

Bernice meet me at recess I have something very important to tell you.

That was all there was on that page. The next one had on it:

Why has south eastern Alaska so many caning factories?

Because there's so much salmon.

Why has it valuable forests?

Because it has the right climate.

What has our government done to make life easier for the Alaskan Eskimos?

Look it up for tomorrow!!!

Phoebe Weatherfield Caulfield Phoebe Weatherfield Caulfield Phoebe Weatherfield Caulfield Phoebe W. Caulfield Phoebe Weatherfield Caulfield, Esq. Please pass to Shirley!!!! Shirley you said you were Sagittarius but your only Taurus bring your skates when you come over to my house. I sat there on D. B.'s desk and read the whole notebook. It didn't take me long, and I can read that kind of stuff, some kid's notebook, Phoebe's or anybody's, all day and all night long. Kid's notebooks kill me. Then I lit another cigarette — it was my last one. I must've smoked about three cartons that day. Then, finally, I woke her up. I mean I couldn't sit there on that desk for the rest of my life, and besides, I was afraid my parents might barge in on me all of a sudden and I wanted to at least say hello to her before they did. So I woke her up.

She wakes up very easily. I mean you don't have to yell at her or anything. All you have to do, practically, is sit down on the bed and say, "Wake up, Phoebe," and bingo, she's awake.

"Holden!" she said right away. She put her arms around my neck and all. She's very affectionate. I mean she's quite affectionate, for a child. Sometimes she's even too affectionate.

I sort of gave her a kiss, and she said, "Whenja get home?"

She was glad as hell to see me. You could tell.

"Not so loud. Just now. How are ya anyway?" "I'm fine. Did you get my letter? I wrote you a five-page — " "Yeah — not so loud. Thanks."

She wrote me this letter. I didn't get a chance to answer it, though. It was all about this play she was in school. She told me not to make any dates or anything for Friday so that I could come see it. "How's the play?" I asked her. "What'd you say the name of it was?" "'A Christmas Pageant for Americans.' It stinks, but I'm Benedict Arnold. I have practically the biggest part," she said. Boy, was she wide-awake. She gets very excited when she tells you that stuff. "It starts out when I'm dying. This ghost comes in on Christmas Eve and asks me if I'm ashamed and everything. You know. For betraying my country and everything. Are you coming to it?" She was sitting way the hell up in the bed and all. "That's what I wrote you about. Are you?"

"Sure I'm coming. Certainly I'm coming."

"Daddy can't come. He has to fly to California," she said. Boy, was she wide-awake. It only takes her about two seconds to get wide-awake. She was sitting — sort of kneeling — way up in bed, and she was holding my goddam hand. "Listen. Mother said you'd be home Wednesday," she said. "She said Wednesday."

"I got out early. Not so loud. You'll wake everybody up."

"What time is it? They won't be home till very late, Mother said. They went to a party in Norwalk, Connecticut," old Phoebe said. "Guess what I did this afternoon! What movie I saw. Guess!"

"I don't know — Listen. Didn't they say what time they'd — " "The Doctor," old Phoebe said. "It's a special movie they had at the Lister Foundation. Just this one day they had it — today was the only day. It was all about this doctor in Kentucky and everything that sticks a blanket over this child's face that's a cripple and can't walk. Then they send him to jail and everything. It was excellent."

"Listen a second. Didn't they say what time they'd — " "He feels sorry for it, the doctor. That's why he sticks this blanket over her face and everything and makes her suffocate. Then they make him go to jail for life imprisonment, but this child that he stuck the blanket over its head comes to visit him all the time and thanks him for what he did. He was a mercy killer. Only, he knows he deserves to go to jail because a doctor isn't supposed to take things away from God. This girl in my class's mother took us. Alice Holmborg, She's my best friend. She's the only girl in the whole — " "Wait a second, willya?" I said. "I'm asking you a question. Did they say what time they'd be back, or didn't they?"

"No, but not till very late. Daddy took the car and everything so they wouldn't have to worry about trains. We have a radio in it now! Except that Mother said nobody can play it when the car's in traffic."

I began to relax, sort of. I mean I finally quit worrying about whether they'd catch me home or not. I figured the hell with it. If they did, they did.

Chapter 6　The Literature since World War II

You should've seen old Phoebe. She had on these blue pajamas with red elephants on the collars. Elephants knock her out. "So it was a good picture, huh?" I said.

"Swell, except Alice had a cold, and her mother kept asking her all the time if she felt grippy. Right in the middle of the picture. Always in the middle of something important, her mother'd lean all over me and everything and ask Alice if she felt grippy. It got on my nerves."

Then I told her about the record. "Listen, I bought you a record," I told her. "Only I broke it on the way home." I took the pieces out of my coat pocket and showed her. "I was plastered," I said.

"Gimme[3] the pieces," she said. "I'm saving them." She took them right out of my hand and then she put them in the drawer of the night table. She kills me.

"D. B. coming home for Christmas?" I asked her.

"He may and he may not, Mother said. It all depends. He may have to stay in Hollywood and write a picture about Annapolis."

"Annapolis, for God's sake!"

"It's a love story and everything. Guess who's going to be in it! What movie star. Guess!"

"I'm not interested. Annapolis, for God's sake. What's D. B. know about Annapolis, for God's sake? What's that got to do with the kind of stories he writes?" I said. Boy, that stuff drives me crazy. That goddam Hollywood.

"What'd you do to your arm?" I asked her. I noticed she had this big hunk of adhesive tape on her elbow. The reason I noticed it, her pajamas didn't have any sleeves.

"This boy, Curtis Weintraub, that's in my class, pushed me while I was going down the stairs in the park," she said. "Wanna[4] see?" She started taking the crazy adhesive tape off her arm.

"Leave it alone. Why'd he push you down the stairs?"

"I don't know. I think he hates me," old Phoebe said.

"This other girl and me, Selma Atterbury, put ink and stuff all over his windbreaker."

"That isn't nice. What are you — a child, for God's sake?"

"No, but every time I'm in the park, he follows me everywhere. He's always following me. He gets on my nerves."

"He probably likes you. That's no reason to put ink all — " "I don't want him to like me," she said.

Then she started looking at me funny. "Holden," she said, "how come you're not home Wednesday?"

"What?"

Boy, you have to watch her every minute. If you don't think she's smart, you're

241

mad.

"How come you're not home Wednesday?" she asked me.

"You didn't get kicked out or anything, did you?"

"I told you. They let us out early. They let the whole — " "You did get kicked out! You did!" old Phoebe said. Then she hit me on the leg with her fist. She gets very fisty when she feels like it. "You did! Oh, Holden!" She had her hand on her mouth and all. She gets very emotional, I swear to God.

"Who said I got kicked out? Nobody said I — " "You did. You did," she said. Then she smacked me again with her fist. If you don't think that hurts, you're crazy. "Daddy'll kill you!" she said. Then she flopped on her stomach on the bed and put the goddam pillow over her head.

She does that quite frequently. She's a true madman sometimes.

"Cut it out, now," I said. "Nobody's gonna kill me.

Nobody's gonna even — C'mon, Phoebe, take that goddam thing off your head. Nobody's gonna kill me."

She wouldn't take it off, though. You can't make her do something if she doesn't want to. All she kept saying was, "Daddy's gonna kill you." You could hardly understand her with that goddam pillow over her head.

"Nobody's gonna kill me. Use your head. In the first place, I'm going away. What I may do, I may get a job on a ranch or something for a while. I know this guy whose grandfather's got a ranch in Colorado. I may get a job out there," I said. "I'll keep in touch with you and all when I'm gone, if I go. C'mon. Take that off your head. C'mon, hey, Phoebe. Please. Please, willya?"

She wouldn't take it off, though I tried pulling it off, but she's strong as hell. You get tired fighting with her. Boy, if she wants to keep a pillow over her head, she keeps it. "Phoebe, please. C'mon outa there," I kept saying. "C'mon, hey... Hey, Weatherfield. C'mon out."

She wouldn't come out, though. You can't even reason with her sometimes.

Finally, I got up and went out in the living room and got some cigarettes out of the box on the table and stuck some in my pocket. I was all out.

Notes

1. **foyer**: a lobby or an anteroom, as of a theater or hotel.
2. **swell**: (AmE.) very good.
3. **gimme**: give me.
4. **wanna**: want to.

Study Questions

1. Why did Holden steal into his own home?

2. What is Holden's greatest complaint about most people in society?
3. Did Old Phoebe care about Holden? Why?

Essay Topics
1. How does *The Catcher in the Rye* relate to current society? Is the novel still relevant?
2. Discuss the novel as a coming-of-age story. How does Holden's character change during the course of the novel?

6.5 Elizabeth Bishop

6.5.1 About the author

Elizabeth Bishop (1911-1979) was born in Worcester, Massachusetts. Her early childhood was marked by a succession of tragic events. Her father died when she was eight months old. Her mother became mentally ill and was permanently committed to an institution when Elizabeth was only five years old. Effectively orphaned during her very early childhood, she was taken at first by her maternal grandparents, who lived in Nova Scotia, Canada. After some years, however, her paternal grandparents took charge of  her. Under their guardianship, Bishop was sent to the Walnut Hills School for Girls. Then she entered Vassar College in the fall of 1929, planning to be a composer. She gave up music and switched to English. In the spring of 1934, Bishop met and became friends with poet Marianne Moore, through whose influence, Bishop came to see poetry as an available, viable vocation for a woman. After graduating, Bishop lived in New York and traveled extensively in France, Spain, Ireland, Italy, and North Africa. Her poetry is filled with descriptions of her journeys and the sights she saw. Robert Lowell met Bishop at a dinner party, a meeting that marked the beginning of a crucial, if complicated, friendship.

The first volume of her poetry, *North and South*, was published in 1946. It contained some of her best-known poems, including "The Map", "The Man-Moth" and "The Fish". In 1955 she published her second volume of poetry, *North and South — A Cold Spring*, which won the 1956 Pulitzer Prize. Bishop's third collection of poems, *Questions of Travel*, came out in 1965, which includes both reflections on her childhood experiences and poems about her new home in Brazil. In 1969 Bishop published *Complete Poems*, a volume that included all of her previously published poems and several new pieces. This book won the National Book Award for 1970. Her final poetry volume, *Geography III*, was published in 1976.

Bishop fashioned a body of poetry remarkable for the transparency of expression, warmth of tone, and a singular blend of sadness and good humor. Her poetry is marked by precise descriptions of the physical world and an air of poetic serenity, with underlying themes of the human experiences of grief and longing and of the struggle to find a sense of belonging. Her style of writing was known for its highly detailed and objective, distant point of view and for its reticence on the sordid subject matter that obsessed her contemporaries. Her outstanding craft, brilliant descriptive power, and subtle organization of her work are highly praised. She is now firmly established as one of the principal poets of the generation that came of age in the shadow of the great modernist masters.

6.5.2 "The Fish"

I caught a tremendous fish
and held him beside the boat
half out of water, with my hook
fast in a corner of his mouth.
He didn't fight.
He hadn't fought at all.
He hung a grunting weight,
battered and venerable
and homely. Here and there
his brown skin hung like strips
like ancient wall-paper,
and its pattern of darker brown
was like wall-paper:
shapes like full-blown roses
stained and lost through age.
He was speckled with barnacles[1],
fine rosettes[2] of lime,
and infested
with tiny white sea-lice,
and underneath two or three
rags of green weed hung down.
While his gills were breathing in
the terrible oxygen
— the frightening gills,
fresh and crisp with blood,
that can cut so badly —
I thought of the coarse white flesh

packed in like feathers,
the big bones and the little bones,
the dramatic reds and blacks
of his shiny entrails[3],
and the pink swim-bladder[4]
like a big peony.
I looked into his eyes
which were far larger than mine
but shallower, and yellowed,
the irises backed and packed
with tarnished tinfoil
seen through the lenses
of old scratched isinglass[5].
They shifted a little, but not
to return my stare.
— It was more like the tipping
of an object toward the light.
I admired his sullen face,
the mechanism of his jaw,
and then I saw
that from his lower lip
— if you could call it a lip —
grim, wet and weapon-like,
hung five old pieces of fish-line,
or four and a wire leader[6]
with the swivel still attached,
with all their five big hooks
grown firmly in his mouth.
A green line, frayed at the end
where he broke it, two heavier lines,
and a fine black thread
still crimped from the strain and snap
when it broke and he got away.
Like medals with their ribbons
frayed and wavering,
a five-haired beard of wisdom
trailing from his aching jaw.
I stared and stared
and victory filled up

the little rented boat,
from the pool of bilge[7]
where oil had spread a rainbow
around the rusted engine
to the bailer[8] rusted orange,
the sun-cracked thwarts[9],
the oarlocks on their strings,
the gunnels[10]— until everything
was rainbow, rainbow, rainbow!
And I let the fish go.

Notes

1. **barnacles**: small saltwater shellfish that attach themselves to underwater objects and other animals.
2. **rosettes**: rose-shaped patterns.
3. **entrails**: inner organs.
4. **swim-bladder**: gas-filled sac in most bony fishes that enables them to maintain or change depth in water.
5. **isinglass**: thin sheets of transparent mica, a crystallized mineral.
6. **leader**: short piece of line used to attach a hook to fish line.
7. **bilge**: dirty, stagnant water that collects in the bottom of a boat.
8. **bailer**: device for removing water from a boat.
9. **thwarts**: seats for rowers.
10. **gunnels**: upper edges of the sides of a boat.

Study Questions

1. Why did the fish surrender so tamely?
2. What do you think all of the colors and the eventual rainbow have to do with what's going on in the poem?
3. Why does the speaker let the fish go?
4. What is the major theme of the poem?

6.6 Robert Lowell

6.6.1 About the author

Robert Lowell (1917-1977) was born in Boston, Massachusetts. He was educated at private schools and at St. Mark's preparatory school. Then he attended Harvard for two years. His passion for poetry took him to Kenyon College, in Ohio, where poet John Crowe Ransom was teaching a generation of critics and creators. Lowell graduated in

Classics from Kenyon in 1940. Then he spent a year, taking graduate courses at Louisiana State University.

Immensely talented and thoughtful, Lowell achieved early success as a poet by publishing *Lord Weary's Castle*, which won the Pulitzer Prize in 1947. In *Lord Weary's Castle*, by blending oppositions to war, to the Puritan ethic, and to materialism and greed, he examined his own worldweariness in verse that is highly crafted, heavy, and dense with symbols.

Partly in response to his frequent breakdowns, and partly due to the influence of some younger American poets, who were writing in a much more open and direct style, Lowell suddenly and drastically changed his style in the midfifties. He began to write more directly from personal experience, and loosened his adherence to traditional meter and form. The result was a watershed collection, *Life Studies* (1959), which became one of the most influential volumes of post-World War Ⅱ poetry and won the National Book Award for the best book of poetry published that year. This new poetry, which has come to be called confessional poetry, is informal and autobiographical; its diction is casual and colloquial, its sound patterns tend to be almost prosaic. Thus, Lowell helped poetry discover a new way of speaking, a new reason for its existence.

Lowell was considered by many to be the most important poet in English of the second half of the twentieth century. In his poetry Lowell expressed the major tensions — both public and private — of his time with technical mastery and haunting authenticity. He continued to develop his work with sometimes uneven results, all along defining the restless center of American poetry, until his sudden death from a heart attack at age 60. Among his other poetry collections are *For the Union Dead* (1964), *Near the Ocean* (1967), *Notebook: Nineteen Sixty-Seven to Nineteen Sixty-Eight* (1969), *The Dolphin* (1973; Pulitzer Prize), *Day by Day* (1977), and *Last Poems* (1977).

6.6.2 "Skunk Hour[1]"

Nautilus Island's[2] hermit
heiress still lives through winter in her Spartan[3] cottage;
her sheep still graze above the sea.
Her son's a bishop. Her farmer
is first selectman[4] in our village;
she's in her dotage[5].

Thirsting for
the hierarchic privacy[6]
of Queen Victoria's century[7],
she buys up all
the eyesores facing her shore,
and lets them fall.

The season's ill —
We've lost our summer millionaire[8],
who seemed to leap from an L. L. Bean[9]
catalogue. His nine-knot yawl[10]
was auctioned off to lobstermen.
A red fox stain covers Blue Hill[11].

And now our fairy
decorator brightens his shop for fall;
his fishnet's filled with orange cork,
orange, his cobbler's bench and awl[12];
there is no money in his work,
he'd rather marry.

One dark night,
my Tudor Ford[13] climbed the hill's skull;
I watched for love-cars. Lights turned down,
they lay together, hull to hull,
where the graveyard shelves on the town...
My mind's not right.

A car radio bleats,
"Love, O careless Love..." I hear
my ill-spirit sob in each blood cell,
as if my hand were at its throat...
I myself am hell[14];
Nobody's here —

only skunks[15], that search
in the moonlight for a bite to eat.
They march on their soles up Main Street:

white stripes, moonstruck eyes' red fire
under the chalk-dry and spar spire
of the Trinitarian Church[16].

I stand on top
of our back steps and breathe the rich air —
a mother skunk with her column of kittens swills the
garbage pail.
She jabs her wedge-head in a cup
of sour cream, drops her ostrich tail,
and will not scare.

Notes
1. This poem is Lowell's response to Elizabeth Bishop's "The Armadillo".
2. **Nautilus Island**: an island off the coast of Castine, Maine; "nautilus" is also a sea creature.
3. **Spartan**: it describes something simple or severe. The word "Spartan" comes from the ancient Greek soldiers of Sparta, who were rough and tough and didn't need much to get by.
4. **selectman**: elected councilor in New England (USA) towns.
5. **in her dotage**: here means she's in the last phase of her life.
6. **hierarchic privacy**: the privacy of a queen — where she's above everyone, so nobody can bug her.
7. **Queen Victoria's century**: here refers to the "Victorian era", which is known for being kind of stuffy and prudish.
8. **We've lost our summer millionaire**: rich people have summer homes there, but leave during the cold months.
9. **L. L. Bean**: a mail-order house in Maine, selling sporting and camping goods.
10. **nine-knot yawl**: a kind of sailboat that can go as fast as nine knots.
11. **A red fox stain covers Blue Hill**: it's probably late-to mid-fall, and the leaves on Blue Hill (a place in the town) are probably changing colors.
12. **cobbler's bench and awl**: "cobbler" is someone who fixes shoes; an "awl" is a type of tool for poking holes in leather.
13. **Tudor Ford**: a type of old car; Tudor (two-door).
14. **I myself am hell**: he's the cause of his own agony. This is a quotation from Satan in Book IV of John Milton's *Paradise Lost*.
15. **skunks**: a small and badly smelling rat-like animal.
16. **Trinitarian Church**: a three-in-one Catholic church.

Study Questions

1. What is the implication of the title?
2. Who is the speaker? What exactly do you think is the speaker afflicted by?
3. How does the line "my mind's not right" affect your reading of the poem?
4. Why does the poem end on the image of the skunk?

6.7 Theodore Roethke

6.7.1 About the author

Theodore Roethke (1908-1963) was born in Saginaw, Michigan. As a child, he spent much time in the greenhouse owned by his father and uncle. He received his education first at Aurthur Hill High School, then at the University of Michigan. In 1923 his father died of cancer, an event that would forever shape his creative and artistic outlooks. Long after that traumatic event, Roethke struggled with depression and mental illness. The hard economic times of the Great Depression forced Roethke to take up a teaching career. He taught at various colleges and universities, including Lafayette, Pennsylvania State, and Bennington, and worked last at the University of Washington.

His first volume of verse, *Open House* (1941), took ten years to write. Roethke fashioned his poems from intense memories of his childhood and boyhood in Michigan. Images of growth and decay can be found in all of his poetic works, including *Open House* (1941), *The Lost Son* (1948), *The Waking* (1953), and *Words for the Wind* (1958). His finest poetry was a journey of personal memory, a process of recovery of his vivid childhood impressions in Saginaw. Stylistically his work ranged from witty poems in strict meter and regular stanzas to free verse poems full of mystical and surrealistic imagery. Building on modernist stream-of-consciousness narrative techniques, Roethke achieved an arresting poetic performance in an associative, and often surreal, verbal style, one that depicted primal and psychic states of mind. Roethke's pioneering explorations of nature, regional settings, and personal confessionalism have secured his reputation as one of the most distinguished and widely read American poets of the twentieth century.

6.7.2 "My Papa's Waltz[1]"

> The whiskey on your breath
> Could make a small boy dizzy;
> But I hung on like death:
> Such waltzing was not easy.

We romped[2] until the pans
Slid from the kitchen shelf;
My mother's countenance[3]
Could not unfrown itself[4].

The hand that held my wrist
Was battered on one knuckle;
At every step you missed
My right ear scraped a buckle[5].

You beat time[6] on my head
With a palm caked hard by dirt,
Then waltzed me off to bed
Still clinging to your shirt.

Notes
1. The poem is written in iambic trimeter, with a simple *abab* rhyme scheme.
2. **romped**: played about; (American student slang) dance.
3. **countenance**: Here means face, or expression.
4. **could not unfrown itself**: could not stop frowning.
5. **My right ear scraped a buckle**: the son's right ear scrapes against the father's belt buckle.
6. **beat time**: Here refers to a musical beat.

Study Questions
1. What do you think this father did for a living?
2. Do you think that, for the boy, this dance was happy, scary, or something in between? Why?
3. What is the relationship between father and son?
4. What is the major theme of the poem?

6.8 Allen Ginsberg

6.8.1 About the Author
Allen Ginsberg (1926-1997) was born in Newark, New Jersey. He grew up in a relatively poor Jewish neighborhood in nearby Paterson. He attended Newark's Central High School and then East Side High School, where he discovered the poetry of Walt Whitman, which sparked his interest in becoming a poet. In 1943, he started attending Columbia University for the purpose of becoming a lawyer like his brother. At Columbia,

he joined a circle of friends that included Kerouac, Burroughs, and Neal Cassady. These new found friends exposed him to drugs, crime, sex and literature, and fostered his artistic and philosophical development. A decade later, each of the group would contribute greatly to the Beat movement. Following graduation, Ginsberg returned home, where for five years he worked for an ad agency. It was also during this time that Ginsberg began to study poetry under William Carlos Williams, who taught him to emulate the voice of the common American and to focus on strong visual images.

Upon leaving New York, Ginsberg moved out to San Francisco. In 1955 he participated in a reading at Six Gallery and delivered a thundering performance of his new poem, *Howl*, which became one of the symbols of the liberation of American culture in the 1950s from an academic formalism and political conservatism. His next books *Reality Sandwiches* (1963) and *Planet News* (1969) solidified his status as a counterculture hero of the West during the 1960s. *The Fall of America*, which registers a sustained protest against the Vietnam War in particular and the spiritual emptiness of the West in general, received the National Book Award for 1972. Ginsberg's *Collected Poems* (1984) is a kind of spiritual autobiography. His other books include *Collected Poems: 1947-1980*, *White Shroud: Poems 1980-1985*, and *Cosmopolitan Greetings: Poems 1986-1992*.

In the following decades, Ginsberg succeeded in forming a bridge between the Beat movement of the 1950s and the Hippies of the 1960s. As the leading figure of the Beats, Ginsberg was involved in countless political activities, including protests against the Vietnam War. His willingness to state his controversial views in public was an important factor in the development of the revolutionary state of mind that America developed during the 1960s. Ginsberg's poetry was strongly influenced by Modernism, Romanticism, the beat and cadence of jazz, and Jewish background. He embraced Eastern philosophies and African American culture, used the raw materials of life as the basis for his art, and subverted numerous societal and middle-class conventions in order to achieve spiritual, political, and sexual liberation. Ginsberg's poetry is informal, discursive, and often repetitive. Its immediacy, honesty, and explicit sexual subject matter frequently give it a spontaneous composition with attention paid to the natural wanderings of the mind and the rhythms of breathing.

6.8.2 An Excerpt from "Howl"

I

I saw the best minds of my generation destroyed by madness, starving
    hysterical naked,

Chapter 6 The Literature since World War II

dragging themselves through the negro streets at dawn looking for an
    angry fix,
angelheaded hipsters[1] burning for the ancient heavenly connection to the
    starry dynamo in the machinery of night,
who poverty and tatters and hollow-eyed and high sat up smoking in the
    supernatural darkness of cold-water flats floating across the tops
    of cities contemplating jazz,
who bared their brains to Heaven under the El[2] and saw Mohammedan[3]
    angels staggering on tenement roofs illuminated,
who passed through universities with radiant cool eyes hallucinating[4]
    Arkansas and Blake-light[5] tragedy among the scholars of war,
who were expelled from the academies for crazy & publishing obscene
    odes on the windows of the skull,[6]
who cowered in unshaven rooms in underwear, burning their money in
    wastebaskets and listening to the Terror through the wall,
who got busted in their pubic beards returning through Laredo[7] with a
    belt of marijuana for New York,
who ate fire in paint hotels or drank turpentine in Paradise Alley[8],
    death, or purgatoried their torsos night after night
with dreams, with drugs, with waking nightmares, alcohol and cock and
    endless balls,
incomparable blind; streets of shuddering cloud and lightning in the mind
    leaping toward poles of Canada & Paterson,[9] illuminating all the
    motionless world of Time between,
Peyote solidities of halls, backyard green tree cemetery dawns, wine
    drunkenness over the rooftops, storefront boroughs of teahead
    joyride neon blinking traffic light, sun and moon and tree vibrations
    in the roaring winter dusks of Brooklyn, ashcan rantings and kind king light of
mind,
who chained themselves to subways for the endless ride from Battery to
    holy Bronx[10] on benzedrine until the noise of wheels and children
    brought them down shuddering mouth-wracked and battered
    bleak of brain all drained of brilliance in the drear light of Zoo,
who sank all night in submarine light of Bickford's[11] floated out and sat
    through the stale beer after noon in desolate Fugazzi's[12], listening
    to the crack of doom on the hydrogen jukebox,

who talked continuously seventy hours from park to pad to bar to Bellevue[13] to
    museum to the Brooklyn Bridge,
a lost battalion of platonic conversationalists jumping down the stoops
    off fire escapes off windowsills off Empire State out of the
    moon,
yacketayakking[14] screaming vomiting whispering facts and memories
    and anecdotes and eyeball kicks and shocks of hospitals and jails
    and wars,
whole intellects disgorged in total recall for seven days and nights with
    brilliant eyes, meat for the Synagogue[15] cast on the pavement,
who vanished into nowhere Zen New Jersey leaving a trail of ambiguous
    picture postcards of Atlantic City Hall,
suffering Eastern sweats and Tangerian bone-grindings and migraines
    of China[16] under junk-withdrawal in Newark's bleak furnished
    room,
who wandered around and around at midnight in the railroad yard
    wondering where to go, and went, leaving no broken hearts,
who lit cigarettes in boxcars boxcars boxcars racketing through snow
    toward lonesome farms in grand-father night,
who studied Plotinus Poe St. John of the Cross[17] telepathy and bop
    kabala[18] because the cosmos instinctively vibrated at their feet in
    Kansas,
who loned it through the streets of Idaho seeking visionary indian angels
    who were visionary indian angels,
who thought they were only mad when Baltimore gleamed in
    supernatural ecstasy,
who jumped in limousines with the Chinaman of Oklahoma on the
    impulse of winter midnight streetlight smalltown rain,
who lounged hungry and lonesome through Houston seeking jazz or sex
    or soup, and followed the brilliant Spaniard to converse about
    America and Eternity, a hopeless task, and so took ship to Africa,
who disappeared into the volcanoes of Mexico leaving behind nothing
    but the shadow of dungarees and the lava and ash of poetry
    scattered in fire place Chicago,
who reappeared on the West Coast investigating the F. B. I.[19] in beards
    and shorts with big pacifist eyes sexy in their dark skin passing
    out incomprehensible leaflets,
who burned cigarette holes in their arms protesting the narcotic tobacco
    haze of Capitalism,

Chapter 6 The Literature since World War II

who distributed Supercommunist pamphlets in Union Square[20] weeping and undressing while the sirens of Los Alamos[21] wailed them down, and wailed down Wall[22], and the Staten Island ferry also wailed,

who broke down crying in white gymnasiums naked and trembling before the machinery of other skeletons,

who bit detectives in the neck and shrieked with delight in policecars for committing no crime but their own wild cooking pederasty and intoxication,

...

and who therefore ran through the icy streets obsessed with a sudden flash of the alchemy of the use of the ellipse the catalog the meter & the vibrating plane,

who dreamt and made incarnate gaps in Time & Space through images juxtaposed, and trapped the archangel of the soul between 2 visual images and joined the elemental verbs and set the noun and dash of consciousness together jumping with sensation of Pater Omnipotens Aeterna Deus[23]

to recreate the syntax and measure of poor human prose and stand before you speechless and intelligent and shaking with shame, rejected yet confessing out the soul to conform to the rhythm of thought in his naked and endless head,

the madman bum and angel beat in Time, unknown, yet putting down here what might be left to say in time come after death,

and rose reincarnate in the ghostly clothes of jazz in the goldhorn shadow of the band and blew the suffering of America's naked mind for love into an eli eli lamma lamma sabacthani[24] saxophone cry that shivered the cities down to the last radio

with the absolute heart of the poem of life butchered out of their own bodies good to eat a thousand years.

Notes

1. **hipsters**: hippies; a person who is unusually aware of and interested in new and unconventional patterns (as in jazz or fashion).
2. **El**: elevated railway; an urban railway that operates chiefly on an elevated structure.
3. **Mohammedan**: of or relating to the Arabian prophet Muhammad or to the religion he founded.
4. **hallucinate**: to see or hear things that are not really there.
5. **Blake-light**: Here it refers to Ginsberg's apocalyptic (启示录的) vision of the English

poet William Blake.

6. **who were expelled... of the skull**: in 1945, his sophomore year, he was expelled from Columbia University for he had drawn some obscene picture and phrases in the dust of his dormitory windows to draw the attention of a neglectful cleaning woman to the grimy state of his room. In 1948, to avoid prosecution as an accomplice of theft, Ginsberg had to plead insanity and spent eight months in Columbia Psychiatric Institute.
7. **Laredo**: a city in southern Texas on the Rio Grande.
8. **Paradise Alley**: a tenement courtyard in New York's East Village, setting of Jack Kerouac's *The Subterraneans*.
9. **Paterson**: Ginsberg's hometown.
10. **from Battery to holy Bronx**: Battery Park and Bronx Zoo are opposite terminuses of a New York subway line.
11. **Bickford's**: all-night cafeteria where Ginsberg worked when he was a college student.
12. **Fugazzi's**: bar frequented by the Beats.
13. **Bellevue**: New York mental hospital.
14. **yacketayakking**: incessant chatter.
15. **Synagogue**: a building where Jewish people meet for religious worship.
16. **Eastern sweats... of China**: African Asian sources of drugs.
17. **Plotinus Poe St. John of the Cross**: Plotinus (205-270), Roman philosopher of Egyptian birth, established the Neo-platonic school in Rome (244); he used the metaphysical myth of Plato to create a mystic religion of union with the One through contemplation and ecstatic vision. Edgard Allan Poe (1809-1849), American poet and author of supernatural tales. St. John of the Cross (1542-1591), Spanish Carmelite monk and poet, his mystical verse gives expression to the supreme type of one kind of Christian experience.
18. **bop kabala**: a mystical tradition of interpretation of Hebrew scripture.
19. **F. B. I.**: Federal Bureau of Investigation.
20. **Union Square**: a public gathering spot in New York.
21. **Los Alamos**: atomic bomb development center in New Mexico.
22. **Wall**: Wall Street or Wailing Wall in Jerusalem.
23. **Pater Omnipotens Aeterna Deus**: (Latin) "Father omnipotent, eternal God" from a letter of the French painter Paul Cezanne in which he commented on the nature of art.
24. **eli eli lamma lamma sabacthani**: Christ's last words on the Cross: "My God, my God, why hast thou forsaken me?"

Study Questions

1. It is said that in reading Ginsberg's *Howl* one may sense the style of *Leaves of Grass* of Walt Whitman, William Carlos Williams' treatment of rhythm and meter and Kerouac's "frank talk" and "oceanic prose". Do you agree?
2. In an explanation of *Howl*, Ginsberg says: "My feeling is for a big long cranky statement... not the way you would think it — i. e., we think rapidly, in visual images as well as works, and if each successive thought were transcribed in its confusion,... you get a slightly different prosody than if you were talking slowly." Do you feel the same as Ginsberg says after reading *Howl*?
3. *Howl* means to make a prolonged, hollow, wailing call like a wolf. Do you have the same feeling in reading the poem?

6.9 Sylvia Plath

6.9.1 About the Author

Sylvia Plath (1932-1963) was born into a middle-class family in Jamaica Plain, Massachusetts. Her father, a college professor and expert on bees, died when she was eight. His death profoundly affected her later life, marriage, and poetry. Left fatherless, Plath lived with her mother's parents and attended school in Winthrop. In 1950, Plath earned a scholarship to Smith College and majored in English literature and composition. Both sensitive and intelligent, Plath was a model student, earning straight A's and winning the best prizes at school. Her first awarded story, "Sunday at the Mintons," was published in 1952 while she was at college. However, Plath was a perfectionist, whose drive for success proved intense and burdensome. In 1953, she suffered a nervous breakdown and tried to commit suicide, which took her six months to recover.

Plath returned to college in 1954 and graduated in 1955. Then she won a Fulbright scholarship to study at Cambridge University in England, where she met and married poet Ted Hughes. The couple settled for a while in an English country village in Devon. In 1957, Plath returned to America and began teaching at Smith. After spending two years in the United States, the couple moved again to England in 1959. When Plath was 28, her first book, *The Colossus* (1960), was published. In the same year, she gave birth to her first child, and her second child was born in 1962. Her health and emotional stability declined with the birth of the second child. She was further antagonized by her husband's adulteries. She separated from Hughes in 1962.

The winter of 1962 — 1963 found Plath living in a small London flat, now with two children, ill with flu and low on money. The hardness of her life seemed to increase her need to write, and she often worked between four and eight in the morning, before the children woke. In the two months after the marriage broke apart, Plath wrote brilliant poems of anguished self-expression, including "Daddy," "Lady Lazarus," "Ariel," "The Bee Meeting," "Stings," and "Medusa." In these last poems, death is given a cruel physical allure, and psychic pain becomes almost tactile. The family burdens and her husband's betrayal produced in Plath exhaustion, depression and tension, which led to her final suicide in 1963.

Two years after Plath's death, *Ariel* (1965), a collection of some of her last poems, was published. The book astonished the literary world with its power, and became one of the best-selling volumes of poetry published in England and America in the 20th century. Her other works include: *The Bell Jar* (1963), *Crossing the Water* (1971), *Winter Trees* (1972), *Johnny Panic and the Bible of Dreams* (1977), and *Collected Poems* (1981), the last of which won her a posthumous Pulitzer Prize for poetry in 1982. Plath has been considered a deeply honest writer, whose ceaseless self-scrutiny has given a unique point of view to psychological disorder and to the theme of the feminist-martyr in a patriarchal society. As one of the great metaphor-makers in the twentieth century, Plath used words and forms with a fierce beauty that has no exact parallel in English-language poetry. Her best-known poems are noted for their brilliant imagery, which moves her poetry far beyond the personal. Even what reads like autobiographical detail in poems like "Daddy" and "Lady Lazarus" is actually a dramatized performance based only loosely on her own life. She is widely regarded as one of the first feminist poets and an icon of the women's movement in the United States.

6.9.2 "Mirror[1]"

I am silver[2] and exact. I have no preconceptions[3].
Whatever I see I swallow immediately
Just as it is, unmisted[4] by love or dislike.
I am not cruel, only truthful —
The eye[5] of a little god, four-cornered.
Most of the time I meditate on the opposite wall.
It is pink, with speckles[6]. I have looked at it so long
I think it is part of my heart. But it flickers.
Faces and darkness separate us over and over.

Now I am a lake. A woman bends over me,
Searching my reaches for what she really is.
Then she turns to those liars, the candles or the moon[7].

I see her back, and reflect it faithfully.
She rewards me with tears and an agitation[8] of hands.
I am important to her. She comes and goes.
Each morning it is her face that replaces the darkness.
In me she has drowned a young girl, and in me an old woman
Rises toward her day after day, like a terrible fish.

Notes

1. The poem is composed of two stanzas, each containing nine lines; in this way, the form of the poem may be viewed as representation of a mirror's image — with each stanza reflecting the other.
2. **silver**: here refers to the coating on the back of a glass mirror.
3. **preconception**: an opinion or conception formed in advance of adequate knowledge or experience, especially a prejudice or bias.
4. **unmisted**: something that does not dims, obscures, or blurs.
5. **eye**: the reflecting surface.
6. **speckles**: a small speck, spot, or mark, as on skin.
7. **those liars, the candles or the moon**: because candles and moonlight provide only dim illumination, they "lie" about what they see.
8. **agitation**: the act or process of agitating; state of being agitated.

Study Questions

1. What is the significance of personifying the mirror by the poet?
2. What effect does this poem's point of view have on its theme?
3. Why is the "lake" important to the woman in this poem?
4. What is the irony in the relationship between the mirror and the woman?

6.10 Robert Hayden

6.10.1 About the author

Robert Hayden (1913-1980) was born into a poor family in Detroit, Michigan. His parents got separated before his birth and he was thus taken in by a foster family next door. Hayden grew up in a Detroit ghetto. He had an emotionally turbulent childhood as he shuffled between the home of his parents and that of a foster family. He also suffered from severe visual problems which prevented him from taking part in different activities such as sports. The constant negligence from his family and friends forced him to read voraciously which developed his intellectual abilities to a higher level. After graduation from high school in 1930, he worked a number of odd jobs. With the help of a

scholarship, he attended Detroit City College from 1932 to 1936. His job as writer and researcher for the Detroit branch of the Federal Writers Project of the Works Progress Administration from 1936 to 1939 provided him with essential material and reading skills that would fuel much of his artistry.

In pursuit of a master's degree at the University of Michigan, Hayden studied under W. H. Auden, who directed his attention to issues of poetic form, technique, and artistic discipline. In June 1940, he married Erma Inez Morris, a concert pianist and music teacher, forming a bond of great depth and closeness that would last for the rest of his life. He also published his first volume of poetry, *Heart-Shape in the Dust*, in 1940. After finishing his degree in 1942, he embarked on an academic career, teaching at Michigan and Fisk Universities. Throughout decades of neglect and scorn, he clung steadfastly to his artistic and human values. Hayden's poetry started gaining international recognition in 1960s. In 1966, he received the grand prize for poetry at the First World Festival of Negro Arts in Dakar, Senegal for his book *Ballad of Remembrance*. His other works included *The Lion and the Archer* (1948), *Figures of Time: Poems* (1955), S*elected Poems* (1966), *Words in the Mourning Time* (1970), *Night-Blooming Cereus* (1972), *Angle of Ascent* (1975), *American Journal* (1978 and 1982), and *Collected Poems* (1985).

Hayden produced a body of work whose artistry and emotional richness placed him at the front rank of an especially talented generation of American poets. His work generally addressed the plight of African-Americans, often using his earlier home of Detroit ghetto as a backdrop theme. As a symbolist poet using historical fact to make the synaptic leap into the consciousness behind events, Hayden explored America's identity with a probing searchlight. His work is full of dramatic tension, edged by irony, and tempered by religious emotions as echoes of the human spirit. African heritage, slavery, and Civil War history anchor many of his poems in the shared experience of the African-American past. Artistically, what distinguished Hayden most was his fusing of history and symbol, of the natural and the spiritual, to achieve an intensification of reality that triggers flashes of social insight, with unity as a touchstone of truth.

6.10.2 "Those Winter Sundays[1]"

> Sundays too my father got up early
> and put his clothes on in the blueblack cold[2],
> then with cracked hands that ached

from labor in the weekday weather made
banked³ fires blaze. No one ever thanked him.

I'd wake and hear the cold splintering, breaking⁴
When the rooms were warm, he'd call,
and slowly I would rise and dress,
fearing the chronic angers⁵ of that house,

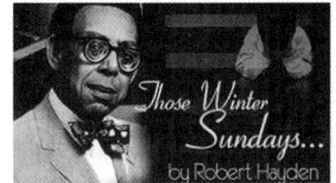

Speaking indifferently to him,
who had driven out the cold
and polished my good shoes as well.
What did I know, what did I know
of love's austere⁶ and lonely offices⁷?

Notes
1. This is a fourteen-line lyric poem written in free verse. Its title is taken from a song in George and Ira Gershwin's opera *Porgie and Bess*.
2. **blueblack cold**: here Hayden uses a technique called synesthesia, that is, to use one sense (like sight) to describe another (like touch); for example, "cold" is something one feels, but Hayden describes it as something one sees (a color). "Blueblack" makes the image both tactile and visual. "Blueblack" might be describing what the sky looks like outside the window or how the room looks in the early light.
3. **banked**: here means a fire that is burning very low and covered in ashes.
4. **hear the cold splintering, breaking**: Hayden uses synesthesia again here to describe the cold. "Splintering" makes the image both audible and visual.
5. **chronic angers**: The "chronic angers" bespeak the unhappiness of the domestic situation and an emotional heat or chill that brings no comfort. "Chronic" means habitual or frequently recurring.
6. **austere**: strict, severe; it can also mean a place that is bare — no decorations or personal touches.
7. **offices**: here it means a duty or task that one is either assigned or chooses to do.

Study Questions
1. What kind of emotion is expressed in this poem?
2. How does the setting contribute to the tone of the poem?
3. How would you describe the relationship between speaker and his father?
4. Why does the speaker repeat "What did I know, what did I know"?
5. What is the central theme of this poem?

Appendix I Sample Test Paper

I. **Multiple Choice** (1 × 20 = 20%)

Directions: *In this part, there are 20 statements or questions; in each of them, there are four choices marked by A, B, C and D. Choose the ONE answer that is most suitable to the statement or question.*

1. What as a cultural heritage exerted great influence over American moral values and American literature as well?
  A. nationalism   B. rationalism   C. individualism   D. Puritanism

2. What is the main theme in Irving's short story "Rip Van Winkle"?
  A. Strong desire for national independence from the British rule.
  B. Strong desire of women's emancipation from men's domination.
  C. Nostalgia for the unrecoverable past.
  D. Nostalgia for the pastoral life in New England before the Revolutionary War.

3. "Nothing is at last sacred but the integrity of your own mind" is a famous quote from ____'s writings.
  A. Walt Whitman   B. Henry David Thoreau
  C. Herman Melville   D. Ralph Waldo Emerson

4. Henry David Thoreau's work, ____, has always been regarded as a masterpiece of the New England Transcendental Movement.
  A. *Nature*   B. *Walden*   C. *The Pioneers*   D. *Song of Myself*

5. Moby Dick, the white whale, as a symbol may stand for all the followings things except ____.
  A. agent of an evil force
  B. instrument of God's vengeance upon evil man
  C. power of nature
  D. divine love

6. Whitman's poems are characterized by all the following features except ____.
  A. the strict poetic form   B. the free and natural rhythm
  C. the easy flow of feelings   D. the simple and conversational language

7. Which of the following features of American Romanticism is different from that of British Romanticism?
  A. Expression of the artist's imaginations, emotions, impressions, or beliefs.
  B. To see nature as a source of mental cleanness and spiritual understanding.
  C. Love for the remote, supernatural, mysterious, exotic and illogical quality of things.

D. A strong sense of optimism and the mood of "feeling good" of the whole nation.

8. Hawthorne is generally preoccupied with such issues as ___ in his writings.
    A. cultural conflicts of different races   B. pursuit of material interest
    C. sin and evil in man's heart   D. social injustice and inequality

9. Which of the following statements about *Scarlet Letter* is not true?
    A. It explores man's never-ending search for satisfaction of materialistic desires.
    B. It relates the conflict between intellect and natural emotion.
    C. It is about the effect of the sin on the people involved and the society as a whole.
    D. It analyzes the inward tensions or internal conflicts of the characters.

10. During the nineteenth century, American literature produced only one female poet, whose name is ___.
    A. Anne Bradstreet   B. Elizabeth Bishop
    C. Emily Dickinson   D. Sylvia Plath

11. The statement that a boy's journey on the Mississippi River is one to freedom and moral growth may well sum up the major theme of ___.
    A. Stowe's *Uncle Tom's Cabin*
    B. James's *The Portrait of A Lady*
    C. Dreiser's *Sister Carrie*
    D. Mark Twain's *Adventures of Huckleberry Finn*

12. In fiction writing, Henry James's primary concern is to present the ___.
    A. inner life of human beings   B. American Civil War and its effects
    C. life on the Mississippi River   D. Calvinistic view of original sin

13. Theodore Dreiser belonged to the school of literary ___, which emphasized heredity and environment as important deterministic forces shaping individual characters.
    A. humanism   B. naturalism   C. determinism   D. realism

14. The following works are all related to the subject of escaping from the society and returning to nature except ___.
    A. Dreiser's *Sister Carrie*
    B. Copper's *Leather-Stocking Tales*
    C. Thoreau's *Walden*
    D. Mark Twain's *The Adventures of Huckleberry Finn*

15. The novelistic technique of projecting the narrative through feelings and thoughts of the characters reached a perfected form in the works of ___.
    A. Washington Irving   B. William Dean Howells
    C. Henry James   D. Herman Melville

16. Chinese poetry and philosophy has exerted great influence over ___.
    A. Robert Frost   B. Ezra Pound
    C. Langston Hughes   D. Theodore Roethke

17. The Hemingway Code heroes are best remembered for their ___.

A. masculinity B. pessimistic view of life
C. war experiences D. indestructible spirit

18. In *The Sound and the Fury*, Faulkner adopted a writing technique called ____, in which the whole story was presented with interior monologues of the characters.

A. Expressionism B. Naturalism
C. stream-of-consciousness D. symbolism

19. Who always used "i" instead of "I" to refer to himself as a protest against self-importance?

A. E. E. Cummings. B. Robert Hayden.
C. Robert Lowell. D. Allen Ginsberg.

20. Which of the following American writers is not a Nobel Prize winner?

A. Eugene O'Neill B. F. Scott Fitzgerald
C. Ernest Hemingway D. William Faulkner

II. Define the literary terms listed below (10 × 2 = 20%)

1. American Puritanism
2. The Lost Generation

III. Reading comprehension (5 × 4 = 20%)

Directions: *Read each of the following quotations carefully and then try to give brief answers to the questions.*

1. "I celebrate myself, and sing myself.
And what I assume you shall assume,
For every atom belonging to me as good belongs to you."

Questions
1) Identify the poem and the poet.
2) What does "myself" stand for?
3) What idea do the quoted lines express?

2. "We passed the School, where Children strove
At Recess — in the Ring —
We passed the Fields of Gazing Grain —
We passed the Setting Sun — "

Questions
1) Identify the poem and the poet.
2) What do "the School," "the Fields" and "the Setting Sun" stand for?
3) What idea does the quoted passage express?

3. "The apparition of these faces in the crowd;

Petals on a wet, black bough."

Questions

1) Identify the poem and the poet.

2) What does the word "apparition" mean?

3) What idea does the poem express?

4. "The Negro man went in and out with the market basket, but the front door remained closed. Now and then we would see her at the window for a moment, as the men did that night when they sprinkled the lime, but for almost six months she did not appear on the streets."

Questions

1) Identify the work and the author.

2) In the sentence: "for almost six months she did not appear on the streets," whom does "she" refer to?

3) Why did the front door remained closed?

IV. Give brief answers to the following questions (10 × 2 = 20%)

Directions: *In this part you are given 2 questions. You are asked to give only a brief answer, explaining what you know about it. You should use no more than 100 words for each answer, and you should, therefore, concentrate on those essential points.*

1. Whitman has made radical changes in the form of poetry by choosing free verse as his medium of expression. What are the characteristics of Whitman's free verse?

2. Mark Twain and Henry James are both considered to be great realistic writers. What are the differences between them in the aspects of theme and language?

V. Topic Discussion (20%)

Directions: *In this part you are asked to write a short essay on the given topic. You should write no more than 150 words on the topic. Therefore, you should concentrate on those important points. Try your best to be logical in your essay and keep your writing clear and tidy.*

Discuss the symbolical meaning of the "rose" in Faulkner's "A Rose for Emily"?

Keys

I. **Multiple Choice** (1 × 20 = 20%)

DCDBD ADCAC DABAC BDCAB

II. **Define the literary terms listed below** (10 × 2 = 20%)

1. **American Puritanism**

American Puritanism refers to the beliefs and practices of those Puritans who came out of different reasons to the New Continent and settled in what is now the United States. American Puritans accepted as their theological foundation the Calvinistic doctrine of predestination, original sin, total depravity, and salvation of a selected few through a special infusion of grace from God. Being a group of seriously religious people, they had a strong sense of mission and very idealistic, for they thought they were the people God chose and sent to the New World to purify the beliefs and practices of the Church of England, from which they had separated themselves, and built in America a new church. On the other hand, they were very practical, for the struggle of survival in the New World had taught them to work hard for profits and material success, which they believed was a sign of God's benevolence. Puritans in America were living a very disciplined and simple style of life, devoid of earthly joy and extravagancy, so they are often criticized. But as a philosophy of life and a culture heritage, American Puritanism has produced an everlasting influence on the American life, and especially the American mind.

2. **The Lost Generation**

"The Lost Generation" is a term now critically used to refer to a group of young American expatriates, basically speaking, who were writing chiefly in the 1920s. When the First World War broke out, many young men volunteered to take part in "the war to end wars" only to find that modern warfare was not glorious or heroic as they thought it to be. When they came back home after the war, they were only disillusioned and disgusted by the frivolous, greedy, and heedless way of life in America. So they left America again. With the help of an American woman writer, Gertrude Stein, also an expatriate, they formed a community of writers and artists in Paris, involved with other European novelists and poets in their experimentations on new modes of thought and expression. Later on this group of writers was addressed as a "lost generation" by Stein. Literally speaking, these writers were cut off from their native land and their past in America. Spiritually, they felt "lost" because of their traumatic war experiences, their disillusionment and their inability to cope with the new era when the whole world had turned to a spiritual wasteland. Among those great figures in "the Lost Generation" are Ezra Pound, Ernest Hemingway, F. Scott Fitzgerald, etc. In their works, there is a strong sense of loss, confusion and despair they felt about the war and their personal experiences. However, the literary innovation they demonstrated in their writings to break away from the tradition is remarkable and monumental.

III. Reading comprehension (5 × 4 = 20%)

1.
1) Walt Whitman: "Song of Myself".
2) An individual.
3) The poet is celebrating individualism and nationalism in this poem. In the later part of the poem, the poet pretends to be (or assume) many other people. When the poet is celebrating himself, he is in fact celebrating all the people he assumes. The self and the other here are united to form a new identity: the individual as representative of American nationality.

2.
1) Emily Dickinson: (712) "Because I could not stop for Death".
2) The three stages of life: childhood, adulthood and old age.
3) In this stanza the first person plural "we" refers to the speaker and the personified death. The two are on their way to the tomb. This trip can be understood as a process of one's whole life, or as an inevitable journey to death.

3.
1) Ezra Pound: "In a Station of the Metro".
2) A visible appearance of something not present.
3) The image of faces in the crowd is sharpened and intensified through the second — metaphoric — image, that is, "petals on a wet, black bough." The intent of the two lines is not only to present a picture to the visual sense, but also to recreate the dreamy sensation that attended the original perception.

4.
1) William Faulkner: *A Rose for Emily*.
2) Miss Emily Grierson.
3) It is an indication of Emily's denial of any social contact with the outside world; it might also indicate that there must be something fishy about the house. Born into an old noble family, Emily could not accept the way of doing things in the changing world, so she shut herself up intentionally to show her resistance and denial.

IV. Give brief answers to the following questions (10 × 2 = 20%)

1.
1) It is flexible and variable in form, adhering to no metrical pattern or the conventional rhyming system.
2) The poetic lines are simple and prose-like, varying in length, which allows him to express his ideas freely.
3) Whitman also applies oral English in his free verse to make it an effective way to express freely the feelings of common people.

2.
1) Mark Twain is famous for his local color, showing his concern for the local people, local scenery and local life; whereas Henry James is famous for his "international theme," showing his concern for the cultural conflicts between Old Europe and New America.
2) Mark Twain's language is fresh, vigorous, humorous, with a variety of bribe dialects, colloquial and vernacular expressions. He depicts the life picture of the American lower-class. Whereas Henry James's language is elegant, elaborate, exquisite, indirect and subtle. He depicts the life picture of the American upper-class people who possess both wealth and leisure.

V. Topic Discussion (20%)

1) Rose is always interpreted conventionally as a symbol of love. It might be applied here in this story when we think that Emily has been trying to win the love of a Northerner and finally she gets it.

2) But actually, "rose" is used here in a rather ironical sense, for Emily kills the man so as to keep forever the love she "obtains". At the time when the town people find Homer Barron's body, they also find the valance curtains of faded rose color, the rose-shaded lights in the room. Hence, as an ironic romantic tribute to Emily, rose has become a symbol of decay and death.

3) Besides, rose could possibly stand for the pity, sympathy, or the lament that the narrator, "we", or the reader, shows for Emily Grierson and all those who are imprisoned in the past and fail to adapt to the change.

4) In a word, "rose" has been intentionally chosen by the author to objectify his complicated and emotional involvement in the South and in the people who grow up and live there ever since.

Appendix II Acknowledgments

Acknowledgments must be made to the following works, from which we have benefited a lot in the course of editing *An Introductive Course Book of English and American Literatures*.

Baym N, et al. The Norton Anthology of American Literature [M]. 3rd ed. New York: W. W. Norton and Company, Inc., 1989.

Booz E B. A Brief Introduction to Modern American Literature [M]. Shanghai: Shanghai Foreign Language Education Press, 1982.

Brooks C. American Literature: the Makers and the Making [M]. New York: St. Martin's Press, 1973.

Brooks C. Understanding Fiction [M]. Beijing: Foreign Language Teaching and Research Press, 2005.

Brooks C. Understanding Poetry [M]. Beijing: Foreign Language Teaching and Research Press, 2005.

Chang Yaoxin. A Survey of American Literature [M]. Tianjing: Nankai University Press, 1996.

Cunliffe M. The Literature of the United States [M]. Hongkong: World Today Press, 1975.

Elliott E. Columbia Literary History of the United States [M]. New York: Columbia University Press, 1988.

Hart J D. The Oxford Companion to American Literature [M]. 5th ed. Oxford: Oxford University Press, 1983.

Head D. The Modernist Short Story—A Study in theory and Practice [M]. Cambridge: Cambridge University Press, 1992.

High P B. An Outline of American Literature [M]. London: Longman Group Ltd., 1986.

Hu Yintong and Liu Shushen. A Course in American Literature [M]. Tianjing: Nankai University Press, 1996.

Modnick F. An Introduction to American Literature [M]. Kaifeng: Henan University Press, 1988.

Rosenthal M L. The Modern Poets—A Critical Introduction [M]. Beijing: Foreign Language Teaching and Research Press, 2004.

Wu Weiren. History and Anthology of American Literature [M]. Beijing: Foreign Language Teaching and Research Press, 1996.

Zhang Boxiang. Selected Readings in English and American Literatures [M]. Beijing: Foreign Language Teaching and Research Press, 1998.